A

Political

Journey

in the

Pacific

Islands

■

MALCOMSON

Poseidon Press

Simon & Schuster Building
Rockefeller Center
1230 Avenue of the Americas
New York, New York 10020

POSEIDON PRESS is a registered trademark
of Simon & Schuster Inc.

POSEIDON PRESS colophon is a trademark
of Simon & Schuster Inc.

Designed by Barbara M. Bachman

Manufactured in the United States of America

10 9 8 7 6 5 4 3 2 1

Library of Congress Cataloging in Publication Data
Malcomson, Scott L.
    Tuturani : a political journey in the Pacific Islands / Scott L.
Malcomson.
        p.   cm.
    Includes bibliographical references.
    1. Oceania—Politics and government.   2. Oceania—Social
conditions.   3. Oceania—Social life and customs.   4. Malcomson,
Scott L.—Journeys—Oceania.   I. Title.
DU29.M22   1990
995—dc20   90-7569
                    CIP

ISBN 0-671-69209-7

T u t u r a n i

is the word for white people
in the Raga language of
North Pentecost, Vanuatu—
a nation of some eighty inhabited islands formerly
governed by France and
Britain as the New Hebri-
des. Literally "stay stay
day," *tuturani* is usually defined by its figurative meaning: "a ship appeared in the
evening, and in the morning
it was still there." Which
suggests "the people who
appeared one day and never
went away."

Contents

III La Franconésie

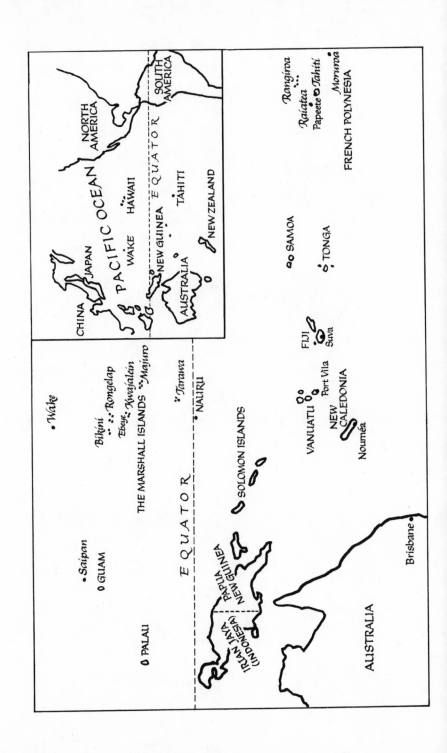

Introduction

"What island are you from?" the Marshall Islander asked with polite interest.

"New York."

"Ah! That's a good island, isn't it? Bigger than here?"

I tried to explain a little about New York, without much success. "Eight million people" is a figure so large that it's practically meaningless, like saying "trillion-dollar deficit" to the average American. It was nice, anyway, to find someone whose opinion of my home I basically shared: a good island, fairly large.

Travel, as they say, broadens the mind. It can also be profoundly destabilizing. One risks ending up in a world of islands, some bigger than others, but all of them hushed at their edges by the same indifferent tide. Questions that usually can be silenced at home become insistent and immediate elsewhere. For instance, What does it mean to be white? Or black?

12 How does a collection of people make themselves into a na-
■ tion-state? Why should they want to? What are the distinctions
between civilized (developed, modern) and uncivilized (developing, primitive)? What is paradise? Spending enough
time in a world of islands can play with one's ideas about
things like history, civilization, sex, race, economics, nationalism, identity—or rather, it seems to me, it *should* play with
them.

This hasn't always been the case. The literary relationship
between white EuroAmerican culture and its nonwhite ana-
logues around the world began in simple conquest and, to a
remarkable extent, retains an imperial character. Even in its
most exalted forms—belles-lettres memoirs and anthropological monographs—white writing about nonwhite peoples com-
fortably employed terms like "primitive," "savage," and
"backward" well into the 1960s, with the explicit or implicit
assurance that the authors' own cultures were none of the
three. This literature, of course, was born and flourished
against a backdrop of extraordinary and unequal bloodshed.

An evolution of racial consciousness and the flowering of
white guilt in the 1960s and '70s briefly altered the terms
of travel writing and reading, as did the military successes of
nonwhite peoples. Suddenly, there could be such a thing as a
"white Negro"; EuroAmerican writers actually considered
some nonwhite cultures to be superior, cultures that whites
ought to respect and perhaps adore. Though much of this
adulation was condescending, it at least became possible to
admire and condescend at the same time. Some whites, most
of them leftists, began to support the liberation of nonwhite
countries from other whites; the (usually distant) struggles for
decolonization acquired global significance.

Unfortunately, I was too young to enjoy this era. The connection between white America, into which I was born in
1961, and the nonwhite world was, in my experience, extremely confused. The stock characters of racism and enlightenment—southern sheriffs and WASPs, liberal Jews and urban
black insurgents—belonged to other places. Race relations
were not a matter of inverted rhetoric and role reversals,

predictable identities and counter-identities, cherished dangers and ethnic epiphanies. Most of my friends growing up had been third-generation Chinese-American, working and middle class. Our favorite music was sung by black groups, particularly Earth, Wind, and Fire. When we got our drivers' licenses we sometimes liked to drive around white neighborhoods and shoot at "their" shop windows. This was in Oakland, California, home of the Black Panthers (and the Gray Panthers), where the largest ethnic group was black Americans.

When I was eleven years old I placed third in the citywide spelling bee, after which the black superintendent of schools, Marcus Foster, gave what I remember as a warm and moving speech. About a year later (November 1973) he was murdered by, of all things, a primarily white revolutionary group called the Symbionese Liberation Army. In dreams I've relived that murder ever since. My junior-high years were memorable for the semi-organized, lightly armed confrontations between Chinese-Americans and blacks. One learned about the paraphernalia of martial arts—nunchaku and sharpened metal stars. I acted as a mediator, sitting down to arbitrate the conflicts with the school principal, who was Hispanic. It was not a question of mediating abstractions. There was no rationale for the fighting or the hatred; we were just kids and our cruelty was inarticulate. Nothing seemed odd or amiss. The shifting passions of race relations came naturally. They were the air we breathed.

My mother was a social worker, serving elderly middle-class whites; my father was a Baptist minister who claims to this day that he learned all he knows about preaching the Word from black ministers. Dad worked at an old church downtown—a white, liberal, middle-class church in a black and Hispanic neighborhood. Sometimes the family would go to hear him guest-preach at black churches, where he seemed especially happy since the congregation actually listened to his sermons (as opposed to *appreciating* them). The family and I enjoyed these trips. We were able to sing in full voices without overwhelming the worshippers next to us in the pew.

I mention all this because *Tuturani* is about identity and race, as any book by a white person about nonwhite peoples has to be, and there's value in knowing something about the upbringing of a writer who's addressing these subjects. It is useful to remember, for example, that Robert Louis Stevenson sprang from the Scottish upper middle class before traveling to Samoa, that the anthropologist E. E. Evans-Pritchard called Oxbridge home, that Ruth Benedict went to Vassar, or that C. L. R. James and V. S. Naipaul both migrated from Trinidad to London.

More important, I mention my growing-up in Oakland because, however unusual, it had one quality that I think is increasingly characteristic of white-nonwhite relations since the 1960s: it was chaotic. Certainly we all defined ourselves by race; we were obsessed by it, we fought over it. But there were a hundred definitions, and they often changed. They would be contradictory one way, then another. Racial identity was always getting mixed up. So were identities of class, though we weren't as concerned about them (the rich kids generally stayed out of public schools). Not until high school did we have to think of white people as an economic group; they usually had cars of their own and wore expensive clothes. My crowd of Chinese-Americans began to cordon itself off, as did the blacks. When we drove around the nice white neighborhoods with our little air pistol we were shooting at ghosts we despised, resented, and couldn't see. But things were becoming clearer—some of us would go to college, some wouldn't—and our inexplicable passions would eventually turn into politics. Yet even as our differences slowly congealed into definitions I could never forget that they were born in disorder and, to some vague extent, would always remain there. It was only later that I learned about other people's categories and the many and grand theories that were constructed from them.

Racial, cultural, and class identities, not to mention the ideas that accompany them, are getting harder to define these days. The current racial retrenchment in Europe and America—and ethnic divisiveness in less-white regions—may be symptomatic of this. French anti-Arabism, British immigration laws, some white American reactions to Jesse Jackson, or, farther afield, Chinese violence against Africans, Fijian hatred for Indians, Javanese terrorism against Papuans, and Estonian nationalism within the Soviet Union—it all has an air of protesting too much. Ethnic identities have become difficult, at least conceptually, to defend, which may explain why so many bullets are being used toward precisely that end. Shiite versus Sunni versus Kurd, Hutu versus Tutsi, Soviet Balts versus Russians, Serbs versus Croats—such conflicts can be explained as a reaction of the soul against centralization, but I wonder if they aren't also a response to the increasing fragility of centralization itself, particularly the very centralizing and very white-ethnic idea of Civilization.

Civilization was at its most solid during the colonial period, giving to world history a certain clarity, especially in retrospect. There was a similar clarity during the anticolonial period, when lighter-skinned people could be reasonably seen as malevolent, and the absolute assertion of darker-skinned peoples' identities could be seen as an unalloyed good. Now that ethnic identities are very much in play, white writing about the rest of the world has become problematic. In America and Europe the most popular travel writing has formed a sub-genre—featuring writers like P. J. O'Rourke, Denis Boyles, Redmond O'Hanlon, and Mary Morris—that might unkindly be labeled "white writer in danger," and which normally involves a young man or woman exposing himself or herself to the crazy whims, poor plumbing, and exotic logic of darker people for a short but intense period of time. This coincides with a nostalgic enthusiasm for the lifestyle of colonial whites, particularly the African and Indian varieties, that would have been inconceivable during, say, the Mau-Mau rebellion. But neither trend is simply colonial or necessarily neocolonial. "White writers in danger," for the most part, have a sense of humor and irony, suggesting that the authors recognize the feebleness of their judgments and intentions, while colonial-nostalgia films like *Out of Africa* and *White Mischief* read as both hymn and parody, and occasionally as apology.

16 ■ The difficulties of white writing about nonwhites have even reached into academia. Clifford Geertz, the chief philosopher of American anthropology, wrote recently of a "pervasive nervousness" afflicting his colleagues. "They are also harassed by grave inner uncertainties, amounting almost to a sort of epistemological hypochondria, concerning how one can know that anything one says about other forms of life is in fact so. This loss of confidence, and the crisis in ethnographic writing that goes with it, is a contemporary phenomenon and is due to contemporary developments." So the center does not hold, and the ethnographer, not to mention the travel writer, finds himself or herself describing a far periphery for the benefit of those in a nearer one, or else creating a center with terms like "economic development," "the modern world," or "the West." These invented centers have inspired much bizarre writing and thinking about the nonwhite world. Isolated outposts that have never seen a communist are described as platforms for Marxist revolution (New Caledonia, Kiribati, and Vanuatu are examples in this book); a decrepit, miniature steel mill becomes *the* measure of some agricultural Third World country's economic prospects (a particularly common syndrome in sub-Saharan Africa and Latin America); tribesmen sitting around a TV is construed as the death knell of human diversity.

As a journalist I've been preoccupied with the political and economic "centers," the little gyroscopes that whirl within EuroAmerican journalism. After working in Europe and North Africa in addition to the U.S., I began to regard these gyroscopes as tyrannical demons forcing me to ask silly, boring questions of a serious and interesting world. Because I am politically to the left, my particular demons were issues like "What is the U.S. role in [fill in blank] and what are the multinationals doing?" or "Who are the good leftists in this country?" If I had been more mainstream or to the right, the questions would have been different but no more insightful ("What is the extent of communist influence in [fill in blank]?" "How strong is the middle class?"). The more I traveled the more difficult it became to ask these questions.

For one thing, they made me feel ridiculous. I'm convinced
that the main reason foreign correspondents constantly quote
the responses of "Western diplomatic sources" is that Western
diplomats are the only people who believe in the paramount
importance of the questions. I realized that if this were the full
aim and extent of foreign correspondence I'd quickly become
bored and cynical and depressed and probably stay home.

The inspiration for this book came after a 1986 trip to the
Caribbean and Peru. I was in Grenada, for the second-anniver-
sary celebration of the "return of democracy," to write articles
for newspapers in New York and Paris; a visit afterward to
Trinidad, during Carnival, was meant as a vacation. In Grenada I encountered two related problems: how an island (two
islands, actually) with 80,000 people could form itself into a
"nation," complete with legislative archives, a banking system, and patriotic holidays; and how the people of a tiny
ex-colony could construct for themselves a national identity
that made emotional sense. These concerns didn't really interest the people who had paid me to go to Grenada—all they
wanted to know was what the U.S. was up to—but they interested me, and they very much interested the Grenadians.

The issues of race and national identity were alive in Trinidad as well. And because this was Carnival they were combined with a third preoccupation: sex. Carnival is an erotic
event, all about hot rhythms, dancing, drinking, abandon—
and, somewhere in the back, the struggle against slavery and
white domination. Racially there are three elements to Trinidad's Carnival: whites, who seem to come mainly for an exotic
sensual adventure among dark people; black Trinidadians, for
whom Carnival was originally an anticolonial bacchanal and
who still, in costumes and songs, subversively parody white
culture, particularly American; and Indian Trinidadians, who
generally look down upon Carnival as a black excrescence
while organizing and profiting from most of the touristic
events.

During Carnival I became jarringly aware of how crucial
eroticism was and is to race relations. The early literature of
exploration is choked with meditations on sex, culminating

18

perhaps in Louis Antoine de Bougainville's 1768 erotic holiday in Tahiti; the word "penetration" probably appears more often in exploration literature than in any other genre save pornography. Anthropologists would go on to make sex an empirical obsession, devoting great and learned tomes to "the sexual life of savages." It's striking that, despite decades of articles on nocturnal tree frogs and the Mediterranean sea sponge, what most people first associate with *National Geographic* magazine are images of dark, naked bodies. Travel writing today, as well as Third World tourism packages, is still focused on sex; most "white writers in danger" are obliged to have at least one erotic encounter before they can be said to have enough material for a book.

From Trinidad I went to Peru. After four months there, what little remained of my faith in conventional journalistic idioms, not to mention the conventional theories behind them, was pretty much destroyed. The situation in Peru was brutal and extremely complicated; its many ethnic, economic, political, and sexual aspects demanded intense concentration. Quite a few people I knew were killed during those four months. Whatever intellectual obligation I felt to understand my subjects on something like their own terms was greatly strengthened by the massive presence of these particular deaths.

And so I found myself in a world of islands, gradually becoming destabilized by experience. In the process of writing about other places I seemed to be writing myself out of the relatively stable, if threatened, discourses of EuroAmerican culture and many of the ideas supporting them. I seemed to be taking leave of civilization.

The European Enlightenment and the industrial revolution that accompanied and followed it were greatly concerned with writing and organization. Denis Diderot and the French encyclopedists thought they could organize the entire world by writing it down. Economists tried to organize material production and consumption, also by writing it down. Psychoanalysis took a stab at organizing sex and madness. Historians had a special responsibility for organizing the passage of time (they

wrote it down), while politicians, soldiers, and journalists set
about organizing the distribution of power and land.

I don't know when Europeans began regularly to think of
themselves as white. Obviously it happened after they realized
not everyone was as pale as they were. In any case, Gauls,
Angles, Norse, and Lapps eventually determined their shared
whiteness to be a newly significant common bond. Whiteness
was a crucial conceit of civilization; with anthropology, it
crossed over into science. People spoke about science and
civilization and believed in them, though they existed largely
on paper. It's amazing the amount of time and energy that
white, civilized people have spent on figuring out just how
uncivilized everyone else is.

The effort continues today, despite the temporary reversals
of the 1960s, but I think the odds against its success are increasing. Modern civilization isn't what it used to be, and
many of its guardians are indeed shaken by "epistemological
hypochondria." As civilization goes, so goes uncivilization.
New ways must be found of approaching the subject—new
ways of travel writing, of foreign journalism, of anthropology.
This book is intended as an effort in that direction.

A trip to the Pacific islands seemed to me a natural choice.
Over the years, modern, Western civilization has found the
islands to be useful sources of material with which to construct
its own image. Above all, the islands have offered something
close to the State of Nature, that is, the paradise of nonciviliza-
tion (or, as Club Med puts it, "the antidote for civilization").
And there in the State of Nature resided the Noble Savage—
in Samoa for Margaret Mead, in Tahiti for Gauguin and for
Rodgers and Hammerstein—a median figure suspended, geographically and in the imagination, between Africa and Civilization. The islands have been both a provider of pleasant
white myths and a playground for the symptoms of unpleasant
ones: sanguinary wars were fought there, nuclear devices are
still tested among the palms and beaches, geopolitical dramas
are played out (many Pacific islands remain colonies or quasi-
colonies), and the mysterious god of economic development
receives its offerings.

I wondered if, beyond the dreams and depredations of civilization, I might find other things in these islands. Not necessarily antidotes for civilization, but other ways of being. I took my obsessions along, obsessions with race, nationalism, economics, sex. Questions of identity, really. You could say I went to places long considered pre-civilized to find a bit of what post-civilized life might be like.

AMERICA
AT SEA

■ *"It is an irony of history," former U.S. ambassador to the United Nations Donald McHenry wrote in 1975, "that in its foreign policy on dependent territories, the United States was one of the foremost advocates of decolonization and international oversight, except for the small dependent island areas of its own responsibility." He was referring to Micronesia, a vast area of about three million square miles between Hawaii and the Philippines. The 2,142 islands of Micronesia, with a total land area of approximately 900 square miles, were taken from Japan by the United States in the course of World War II. After the war, many Americans advocated annexation. Louisiana Congressman F. Edward Hébert said in 1945, "We fought for them, we've got them, we should keep them. They are necessary to our safety."*

It is a great challenge now to understand the American conception, in 1945, of safety. Although their nation was by far

*the most formidable in the world, many Americans neverthe-
less regarded the future with an obsessive fear. Having tri-
umphed in one great conflict, they were bent on fighting another. By April 1950, U.S. State Department planner Paul
Nitze, in laying down policy for the Cold War, noted that it
"is in fact a real war." That same year the U.S. Joint Chiefs
of Staff, reporting on their country's global position, complained that "Everywhere is weakness." Nuclear weapons
were considered both a cure for weakness and a guarantor of
safety. Unfortunately, they were not, in themselves, safe; as the
U.S. Atomic Energy Commission explained (though not until
1953), "The Commission felt that the [nuclear] tests should be
held overseas until it could be established more definitely that
continental detonations would not endanger the public health
and safety." Here "safety" meant American safety, and "overseas" meant Micronesia.*

*Pursuing its own security, the U.S. had determined to re-
tain control over Micronesia, and does so to this day. With the
exception of Guam, already a U.S. territory, Micronesia was
formed into a "strategic trust territory" in 1947, to be administered by the U.S. on behalf of the United Nations. Beginning with the Northern Mariana Islands in 1978, the Trust
Territory has become divided into quasi-mini-states—
"quasi" because none is really independent of the U.S.,
economically, politically, or culturally; "mini" because the
largest, the Federated States of Micronesia, with forty-one
inhabited islands, has a population of less than 100,000.*

*By UN standards, independence should have been an op-
tion for the Micronesian peoples. But as U.S. ambassador
Warren Austin explained while negotiating the 1947 Trust
Territory agreement, "The United States feels that it must
record its opposition, not to the principle of independence, to
which no people could be more consecrated than the people of
the United States, but to the thought that it could possibly be
achieved within any foreseeable future in this case." The late*

*1940s was a period when American policymakers felt they had
a solid grasp on what "any foreseeable future" might be.
Probably that attitude has changed somewhat since then.
From a Micronesian point of view, however, the basic nature
of American control has changed very little. Micronesia's strategic value, real or imagined, is the main reason that the U.S.
has been willing to pump money into the islands rather than
abandon them. Micronesia's elites have been happy, for the
most part, to cut such a deal, finding it better to take the
money than not. One wonders whether, in the years to come,
America's notion of its own safety will no longer include funding quasi-colonies in the middle of the Pacific.*

*Meanwhile, Micronesians are trying to mold themselves
into "modern" people living in "nations" that have an "identity." Yet many aspects of traditional culture survive, surging
up from a half-remembered past, jostling the conventions of
contemporary nationhood. American congressman Thomas S.
Foley, visiting Micronesia in 1969, said memorably, "Traditional culture violates almost every principle the American
people have ever known." But then, U.S. policy in the islands
has also violated just about every American principle, as well
as mangling the seemingly straightforward concept of
"safety."*

Palau

Palau, with 14,000 people spread over about thirteen inhabited islands, is both the smallest Trust Territory subdivision
and the only one to retain an ill-defined relationship with the
U.S. The State and Defense departments want Palau to be a
"freely associated state," that is, to accept a semi-sovereignty
in which the U.S. would keep control over Palau's defense. A
Compact of Free Association has been presented to Palauan
voters numerous times since 1983—and never approved. The
legal history of these votes (plebiscites, referenda) is extremely
complex. The main issue that has gradually emerged is the
antinuclear clause in Palau's constitution. The U.S. wants
this clause removed so that its nuclear ships might have right
of passage through Palau; it also wants to preserve Palau as
a fallback position if the Philippines were one day to cancel
leases on the huge U.S. bases there. However, the Palauan
constitution requires a 75 percent favorable vote to eliminate

the antinuclear clause, and neither the pro-Compact Palauan government nor the U.S. has convinced 75 percent of Palauans to vote its way. The primary Compact opponents have been opposition politicians, a few antinuke activists, and Palau's matriarchs, whose traditional power is based on controlling the disposition of land—land that the U.S. wants. Palau remains in political limbo. Meanwhile, corruption, traditional rivalry, and economic stagnation have made political violence a regular feature of Palauan life.

■ When George Shultz, then the U.S. secretary of state, visited Palau in 1986, great preparations were made to greet him. Shultz was the highest U.S. official ever to visit Palau. An official brass band was organized and made to practice; various Palauan customs were remembered and reshaped; groups of women prepared dances of welcome. Everyone gathered at the airport. "There was a great sense of expectation," a Palauan friend told me. "But minutes before the plane was supposed to arrive the sky darkened, clouds gathered. A strong wind blew the hats off people's heads. Everyone had to scramble. It started to rain very heavily. People believed all this was a *sign.* Palauans take these things very seriously."

My own arrival in Palau, by contrast, was smooth. I took a taxi into the capital, Koror, because Palau effectively has no public transport. The driver said, "All the politicians are corrupt," and offered to provide me with marijuana. He used to deal drugs, he said, to a young Australian woman who had lived here for several months. She eventually left because one day several young men, who had seen her sunbathing near a local bar, went to her apartment, broke down the door with an axe, and raped and mutilated her.

The driver deposited me at a seedy hotel near a dock. There were two seedy hotels in Koror and three nice ones. The other seedy hotel was considered the stronghold of Koror thugs and supporters of Palau's president, Lazarus Salii. Almost every hotel, restaurant, and bar in Koror was associated with one of

Palau's violent political factions. So I felt lucky to have found
an apolitical hotel.

■ Try to imagine a hot and humid country of 14,000 people
with its own particular language and customs. Add several
layers of colonialism (Spanish, British, and German in the last
century, Japanese and American in this), plus the aspirations
and bureaucratic appurtenances of constitutional democratic
government. Mix in tourists, a large dollop of Cold War geopolitics, Japanese economic expansion, assorted small- and big-
time American mercantile riffraff, illegal drugs and firearms—and you have Palau, whose slight international
notoriety comes from its problematic relationship with the
United States. Like most of Palau's episodes with foreign powers, that relationship was born in pain. The battle for Peleliu,
an island south of Koror, in September 1944 claimed the lives
of some 11,000 Japanese, 1,864 Americans, and 526 Palauans
(10 percent of the Palauan population at that time).

Not an auspicious beginning, but an appropriate one. For
the type of technologically advanced destruction pioneered in
World War II and displayed at Peleliu must have been utterly
mysterious to the Palauans. And so must be the nature of
nuclear weaponry: the immediate devastation is, perhaps, almost comprehensible; but the stealthy murders by radiation,
how can one understand them? Palauans know something
about inexplicable torments, having received them as imports
for over a century—first from the Spanish and British, then
from the Germans, the Japanese after 1914, and the Americans. Each successive invader brought larger guns. But there
is, of course, something different about the particular terror of
radiation.

In any event, Palau's stand on nuclear weapons became a
cause célèbre for the international antinuclear movement,
David battling an American Goliath. I came to Palau with the
briefings and arguments of stateside activists fresh in my head,
but after a few days I despaired of finding many Palauans who

actually cared about nuclear issues. I tried to interview matriarchs but failed. Apparently they weren't the sort of people
who talk to journalists; almost none of them, I was told, spoke
English; and the risks to them of public speaking were apparent. The home of the most prominent anti-Compact matriarch,
Gabriela Ngirmang, had been firebombed a year before.

I'd actually heard Ngirmang speak in New York, months
earlier. A small, thin, stern old woman, she'd sat patiently
while various activists detailed the Palau struggle and its importance in the battle for a nuclear-free Pacific. Finally Ngirmang stood and spoke, through an interpreter, about land—
how the U.S. wanted to take it and she and the other women
leaders were determined not to let them (the Pentagon has
drawn up plans for turning most of Babeldoab, Palau's largest
island, into a military base). Ngirmang didn't say anything
about nuclear weapons. In Palau I asked several people why
this was, and they all gave me the same response: the matriarchs' power is based on controlling the use and inheritance
of land, and it is land that they will defend. The social system
that gives them influence was based on agriculture; today most
Palauans work for the state government—a government run
entirely by men—so control over land is less important and the
matriarchs' position is threatened. For them, the possibility of
a U.S. land-grab simply made a deteriorating situation intoler-
able.

One afternoon I met with Palau's leading antinuclear activist, Roman Bedor, outside his modest house near Koror. We
sat on a log and drank the juice from coconuts. His house was
set back from the road and surrounded by palms and tropical
undergrowth; the waning day brought a cool breeze. A New
York activist had told me Roman Bedor was "the last principled man in Palau," which may account for his being such a
lonely figure in his own country. Big, amiable, and soft-
spoken, Bedor seemed like a courageous man who had been
forced by events to turn his courage inward. The previous
year his father had been shot dead a few yards away with two
bullets probably intended for Roman—a case never solved
and, by the time I arrived, no longer under investigation.

"The Compact will be passed, sooner or later," he sighed.
Bedor painted a picture more complicated than the one I'd
received back home. Palau's constitution, he said, was not (as
advertised abroad) the first in the world to have an antinuke
clause—the Federated States of Micronesia (FSM), of which
Palau was initially a part, had had a similar clause. In fact, that
section was written by Palauans, including Lazarus Salii, who
now, as president, was working feverishly to get his country's
own antinuke clause eliminated. And Palauan politician and
businessman Roman Tmetuchl (muh-*tool*), who was once a
key opponent of the FSM's antinuclear section, was now
fiercely fighting the free-association Compact and President
Salii—and had become, in his own way, antinuclear.

So Salii and Tmetuchl, Palau's most powerful politicians,
had both played both sides of the nuclear fence. Salii had spent
years as Palau's chief negotiator with the U.S. and was perceived as Washington's friend. Chubby and phlegmatic, he
was an inside man, at home in the clubby ambience of decision
making, the conference rooms and hotel bars. Tmetuchl was
more like a pit bull, trim and agile despite being in his sixties;
conversations with him always felt like debates. As a young
man he'd been the interlocutor between Palauans and their
Japanese rulers. He still speaks better Japanese than English.

Bedor described Palauan politics as if it were ancient history. Perhaps he *was* the last principled man in his country. A
child came out to refresh our coconuts but Bedor looked tired
so I said goodbye. I walked along a path among palms and
pandanus. The sun was lowering and I felt slightly afraid. It
was hard to believe so much violence and deceit could occur
in such a small place. Roman Tmetuchl once told me, in a
humorous, anecdotal way, about the time four political com-
petitors, allegedly led by a noted Salii ally, tried to assassinate
him in the late 1970s. One of them had walked up to Tmetuchl's house and asked to see him. A relative went to Tmetuchl's bedroom and announced the visitor. Tmetuchl happened to have a carbine next to his bed—"It was an old gun,
but a good gun," he told me—so he came out of his bedroom
carbine-first and the assassin fled. Tmetuchl ran into the road

and traded shots with the four would-be killers. No one hit much of anything; it was, of course, quite dark.

I heard this story from several people, and everyone agreed on the details, including the identities of the four men who tried to kill him. In another country one might think the police would be involved in an event like this. But Tmetuchl says there was "no reason" to prosecute the assassins, two of whom I saw regularly on the semi-paved, ugly streets of Koror.

The attempt on Tmetuchl was only one of many such incidents, and Roman Bedor's father was not the first or the last Palauan to die for political reasons. Back in the U.S., I had thought this violence was connected to antinuclear idealism; yet most of the Palauans I met seemed more preoccupied with power, money, and the disintegration of their society. So I decided to pursue these issues, and ended up investigating a murder.

■ One evening I had dinner at the home of Johnson Toribiong. Johnson is a Palauan lawyer and has done well for himself; his modern, well-appointed house sits high above Koror and looks across a broad, placid bay to the green slopes of Babeldoab. We sat down in the living room while his wife, Valeria, and their maid prepared dinner. Johnson went over to the TV and sifted through his videotapes. "You should see this video," he said. We settled back on the couches and sipped white wine. On the screen were Palauans dancing and singing, sober dignitaries from small countries walking diplomatically, and, finally, a man of unremarkable appearance approaching a microphone. It was Haruo Remeliik, Palau's first president, at his inauguration in 1981. Johnson moved close to the TV, as if to place himself in the image. "Look at his shoulders," he said. "Look at how he's standing. He knew what was coming, he knew he had to carry a heavy weight. See how he holds his shoulders, like there's something holding him down."

Some four years after the inauguration, at 12:30 A.M., June 30, 1985, Remeliik was killed by four bullets—one in the leg, one in the neck, and two in the head. His body tumbled from the front yard of his house down into a ravine. The moon had been an unusual color the night before, which, according to one Palauan I met, indicated that someone important was about to die. The night of the killing, Palau's few dozen police officers were having a party, and so they were less than pristine upon reaching Remeliik's house. An American law-enforcement trainer, William Stinnett, happened to be in town and took charge of the investigation, which would go on to take a number of bizarre turns.

Two FBI agents joined Stinnett—none of the three spoke Palauan—and together with Palauan police they interviewed an assortment of witnesses. Things moved slowly until two Palauan politicians, Hokkons Baules and Frank Asanuma, produced a young woman of their acquaintance, a heroin user named Mystica Maidesil. Under questioning she named four young men whom she claimed she had overheard discussing the killing. These four men were then charged with murder. Four days later, Maidesil, according to an FBI report, failed a polygraph test and "confessed that she had fabricated her entire account. . . . She acknowledged that she has no idea who actually shot President Remeliik." The charges were dropped.

Maidesil was shipped here and there—Guam, Honolulu, Oregon—and interviewed further by federal agents. Eventually, according to an FBI report, Maidesil stated that "she had made up all the details in her statements because of pressures of continued police questioning and because she wanted to satisfy investigators so that they would leave her alone." Such admissions did not deter the investigators, however, who continued to focus on the four young men and, in November 1985, reinstated charges against three of them—though not, for some reason, against the fourth, who Maidesil originally had said was the actual killer. The murder weapon was never found, nor any other material evidence, nor any direct witnesses to the killing. One person did manage to pick out one of the men from a lineup, saying she had seen him near the murder site that night. The three accused were also linked to two cars—a four-by-four pickup and a black sedan—that had

appeared near the scene of the crime. As a result, they were
charged with assassinating the president and convicted by a
three-judge panel. There was no jury. One of the judges was
a proper judge, the other two were civilians appointed by
Remeliik's successor, Lazarus Salii. The conviction was later
overturned because of insufficient evidence. Mystica Maidesil
was given U.S. working papers and moved to Oregon.

It happened that Maidesil's promoters, Frank Asanuma and
Hokkons Baules, were close political associates of the wily
Lazarus Salii. Salii and Roman Tmetuchl were the main rivals
for the presidency until Mystica Maidesil began her allegations. One of the four men she named was Tmetuchl's son
Melwert, another was Tmetuchl's nephew Leslie Tewid. This
pretty much destroyed Tmetuchl's chances of becoming president; Salii won; and the assassination of President Remeliik
was never solved.

■ To say that Palau degenerated into violence after Remeliik's death would be an understatement. The conflict over
approving the Compact escalated, by 1987, into virtual civil
war. Most of the firebombings, shootings, and other acts of
intimidation were carried out by the rougher portion of
Palau's civil service. President Salii furloughed hundreds
of government workers in the spring of 1987, saying that until
the free-association Compact passed there would be no money
to pay salaries. The angry workers then camped out in front
of Palau's legislature to pressure anti-Compact politicians to
change their positions, giving life in Koror a general feeling
of besiegement. Behind the scenes, Salii's administration was
funding the group—$100,000 went to its leader—and provid-
ing government vehicles when the furloughed workers
needed transport to deliver firebombs or threats.

The simplest and most common explanation for all this is
that the Salii government has been basically a criminal syndi-
cate, involved in every conceivable illicit activity and manipulated by the U.S. government. When Remeliik was still president, he, along with members of the Salii group, negotiated

with International Power Systems Company Ltd. (IPSECO), a British firm, to build a $27.5 million power plant and fuel storage facility. Palau secured $32.5 million from two British banks—National Westminster and County Bank of London—to cover the expenditure plus bank fees and the cost of delayed interest payments. The obvious question was: Where does a nation of 14,000 get $32.5 million, that is, more than twice its annual budget? And the equally obvious answer was: the United States. The U.S. State Department provided crucial support in closing the deal, assuring National Westminster in a confidential cable that money would be available. Once the power-plant deal was signed, in May 1983, the pressure on Palau to pass a Compact of free association, and get the hundreds of millions of dollars that would supposedly go to economic development, became severe.

According to two people close to Remeliik—and only two that I know of—the president, just before his murder, was planning to go on television and reveal the corruption and misjudgment behind the power-plant negotiations (IPSECO paid hundreds of thousands of dollars in gratuities to Salii and his comrades). The conclusion often drawn is that those associated with the deal, all Salii cronies, were also behind the assassination.

Consequently I approached the offices of the president—a small and unimpressive collection of one-story buildings atop a low ridge outside Koror—with some concern. The idea of a country with few people, lots of guns, and no apparent laws was unnerving. Over several evenings I'd been reading a book called *Shakespearean Negotiations* to take my mind off Palau, and this had the perverse effect of making Palau's situation seem reminiscent of *Macbeth*. There was something vaguely medieval about the place: a ruling elite, their arms drenched in the blood of their forefathers and friends, huddling together against the ghosts they know will one day reach out for them.

At the president's office I got as far as his secretary. Apparently she had met journalists before, since her first move was to remove all the papers from her desk. (I had, in fairness, begun reading them as we talked.) She promised to tell the president I had come by, then referred me to Bonifacio Basilius, Salii's representative. Basilius was at that moment in conference with a dozen or so men, some of whom I recognized. They were the core of the Salii group; when Basilius emerged he told me they were holding yet another meeting on how to convince Palauans to pass the free-association Compact. They didn't look pleased to have a visitor.

Basilius was optimistic about the Compact eventually passing and the nation receiving a great deal of money. He took me into his little office, offered a cigarette, and complained about how the international press had been unkind to Palau. He compared it with the Israeli situation, in which far too much attention had been given to the Palestinians (Palau receives some American TV news programs). He said the real problem in his country was dengue fever, a malady, transmitted by mosquitoes, that had already claimed the lives of three Palauans.

Then he explained, without any prompting, that in Palau there are two systems of authority—traditional and, for lack of a better word, modern. "The dual system exists everywhere, even in the villages. Politics on the American model is a very new thing for us." Basilius said there are two main chiefs, the *reklai*, or northern chief, and the *ibedul*, based in Koror and roughly associated with the south. They are nominated by committees of matriarchs, who also nominate the lesser chiefs below the *reklai* and *ibedul* and have the power to remove unsatisfactory leaders. The success of Haruo Remeliik and Lazarus Salii resulted, Basilius said, from their not being tied to either clan. "Culturally, they are no threat to anyone. Haruo played it to the hilt."

Clearly Haruo Remeliik had played *something* to the hilt. Basilius seemed to be trying to communicate some idea of what it was. "The competitiveness of the traditional system ensures good leaders," he said. I mentioned Remeliik's murder and he smiled faintly. "Over twenty-three generations, more than half of the *reklais* died of unnatural causes." I smiled back as if I knew what he was talking about. Basilius finished by saying that U.S. colonialism (his word) had been good for Palau because it introduced the concepts of equality and the right to self-government.

Fortunately a young man named Beketel was hanging around the president's office and offered to drive me the mile back to Koror. Beketel, young and energetic, was Palau's most important journalist, writing articles for the government newsletter; there are no other newspapers or magazines in Palau. We drove along and he said that he'd written the propaganda for Black September (more Middle East echoes), a radical group that had helped run the civil service insurrection in 1987. He apologized for writing things that he didn't believe. I said it was okay, it happens all the time. He seemed genuinely remorseful about it. Beketel dropped me off on Koror's main street then drove toward the jail, where he'd been living since he stabbed an opposition politician a few months before.

■ "In general there are no secrets in Palau," Phil Isaac, Palau's attorney general, said confidently. Many Palauans had told me the same thing, though no one ever said directly who they thought had killed Remeliik. Isaac had been the prosecuting attorney against the three men charged with murdering the president. When the conviction was overturned, one judge went out of his way to criticize the prosecution, and Isaac was bitter about it. He said being the attorney general in Palau was "a real challenge." Drug-law enforcement is difficult, for example, because there are no customs agents, and corruption is hard to fight because there is, effectively, no public auditor and no effort made to determine the legality of contracts. I admitted that I'd spent a day reading through a pile of construction contracts and the relevant laws and, as far as I could tell, every one of the contracts was illegal. (Basically, Palauan law requires the legislature to approve contracts that involve expenditure of government funds. The contracts I saw, for roads and other public works, had the anticipated arrival of free-association Compact money as their written or unwritten premise; no other source of payment existed. Thus state money had been committed without proper government approval.)

I mentioned I was curious about who had killed President Remeliik, and Isaac, though he believed the evidence pointed to the three men, generously allowed me to read through the original police interviews and various other papers. I was struck by a certain coincidence. The two automobiles that had been the decisive evidence in convicting the three men corresponded, in the original descriptions by witnesses, to two automobiles that were said to have been owned or rented by Hokkons Baules, the pro-Salii politician, and Hitler Demei, a local convicted felon (assault with a deadly weapon) and friend of Baules. Isaac said that Demei was a small-time drug dealer; Baules, of course, had helped promote Mystica Maidesil as a witness. He had since become a senator, chairing the Committee on Foreign Affairs.

The first few times I saw Baules and Hitler (as everyone calls him) they were at the Nikko, a lovely Japanese-owned hotel tucked into tropical growth on a hillside near Koror. The Nikko overlooks the Rock Islands, curious mushrooms of limestone and jungle that dot the waters to the west of Koror. Sitting at the Nikko, breathing in the scent of frangipani, I wished I had come to dive among the coral gardens rather than investigate politics, murder, and drug dealing. Koror itself is a painfully unattractive town, its cheap-American-suburbia look relieved only by the occasional bunkerlike Japanese holdover; U.S. State Department wits used to call Koror "the Zoo." More than half of Palau's population lives there, most in near-poverty. The few who live in comfort are usually connected to the government. Palau's biggest exports are marijuana, stamps (to collectors), and fish. Apart from these, people make money by more or less fleecing Japanese investors—who willingly pour excess yen into Micronesia—and working for the government, which employs the vast majority of Palauan wage earners.

One morning at the Nikko I screwed up my courage and asked Hitler if he had killed Remeliik. A large, unfit man with

a wispy beard and easygoing manner, Hitler seemed unsur-
prised by the question. He said he didn't do it. I asked why
he thought some people blamed him and he said, "Maybe it's
because of my name," and smiled. We talked about the black
sedan he'd rented at the time of the murder, which answered
to witnesses' descriptions. He said a friend, Silas Orrukem,
had borrowed it that night. Hitler said he had himself stayed
home to drink beer and watch TV, and Silas had returned
"after the television was over," that is, after the last programs
at eleven o'clock. I told him that the attorney general had said
he was a drug dealer and Hitler, looking hurt, denied it.

Some days later Senator Hokkons Baules agreed to an interview. A forbidding, powerfully built man, he wore his trademark: a short-sleeved, fatigue-green U.S. Army surplus shirt.
I asked him about the attorney general's remark that he was
a drug user; he said it wasn't true, and maybe people were
confusing him with his brother. I didn't know the Palauan
language and Senator Baules's English wasn't too good, so he
had to concentrate hard on each question. His answers were
short. We talked for half an hour about Remeliik's assassination, focusing on where Baules was and what he'd been driving. He said he'd been tooling around in a pickup with his
wife until midnight or so. At 12:15, he said, he called the
police ("I heard something had happened") and was told
about the assassination. (Remeliik wasn't killed until 12:30,
but the time confusion may have just been faulty memory.)
Later in our interview, Baules amended his remarks and said
that he had actually been out with friends at a club, and drove
a silver sedan. He said he didn't think the three accused were
guilty, adding, "There is no evidence."

We were sitting in a Japanese restaurant in Koror and somehow the theme from Carol Reed's *The Third Man* was playing
on the stereo, which made it hard for me not to laugh. I saw
Joseph Cotten's innocent and tragic face, and Orson Welles's
shadow running along the crumbling walls of postwar Vienna.
Then Baules once again had second thoughts (or would they
be "third thoughts"?) and said he had never owned a silver
sedan and that "everyone" thinks the three are guilty. "Haruo

Remeliik was not a man who worried a lot," Baules said. "He was the most relaxed leader. Maybe that's why he was killed. Maybe that was why."

■ After interviewing Baules and Hitler I found myself growing more and more anxious. Through a series of coincidences I'd managed to secure an apartment owned by the *ibedul*. People told me I'd be safe there because everyone would think I was under the *ibedul*'s protection. Nevertheless, I slipped into a pattern of drinking beer in the evenings, rather a lot of beer, to put myself to sleep. I'd lie at night sweating into the sheets and thinking fuzzily about the apartment door, the windows, and bullet trajectories. I tended to rise early, go to a cafe frequented by the anti-Salii opposition, and drink four or five cups of coffee—partly to offset the beer, partly because I wanted very much to be alert. Days and days of this made me jittery; I was the only journalist in Palau (except for the knife-wielding Beketel), which didn't ease matters.

The murder case was becoming both clearer and more vague. I spoke about it with almost everyone I met. I got lost in a forest of imprecations and dark hints. Various Palauans slipped anonymous notes to me, little morsels of obscurity. So-and-so had seen this car at this corner that night; I heard rumors of Filipino assassins, drug money, the CIA, missing flight manifests, missing phone logs, snippets of overheard conversations twice removed. An Australian pilot and gunrunner named Gary Camm loomed in and out of the picture, as did the shadowy Mike Merando, an Italian-American from Ohio who'd served as Salii's "special assistant." (Merando has been named by two American businessmen as having solicited bribes from them; the bribes weren't paid, and the projects didn't go through.) One Palauan involved in the original investigation told me, whispering in the shadows of his own living room, that initially the evidence had led in the direction of government officials, but his boss told him to concentrate on the three suspects instead. Another Palauan told me, in the even dimmer shadows of an especially sleazy bar, that he had been the first person to arrive at the crime scene, was never interviewed by police, and knew that people in the government were involved.

And yet he, like everyone else, was not prepared to say who, exactly, was guilty. Late one afternoon I sat with Johnson Toribiong at a cafe. It was nearly six, and we were starting in on our late-afternoon beers. I told him how strange it was to be in a country that seemed entirely populated by anonymous sources, sources who appeared to know everything and revealed quite a bit less. Johnson was himself one of those sources, so the question was obliquely pointed. "Palauans will always tell you what you want to hear," he said. "They don't hesitate to lie." Johnson and I stared into each other's eyes for what seemed a long time. "Knowledge is power," he said, faintly but with conviction.

■ By chance, Janet McCoy, the former U.S. Trust Territory head and now an Interior Department adviser with responsibility for Micronesia, stopped by Palau while I was there. I was talking to Santos Olikong, speaker of Palau's House of Delegates, in his office when she arrived, along with a U.S. State Department representative and an Interior Department underling. The House of Delegates was in the process of impeaching President Salii's brother, Carlos, a congressman, former House speaker, and head of the Palauan Bar Association, who had received $250,000 from IPSECO. McCoy had flown in to fix things, Carlos being an important pro-Compact ally of the U.S. The three Americans closeted themselves with Olikong; I lounged on a porch outside with the janitors. Eventually the three emerged and I asked if I could take a picture. McCoy gave me that look you find at dinner parties when someone wants to stick a fork in your hand. She said I could photograph her but not the State Department representative or his Interior Department companion. The two of them scurried behind a pillar while I took the picture, in which she just managed to smile. I wondered what the janitors made of seeing two Americans hiding behind a pillar at the House of

Delegates, called the Olbiil Era Kelulau (House of Whispers) in Palauan. As for me, I couldn't explain it.

McCoy had flown in on a military plane with an admiral and his staff. They were ensconced at the Palau Pacific resort outside Koror, taking advantage of a special U.S. government employees' discount. Also in town was William Stinnett, who had headed the Remeliik investigation. That evening I took a taxi out to the resort, hoping to interview Stinnett, McCoy, and anyone else who was willing. The resort was beautiful, gently landscaped, with bungalows nestled here and there in a well-maintained tropical garden. A small road with speed bumps meandered about the grounds and up to the main entrance, which was decorated with sundry, semi-authentic indigenous symbols and tastefully sprinkled with wicker peacock chairs. Banks of ceiling fans turned slowly. Beyond the lobby was a nice restaurant overlooking a large swimming pool where tourists were disporting themselves happily; the pool, in turn, gave onto a gorgeous white-sand beach, monitored by Palauan employees who assiduously picked up the leavings of the hotel's clients.

Happy hour arrived and I met Stinnett in the lobby. He was a handsome and fit man, deeply tanned, exuding a confident smoothness. Unfortunately, Stinnett said, he had spoken to McCoy and she had told him not to talk to me. All he would say was that he knew a lot about the murder but couldn't reveal it, and doubted that he ever would. "Who knows," he said, walking off, "maybe I'll write a book someday." McCoy passed by with the admiral on their way to dinner.

Feeling snubbed, I rode back into Koror and meditated on what little I had learned. Here was a man, William Stinnett, who was in charge of training police officers all over Micronesia, and who had been a central figure in investigating the assassination of a president—by far the most serious crime in Trust Territory history, still unsolved. And this man was telling me that he knew a lot about it but would never reveal anything. What's more, there was a full coterie of high-level U.S. military and executive-branch types on a semisecret jaunt

to this tiny nation of shadows and none of them would talk.
My anxiety was not lessening.

■ I decided to visit Joel Toribiong. Joel is Johnson Toribiong's brother and was raised by Roman Tmetuchl. At the
house Joel was watching TV with Leslie Tewid, Tmetuchl's
nephew and one of the three acquitted of killing Remeliik.
Joel introduced me to Tewid, who seemed very much like a
timid and angry young man trying to besot himself with television. Two weeks earlier I would have been surprised to find
Tewid, who is presumably part of the anti-Compact crowd, at
the home of a rather notorious pro-Compact activist. Now it
appeared almost natural. Joel and I went out on the porch to
talk. Night had fallen and the damp undergrowth rustled and
thumped under a light breeze.

Joel was a bit jumpy; I don't think he had spoken to many
journalists. He'd been convicted, a month or two before, for
shooting at House speaker Santos Olikong's house. He was
also suspected of being an accessory to the murder of Roman
Bedor's father. Joel had been a leader of the civil service
rebels in 1987; he'd helped found Black September, which
went on to burn the property of Compact opponents, write
anonymous threatening letters, and experiment with various
forms of propaganda. I didn't question Joel about his participa-
tion in these activities, since he was perfectly willing to admit
he was a "mob leader." We did discuss what really irritated
him, namely that foreigners—particularly the environmental
organization Greenpeace, which has actively fought the Compact and aided the Palauan opposition—didn't understand
what it was *like* to be a mob leader.

"You're standing up there, trying to figure out what to do
next, and the workers are saying, 'We need money!' and someone will shout, 'Let's go to the Ministry of Finance, there's
money over there!' And what am I supposed to do? Tell them
they can't go? Greenpeace calls me a mob ruler. They don't
know what a mob ruler is."

There was something about the rough democracy of the

44
■
insurrection that Joel liked. He thinks the future of Palau lies
with democracy; the traditional system is wearing away, the
chiefs and matriarchs are losing their grip. "Young Palauans"—though Joel's past thirty, he spends most of his time
with young people—"have a live-and-let-die attitude. There's
nothing to work *for*. Why work? They see that a few politicians make money fast, and the rest scrape along. The elite is
up above, playing politics. But the society doesn't get *moving*."

Joel has a vision of Palau's future: more hotels will go up;
Filipinos, Japanese, and Chinese will get the good jobs and
many of the bad ones; Palauans will be left with menial work,
pushing paper in government offices or making storyboards in
prison. Storyboards are wooden tablets, usually the size of
large serving trays; their images of people, animals, and plants,
carved in relief, illustrate putatively authentic myths. They
were invented by a Japanese folklorist in the 1930s. It was a
clever marketing idea: storyboards are now sold as vestiges of
traditional Palau. Most of them are made by prisoners in the
Koror jail. "One day we're going to run out of boards," Joel
said. "Then they'll just put tattoos on a Palauan's back and
stand him up in front of the resort and say, 'See? Here's a
Palauan.' "

■ One afternoon I visited a Palauan doctor specializing in
mental illness. He said that schizophrenia, drug abuse, and
disabilities associated with neurosis have been increasing in
Palau since the mid-1980s. He attributed the situation to soci-
etal changes. Palau, he said, had gone from a productive society to a consumer society, one dependent on American money
rather than work. "We are depending much more on electricity than we used to depend on the sunlight. We used to be a
very communalistic society rather than individualistic. The
traditional power structure is deteriorating. When we wrote
our constitution, we systematically destroyed our traditional
system." As for drugs, he said that, generally speaking, the
police are seen as part of the business, and the borders are
completely porous.

Another prominent Palauan I spoke to—he also didn't want to be named—agreed that things were collapsing. "It used to be that you didn't see just one person, you saw all of them. Now people work for personal gain." The matriarchs and chiefs still exercised power but it was waning; together with many other Palauans, he confirmed that the matriarchs' reason for opposing the free-association Compact was not the antinuclear issue but a desire to protect their power over land—if (or when) the Compact passes, the U.S. will probably be able to take whatever land it wants. Also, most of the anti-Compact matriarchs are from southern Palau; if the Compact passes, development money will almost certainly go to the North, to the land of the *reklai*.

I talked for a while about secrets and how Palau seemed to have an astonishing number of them. He smiled. "Traditional power was based on having information. For example, the most important thing was land rights. The chiefs and matriarchs decided who got what on the basis of *knowledge*, knowledge that only they had. You have to remember that our system of land ownership is very complex. It is true that this knowledge, these histories, could be manipulated. But the point is that power was seen as a result of having information—and so the more secrets you have, the more powerful you are. Secrets have a special meaning for Palauans."

And when all you have left is secrets and nothing to give them meaning over time, no laws or viable traditions, I suppose what you get is paranoia.

President Lazarus Salii shot himself to death on August 20, 1988. Roman Tmetuchl contested the ensuing election and lost amid allegations of voting fraud. Ngiratkel Etpisan, an obscure politician from the Salii camp—and one loyal to the northern high chief, or reklai—*replaced Salii. The following year, on July 11, 1989, thirteen Palauans were arrested by U.S. agents for involvement in heroin and marijuana transshipment. Among them were former parliamentarians Frank Asanuma and Hokkons Baules, as well as Leslie Tewid and*

Melwert Tmetuchl, both of whom were acquitted in 1987 of President Remeliik's murder. Asanuma received a suspended sentence; the other three are now in prison. According to the original indictment, Melwert Tmetuchl was the "organizer" of the drug ring.

On February 6, 1990, a seventh plebiscite was held on the Compact of free association. The voter turnout of sixty-eight percent set a record low, as did the percentage of voters— fifty-nine—willing to support the Compact. At last count, four distinct proposals were circulating in Palau, each intended in its own way to break the impasse.

Guam

For the Pacific traveler Guam comes as a surprise, if not a shock. Traffic jams, high-rise hotels, good roads, military transport planes and bombers flying here and there. Some 20,000 U.S. military personnel and dependents live on Guam, an unincorporated U.S. territory; the remaining 110,000 residents are predominantly American, Filipino, Japanese, Chinese, and Chamorro. Chamorro is the name given to the original inhabitants of the Mariana Islands, of which Guam is the southernmost and, at 209 square miles, the largest; about 50 percent of the contemporary population are Chamorro. Ferdinand Magellan, who in 1521 was the first European to reach Guam, named it and the other Mariana Islands the Islas de los Ladrones (Islands of Thieves) because the Chamorros stole one of his boats. "Guam" comes from the Chamorro word guahan, "we have." These days the key question on Guam is to whom, exactly, that "we" refers.

■ I arrived in Guam's capital, Agaña, took a second-floor room in a cheap businessman's hotel, and slept for two days. The tensions of Palau had enervated me completely. I felt guilty about having slipped so quickly into fearfulness, and was comforted only by the idea that the Palauans seemed quite fearful themselves. Eventually I woke up, looked out the window, and saw a road, two garbage cans, and two palm trees, all bordering the placid harbor of Agaña. Next to the hotel was a Chinese-run restaurant called Uncle Sam's, which served middle-American staples and Chinese food. I wandered around Agaña to get a feel for the place. Between the hotel and downtown was a large shopping mall, one-story, air-conditioned, with piped-in music, precisely reminiscent of malls in the suburban American West. Downtown Agaña had a few medium-sized office buildings, notably the fifteen-story-or-so Pacific Daily News Building, which housed Micronesia's only daily newspaper—American-owned and -run, its politics nurtured by years of friendship with the U.S. military—and branches of the Federal Bureau of Investigation, the Drug Enforcement Agency, the U.S. Department of the Interior, and other foreign bodies. The roads and sidewalks were well lit and solidly constructed; there were law offices and doctors' offices and barbers. Between downtown and the harbor lay Guam's main highway, leading south to undeveloped highlands and north to Tumon Bay and a row of expensive tourist hotels. Cars zipped up and down, past bars and auto dealerships, giving an impression of great, if unfocused, activity, and of complete, unmitigated Americanness.

■ When Chamorros stole Ferdinand Magellan's skiff on March 6, 1521, Magellan, according to a crew member, "went on shore with forty armed men, burned forty or fifty houses and several boats, killed seven men of the island, and recovered the skiff. Before we had gone on shore, some of our sick men begged us that if we killed men or women, we should bring them their entrails so that the sick men would be cured." The writer doesn't say whether the entrails were brought, but in any case the sick men's request may have been the first suggestion of cannibalism on Guam.

For a century and a half Spanish culture and weaponry made no further contributions to Guam; galleons stopped only occasionally to reprovision on their way to the Philippines. However, in 1662 a young Jesuit, Diego Luis de Sanvitores, visited Guam and felt pity for the Chamorros. After several years of petitioning back home, he acquired approval and funding for a Guam mission. The Jesuit outpost, begun in 1668, was the first mission in Micronesia. According to a contemporary Spanish account, the mission started out well; Chamorros ran forward at the opportunity of receiving baptism. Two years later local attitudes had changed. Apparently a rumor had been circulating that baptismal water was poisonous; it seems likely that local leaders resented Spanish authority. Four years after founding the mission, Sanvitores was murdered by two Chamorros (he's now being considered for canonization). Killings of priests became a regular occurrence, as did massacres of Chamorros. Spanish-Chamorro conflict developed into a full-scale war. The last great anti-Spanish uprising began in 1684; by 1695, the few remaining rebels had been subdued, and the estimated pre-Spanish Chamorro population of 50,000 to 80,000 had been reduced to fewer than 5,000. According to official Spanish figures, the Chamorro population declined further to 1,639 by 1790, and to under 1,000 by 1825. Whatever Chamorro society and culture may have been—extremely little was recorded—they were now destroyed. The few surviving Chamorros, mostly women, children, and the elderly, were herded into camps.

Spain maintained this distant, not very useful colony until 1898, when Guam was ceded to the U.S. under the treaty that ended the brief Spanish-American War. U.S. Navy governors administered Guam until 1950, when President Harry Truman signed an Organic Act giving Guam residents some autonomy. Not until 1968 were they allowed to elect their own governor. Today Guam remains an "unincorporated territory" of the U.S., which means there is no presumption that it will eventually become a state. It also means that, according to Supreme Court decisions, the rights contained in the U.S. Constitution are only available selectively. Protests against the lack of self-government on Guam have been made since at least 1902. Now Guam has presented the U.S. Congress with a draft Commonwealth Act that calls for "Chamorro self-determination," a phrase not calculated to please American legislators. It may, they say, be *un-Constitutional,* a strange argument given that the Constitution is only applied to Guam when it's convenient.

■ I met up with a white American lawyer I'll call Tim at a bar run by an Asian woman named Tiger. She was at the door and told Tim he owed her ten bucks from his last visit, but he only remembered being very drunk. We sat at one end of the bar and Tim flirted with Marge, the Chamorro bartender, and Shin, a Palauan woman at the other end of the bar. Tim said Shin's boyfriend was up for fifteen years on a heroin-trafficking charge, and that she had slept with one of the FBI agents who investigated Remeliik's murder. At this moment she was surrounded by three white men. Behind us, a veteran FBI agent was pouring money into a slot machine and bourbon into himself. Tim said the agent was a big gambler and had gone into airline security because his FBI earnings weren't sufficient to support his habit. Tim also talked a bit about women. He said that, after he had slept with a nonwhite woman, he found white women cold and threatening. "Once you go brown you never go back," he said with a smile.

A second attorney, call him Pete, joined us and we went to Club Texas. Guam has an astonishing number of strip joints and grimy bars. As one academic writer put it, "The American military presence on Guam is, therefore, the crucial factor underlying economic and political considerations in the island's future." At Club Texas the dancers were white and the waitresses were Chamorro and Filipina. The dancers were pretty in a *Playboy* magazine kind of way, so I asked Tim what they were doing here. Surely they could make more money as wives or mistresses, and for less work? "I read somewhere

that girls like these usually hate themselves," Tim said. We
were in a booth, but most of the men were seated on stools
around the edge of the stage; two-thirds of them looked like
GI's (mostly white) and one-third were local men.

A woman in a long white dress danced to the Oak Ridge
Boys song "My Baby Is American-Made." Tim and Pete con-
versed about real estate and politics. Japanese investors are
willing to pay enormous sums for Guam real estate, Tim said.
In just a few years prices have gone from $1,000 per acre to
$15,000. One Japanese group is building condominiums, out-
side Agaña, with three-bedrooms going for $350,000. Local
wages, however, are generally lower than in the poorest of
mainland states (Mississippi). American expatriates are buying
heavily into real estate. Unfortunately for them, there are laws
prohibiting alienation of Micronesian land. One popular way
of circumventing these laws is to marry into the local blood-
line, so to speak, and trade land in your spouse's name. This
was Tim's strategy. "The idea is to sell as soon as the Japs hit
a limit. And if the Japanese economy fucks up, then let them
sort it out."

The political situation is similar. Since there is now some
presumption of Chamorro self-government, most Americans
exert their influence outside of office. The best way to do this
is with money. Judging from my conversations with Tim, Pete,
and other local professionals, corruption is the warp and woof
of Guam politics. They spoke easily of someone *owning* someone else.

Waitresses in scant clothing offered to sit with us if we paid
for their drinks. We declined and went to another bar, Sandy
You's, a cheaper place with more locals and fewer soldiers. A
white dancer was at one end of a long stage wrapping herself
in a feather boa. Three GI's called out, "We're from Washington, where're you from?"

"Kansas," the woman shouted with a smile.

"They're all from Kansas," Tim said.

As the young woman from Kansas started down the runway,
a soldier stretched himself across it, on his back, with a dollar
bill (or maybe it was a ten or a twenty) tightly rolled and

sticking up from his mouth. He was a huge, muscular man. The idea was that she should squat down and he would insert the money into her vagina. She stepped over him and continued dancing. Perhaps there was a rule against this sort of thing. The frustrated GI shouted, "Hey, I guess my money isn't good enough! Isn't my money as good as anyone else's?" He was laughing, and the bill unrolled in his mouth as he laughed.

Pete left; Tim and I went back to Tiger's and played pool. By this time we had drunk quite a lot. Tim was trying to schedule a rendezvous with Marge and not having much luck. He came back to the pool table, feeling confessional. Our conversation had that peculiar time-hopping, boozy logic. Tim said, "Times like this you wonder: What the fuck am I doing here? And why?" I couldn't answer either question. I tried to concentrate on the game, and kept thinking about the soldier with his rolled-up money, and *Once you go brown you never go back.*

■ While in Guam I spent a lot of time with Ron Rivera, head of the Organization of People for Indigenous Rights, which has been the primary group responsible for the cultivation and flowering of Chamorro consciousness—the source of the proposed Commonwealth Act's "Chamorro self-determination" clause. We first met at Uncle Sam's restaurant, along with another, better-educated Chamorro activist. Ron had been quiet during that first meeting, when we discussed the basics of the Chamorro rights movement. I tried to draw him out but he just sat there, a somewhat squat man in his thirties, mustachioed, partially hidden beneath a wide-brimmed straw hat, giving the impression of someone who is thinking rather than talking and prefers to release words when he believes you're ready for them. So I kept telephoning, trying to get him to come out for a drink or something, trying to get him to talk. We met two more times, but always with others around, and Ron kept to himself.

Eventually he suggested we go for a tour of the island. We

drove through Agaña, past the governor's mansion, and south to Cetti Bay, where there was a lookout point. Steep cliffs dropped below us, and beyond them the sea, swelling and heaving in a bright afternoon light. Most of this area, he said, was being sold to developers. Right now it was empty and beautiful. Steep brushland rose behind us to the 1,332-foot summit of Mount Lamlam, Guam's highest point. We got back into the car and drove up the west coast, past a saltwater grotto where Chamorro children were playing, to Umatac. This was where Ron's mother lived, and where Magellan first landed. Umatac was a small and placid village of solid one- and two-story homes. We bought cans of beer at a grocery and gazed out over the tiny bay. It was difficult to imagine Magellan landing 400 years earlier in his galleons, the *Trinidad*, the *Victoria*, and the *Concepción* (not to mention the contested skiff). All we saw on the bay was a Chamorro boy bailing water from a half-submerged dinghy.

The road north of Umatac hugged the coastline, shielded from the water by palms and thick tropical undergrowth. By this time Ron knew the question I wanted him to answer: What is a Chamorro? The apparent facts of "ethnic identity" were obvious but, from an "authenticity" point of view, unfavorable. The Chamorros had been effectively wiped out 400 years ago. There were precious few traces left of Chamorro culture, save for the language, the roots of which are not very clear. Those 800 or so Chamorros still alive in 1825 had intermarried with the Spanish and Filipinos (Filipinos served as an imported buffer group between the Chamorros and the Spanish). I told Ron what an elderly Chamorro man had told me:

"There are no true Chamorros now. We are all mixed up with the Spanish and Filipino. Our ancestors are all dead. Guam is like Hawaii; the kids are basically American. There is no Chamorro culture left. Chamorro is taught in the schools, but so what? It has no use for the ambitious.

"Like my brother. He lives stateside for forty years. I went and visited him, and he didn't know me. That's my brother. I think he still knew how to talk, but he didn't want to talk in

Chamorro, he wanted to talk English. He left when he was ten. Now he doesn't even know me. He's an attorney there.''

I recited this while looking down at my notes because I knew I was causing Ron pain. The jungle passed by on our right and dry hillsides on our left. "Chamorro self-determination is the only choice available for us," Ron said in his gentle voice with its slightly lilting cadence. "The alternative is a slow death, and absorption as a second class.''

"But it seems like 'Chamorro' exists simply in opposition to 'white,' " I said.

"Yes, there is a kind of reverse racism.''

Ron said the Chamorros have been forced to defend themselves—that is, identify themselves—in a negative sense because of discrimination. This has become obvious, gradually, over the last century.

"Intellectually, it's fairly simple. But *emotionally* it's difficult. It requires an understanding that Chamorro self-determination is not simply anti-U.S. ["U.S." being, among other things, a synonym for "white."] I had to work this through, myself, for years. It isn't *a* or *b,* it's more subtle. There are no words for it. It requires an emotional education.''

We pulled over to the side of the highway, walked through a strip of jungle and into a clearing by the sea. This was Ron's land, a small plot he'd purchased with hopes of building a house and moving out of Agaña. There was nothing on it but a slight wooden frame, over which one could hang a tent, and a stone madonna propped uneasily on cement blocks. Ron said his mother had insisted he put it there. I had the feeling of facing too many symbols at once, too many histories that could never be made to add up. Ron's mother, living in the village where Magellan had first landed; Ron's mother telling him to put a Catholic icon on his land, the icon that had inspired Father Diego Luis de Sanvitores until his death at the hands of Ron's distant ancestors. I wondered why Ron had brought me here. He seemed unusually timid, almost resentful as I wandered around, touched the trees, put my hand in the water, and mumbled about how beautiful it all was. We stood on the narrow beach and were silent. One lone house could be seen in the distance, otherwise there was nothing but palms and bushes and sand and ocean. I suppose Ron wanted me to have a bit of emotional education. The beach arced away from us on either side, creating a tiny bay. The water was still and pale blue as far as the reef.

We drove north on the highway then turned across the center of Guam, stopping only once to gaze over one of the vast tracts "owned" by the U.S. military. ("Owned" is the common term, another sign of American influence.) The U.S. government keeps one-third of Guam's land for itself. This is entirely due, of course, to America's odd notions of self-defense. Most of the land, heavily protected by high fences, barbed wire, and patrols, lies fallow, constituting a "security zone" around the actual installations—storage sites for nuclear weapons (there are probably more U.S. nuclear warheads stored on Guam than anywhere outside the lower forty-eight states), tracking and intelligence-gathering stations, barracks, shops, and offices. The military's land is also the best for agriculture, making profitable farming almost impossible on Guam. Seeing this, too, is part of an emotional education.

■ That night I went out on the town hoping to meet people. I stopped in at a music club called Maxim's. A Filipino band was playing American pop songs from the '70s. The club's owner, Jesse Zasse, said he used to book rock 'n roll acts but had quit because the young people, mostly Chamorro, were "so rowdy. Now we're trying to put back the old kind of music." In Guam, the "old kind of music" is slowed-down mainstream American pop played by Filipinos. I went to several other clubs and the situation was the same. I tried to converse with people but didn't have much success. The women I spoke to seemed to assume any advance was a prelude to sex. Nonwhite men didn't show the slightest desire to speak to a white American. And the white men I met were unenthused about the idea of a journalist, except for one Vietnam veteran who poured out his heart, narrated his past crimes—assassinations, drug-running, betrayals—and wept in describing his self-imposed exile, scraping along through the dismal remnants of our country's Asian empire. I walked up Agaña's public beach, which was crowded with young Chamorros standing around their cars, listening to the radio, and drinking. I tried to talk with them, too, but failed.

And so I stumbled along and thought that this place reminded me very much of home. Because here in Agaña I was branded by my color, sex, and nationality in a particular, familiar way. I could only be what I appeared to be, and I felt that emphysema of the imagination that is a constant possibility (even, in the saddest cases, an aspiration) for every white American male—the short breaths that are just enough to sustain life while evading the risks of actually living. For me, at least, the traditional position of the white American male on his home ground offers power, wealth, and a spirit so cramped that its movements can barely be seen: a privileged, paralytic identity. James Baldwin once wrote, "We cannot be free until they are free." The "they" he meant was me and my people.

It made complete and perverse sense that an ethnic group, the Chamorros, should be willing itself into existence in this minuscule corner of my homeland, where I felt my own ethnicity—that is, "American whiteness"—clamping down in all its majestic indifference. The conflation of ethnicity and skin color, after all, is sheer invention, a peculiar idea born in criminal circumstances and struggles for power. Born, ultimately, in slavery, the "peculiar institution." And here were the Chamorros in Guam, "where America's day begins" (as the tourist slogan says), in the thankless position of defining their ethnicity. In the Commonwealth Act, Chamorro-rights advocates were compelled to offer some definition of how one qualifies for Chamorro-ness. The adopted rule stipulates that anyone born in Guam before August 1, 1950, is "Chamorro."

Knocking around Agaña's streets that night had made me depressed, so I opted for the American (and, increasingly, global) solution for depression. I went to the hotel and watched television. On TV was a Fabergé/Brut women's wrestling competition, telecast from somewhere in the U.S. The two wrestlers were Mata the Samoan Headhunter and

Amy the Farmer's Daughter. I experienced a digestive spasm, brought on by cheap irony. The crowd was rooting heavily for Amy. She had blond ponytails and wore a cowgirl-pinup outfit. Mata was dressed in leaves and carried a spear. She was definitely not Samoan; her skin was smudged to make her look darker. After some initial hair-pulling and kicking, Mata started biting Amy. Then she attacked the referee. Soon the security guards came in and dragged her off; she was flailing and screaming. That's the kind of night it was in Guam.

■ I spent several more days in Agaña, talking to government officials and other experts, sketching in a general picture of Guam economics and politics. The influential class of people is divided roughly between nationalists, who want a more independent Guam, and traditionalists, who are happy with the status quo and, when they worry about things, usually focus on crime and the terrifying possibility of U.S. military budget cuts. The Guam elite live in a small world, circumscribed by certain hotels, clubs, and neighborhoods. There's a lot of corruption and spousal infidelity. It was, to me, a boring world, and I found myself thinking often of Ron Rivera and the land, hoping for an emotional rescue I couldn't name.

The nationalists hope to build a economy based on tourism, agriculture, and possibly international finance, which could use Guam as a tax haven (tax-haven status is a common Pacific panacea). The two latter goals might have modest success. Tourism, however, is already booming. Almost all of the tourists are Japanese—another historical irony, considering that Japan took Guam from the U.S. in December 1941, three days after Pearl Harbor, then lost it in August 1944 at a cost of 17,000 lives.

The first direct flight from Tokyo reached Guam in 1969 (the island had been a restricted military zone until 1962). By 1988 there were about half a million Japanese visitors each year, and ambitious plans to expand hotel capacity. The hotels I visited were exceptionally clean and orderly, with guards in

front and meticulous gardens in back, that is, between the
hotels and the beach. I watched the guards stop various people, none of whom had my own lightness of skin; I could go
where I liked, undisturbed.

Most Japanese tourists stay in the strip of hotels that line
Tumon Bay. These hotels are primarily owned and staffed by
Japanese; the Guam package tours are arranged by Japanese
companies; tourists arrive and depart on Japan Air Lines. The
business is almost hermetically sealed, both in terms of the
circulation of tourist money and the experiences tourists have.
In many ways, the Tumon Bay hotels could be anywhere in
the world that has a beach. However, there is one unique
aspect to Guam tourism, an aspect that also has a historical
irony: the Japanese can come here and fire guns.

I first became aware of this while leafing through the
monthly pamphlet *Guam Now.* On page 63 was an intriguing
advertisement. In the upper right corner was a photo of two
smiling young Asian women, one holding an M-16, the other
a single-bolt hunting rifle. Next to the photo it said, "Tourist
Night Club." The rest of the advertisement was in Japanese,
except for "Open weekdays, weekends," "U.S.A.," and "Free
chaser." There were similar advertisements elsewhere in the
pamphlet, but the only one with directions in English was the
Arizona Gun Club, so I went there.

In front of the club stood a small decaying wooden horse
and an even smaller wooden steer; inside were a young American man with thinning hair (the manager), piles of Wild West
paraphernalia, an American flag, a Confederate flag, a brace
of handguns, an Uzi, and no customers. The manager explained that it was still afternoon and most people preferred
to shoot after dinner. There were, he said, about ten gun clubs
on Guam. The majority of the customers were Japanese. He
wasn't sure why they patronized the clubs. "I guess they like
to shoot. I think maybe it has a lot to do with the history of
World War Two."

After dinner I tried two more clubs, variously decorated
with machine guns, Clint Eastwood posters, American and
Confederate flags, and cowboy memorabilia, but couldn't find

anyone who spoke English until I walked into the Wild West. There, at the counter beneath a display of semiautomatic rifles, I met Mike, an instructor fluent in both Japanese and English. We chatted for a while, loudly, over the sound of gunshots. You could see the shooting range through a large viewing window, above which loomed a photo of John Wayne, three rifles, and a cow skull. A crowd of Japanese, two-thirds of them men and most fairly young, stood at the window and watched. Behind them, in the lobby, a woman sat alone on a saddle and played with a noose that was hanging from the rafter above her.

Mike agreed to interpret for me and persuaded a young couple—Guam is a popular spot for Japanese newlyweds—to go out on the rustic Western porch and have a talk. Mike translated: "They say they really have fun. They don't have this experience in Japan. You can't have a license to shoot like in the U.S." Since the end of World War II, apparently, the only gun available to the average Japanese is a rifle for shooting birds, and acquiring even such a humble gun requires extensive applications and government-supervised training. The couple agreed that the Japanese shouldn't have guns because they aren't needed. "We don't have murders or real intense crime. We don't have real killings or anything. Not like the United States." This was their first experience at shooting, and the young woman said they were surprised at how powerful guns were, that their experience watching television hadn't really prepared them. She smiled and said they were afraid they might dream about it, feel the shock, and wake up. They both mimed being asleep then waking with their bodies convulsing and their hands clasped before them holding imaginary guns; they laughed. Mike remembered one twenty-five-year-old woman who wept after shooting her first bullet. He said that often women will get all set up with their guns and eye protectors then, when they hear the others start firing, put down their weapons and walk away.

After we went back inside I saw another woman sitting on the saddle beneath the noose. Two men stood above her with pistols; sometimes they pretended to shoot each other, some-

times they pretended to shoot themselves. It cost from $35 to
$100 to rent a gun on Guam. I thought about renting one
myself but decided against it.

■ Coincidentally, it was also on the Tumon Bay strip that I
met Ron Rivera for our farewell drink. We drank beer in the
fading afternoon, watched tourists troop up and down the
beach, and carried on an excessively abstract conversation
about the future of Guam. Behind us, three thin, long-haired,
white American boys were tuning instruments for that night's
gig and mumbling. I wanted to know what Guam might be
like under the leadership of people like Ron. We agreed that
young Chamorros, however militant they might become on
questions of ethnic identity, would never be eager farmers,
even if the U.S. were to give up the good land. So a future
Guam economy, regardless of who's in power, would probably be based on tourism, finance, and light industry, none of
which is particularly conducive to Chamorro-ness. But then,
what is? Modern Chamorro-ness is largely based on the experience of oppression, so if you take away oppression, what will
you have?

Ron said, characteristically, "You try to imagine the future.
But there are no words for what we want." We both laughed
quite a bit as the sun was setting and the musicians banged and
plunked. A pleasant breeze blew through the club, which was
a bunch of cheap tables gathered under a metal roof. Ron was
not disposed toward the established foreign concepts of cultural identification—whether black nationalism or Chicano
power or *négritude*—so our discussion was bound to be vague.
The language of cultural emotion was unassuming. I realized
this wasn't America after all.

That night we went to a cockfight. Ron had raised cocks and
frequented the fights. The arena, sheltered under a tin roof,
was a dusty oval, about thirty feet wide at its greatest diameter,
protected by a high fence and surrounded by a semicircle of
bleachers. Ron said the cockfights are "very Chamorro" (and
exclusively male); I was one of about five discernibly Cauca-

sian spectators in a crowd of maybe 200. At either end of the oval, a man knelt with his fighting cock. As the fight neared, the two men would bring the cocks forward, holding them tightly, placing them near each other to get them agitated. Ron said people made bets based on the size of the bird, its history, its owner's history, or sometimes just its color. There were, of course, even less scientific betting methods (birthdays, the moon). Each bird had a blade tied to one leg, positioned where a claw would normally be. Specialists in blade-choice and blade-tying were there, in a preparation area behind the grandstands, as was a specialist in repairing birds after their fights.

Getting the birds agitated was an extended process, progressing along with the agitation of the bettors. Men circulated in front of the arena's fence, facing the grandstands, taking bets. To bet, one exchanged hand signals with one of these men, indicating the bird, the amount, and the odds, then threw wadded-up money to him once an agreement had been made. I'd never seen the phrase "throwing money away" illustrated so vividly. The birds were now ready to kill; the shouts of men became a roar; bills rained down from the stands. The owners released their birds and the cocks rushed forward, ruffling their wings, puffing their breasts, pecking at each other's heads. Cocks naturally have a claw protruding hindward from each leg; in fighting, they jump up and try to cut their opponents. The steel blade makes this much more effective. I stood with Ron and a relative of his, our fingers grasping the fence, a few feet from the birds. The fight took less than a minute. One bird was left in the dust, dying, his breast heaving. The other staggered about, dazed and victorious. Blood spattered the arena and some of us as we pulled away from the fence. Ron and I returned to the stands, saying little. I've seen blood sports many times and find it hard to say much about them. To me they are a way of educating the emotions about one's own species, which is often a wordless task.

Saipan

An alert American consumer might find, on the tag of his or her sweater, the legend "Made in the Commonwealth of the Northern Mariana Islands." Since 1978 the Northern Marianas has been one of the United States' two commonwealths, along with Puerto Rico. It somehow comes under Headnote 3 (A), a trade provision that has its roots in Danish law. Some of the Caribbean Virgin Islands were controlled by Denmark until 1917, when they were sold to the United States. Danish colonial law had permitted exemptions from customs duties for some Virgin Islands products. The notion was retained by the U.S., and over fifty years later had the unanticipated result of benefitting islanders on the other side of the globe. This is as close as the U.S. has come to developing any of its Trust Territory dependencies.

■ Lydia Romisher seemed like someone who can't swim and suddenly finds herself well beyond the breakers, at dusk, catching glimpses of a distant and empty beach. Around her stood stacks of paper, four, five, six feet high. Among these stacks her underlings burrowed, pulling out a piece of paper, looking at it, putting it back somewhere else. Romisher's Office of Economic Development, Department of Commerce and Labor, was a pyromaniac's dream.

We escaped into her office, where she was slightly calmer. A middle-aged, attractive woman, dressed in the style of an American bureaucrat, Romisher had been Saipan's director of economic development for only a few months. She faced a Sisyphean task. "It's so frustrating. In economic development we need information, and we don't have it. When I started, I asked the person in charge of the garment industry for basic information and she didn't have it." After tourism, garment manufacture is Saipan's major industry, with twenty-four factories on the island and more under construction.

Romisher said most of the stacks of paper lurking outside her office were applications for business licenses. For $50 just about anyone could get a business license. "Until recently, you could renew licenses without having paid taxes. In the first year of business you don't have to file a finance report. You don't even have to say where your business will be located." Romisher tended to stare ahead rather blankly between statements; she also had a slight tremble. "When I started here we randomly called business phone numbers. Most of them were dead."

Romisher staggered off into the thicket of applications, leaving me with a pile of statistical documents. All of them were dated and most were useless. Official economic statistics always tend toward the fictional, but in my experience these set a new standard. Yet a few generalities were clear: roughly half the population were foreign workers—Filipinos, Chinese, Japanese—brought in on temporary visas to assemble garments or work in hotels and restaurants. Most permanent residents—Chamorros and, to a lesser extent, Micronesians from the Caroline Islands to the south—worked for the government. This is what economists mean when they refer to a "capitalist platform." It isn't an environment conducive to the keeping of records.

I left the Office of Economic Development and explored the Commonwealth of the Northern Marianas government offices. The buildings, and the headquarters of the Trust Territory of the Pacific Islands, are perched atop a ridge that runs the length of Saipan. The oldest buildings once had been part of a Central Intelligence Agency base. From 1951 to 1962, this was where the CIA trained Chinese "nationalist" fighters, who hoped to retake China under the leadership of Chiang Kai-shek, as well as "advisers" en route to Vietnam. After the CIA's departure, the Trust Territory administration took over its headquarters; a small Office of Transition remains there today. For decades after World War II, the hilltop complex had the only regular supply of water and power on the island.

In acquiring the Trust Territory in 1947 the United States was obligated, in the words of its United Nations mandate, to "promote the development of the inhabitants of the trust territory toward self-government or independence . . . to promote the social advancement of the inhabitants, and . . . to promote the educational advancement of the inhabitants." For nearly fifteen years, however, extremely little advancement was made. What development did occur came as a by-product of U.S. military needs—the testing of nuclear and other weapons in the Marshall Islands, on the Trust Territory's eastern edge, and CIA training on Saipan.

After World War II there were eleven trust territories, all farmed out by the UN to various colonial powers. By the Kennedy years, American suzerainty over the islands was more and more of an embarrassment. Eight of the original eleven territories had become independent or absorbed into neighboring states, leaving only Papua New Guinea, the tiny central Pacific island of Nauru—both administered by Australia—and Micronesia.

President Kennedy appointed a commission, headed by Harvard economist Anthony M. Solomon (later assistant secretary of state for economic affairs), to investigate the situa-

66 tion. The Solomon Report, submitted in October 1963, is an
■ absorbing document. Being classified, it was written with uncommon honesty and clarity. "In the almost twenty years of
United States control," the commission states, "physical facilities have further deteriorated in many areas, the economy has
remained relatively dormant and in many ways retrogressed,
while progress toward social development has been slow. The
people remain largely illiterate and inadequately prepared to
participate in political, commercial and other activities of
more than a rudimentary character." The report notes that
"per capita Micronesian incomes were almost three times as
high before the war [under Japanese government] as they are
now" and that the Trust Territory had experienced "an overall net capital disinvestment."

The commission believed that the Micronesians were "not
unintelligent," but nevertheless in dire need of tutelage.
Without such tutelage, the Micronesians might stand in the
way of American goals as presented in President Kennedy's
National Security Action Memorandum 145, "which set forth
as United States policy the movement of Micronesia into a
permanent relationship with the United States within our political framework." Kennedy's memorandum violated at least
the spirit of the 1947 UN–U.S. agreement, but the Solomon
commission believed that, with a little effort, United Nations
requirements could be made "an academic issue." And so the
commission set out to determine how to arrange the "favorable outcome of a plebiscite in Micronesia." Its main sugges-
tions were:

—to fund "the minimum capital investment and operating
program needed to insure a favorable vote in the plebiscite,"
retaining some additional funds to be spent as "inducements
. . . to offer as a reward for a favorable vote"
—"to permit Japanese businessmen, technicians and fishing
vessels into non-sensitive areas of the Trust Territory, which
would supply a very great stimulus to economic development
at no cost to the United States"

—to encourage "a viable economy based on American residents and tourists"

—to introduce into the school system "United States oriented curriculum changes and patriotic rituals"

—to create a governmental organization in the territory that gives "a reasonable appearance of self-government . . . but on the other hand retains adequate [U.S.] control through the continuation of an appointed United States High Commissioner"

—to deploy public-affairs officers "responsible for the development of favorable political attitudes toward the United States"

—and finally, to ensure "the safety valve of legally unlimited (and possibly financially-aided) immigration to the United States."

I quote the Solomon Report at such length because it has been the blueprint for U.S. Micronesia policy ever since, in attitude if not always in details. The U.S. government never had the slightest intention of giving the Micronesians any meaningful independence, whether economic or political. "We cannot give the area up," the report states. And yet the expense of maintaining a colony scattered over an ocean area roughly the size of the continental U.S. had to be minimized. Consequently, the commission realized the need for limited and timely development expenditures, which would create political sympathy among Micronesians, though "it is the Mission's conclusion that those programs and the spending involved will not set off a self-sustaining development process of any significance." The commission recommended that economic aid be heavily front-loaded so that political "advantage be taken of the psychological impact of the capital investment program before some measure of disappointment is felt." In the long term, of course, it would be up to Japanese and American investors to run the economy, with some local autonomy allowed as a sop to Micronesian pride, and ample encouragements provided for emigration. The report cites

Australian plans, later abandoned, to resettle the entire population of Nauru. (Nauru is now independent and has, argua-
bly, the world's highest per capita income, thanks to phosphate deposits.)

One afternoon, twenty-five years after the Solomon Report,
I met Chuck Jordan, head of the Trust Territory Office of
Transition, in one of the former CIA buildings. It was Chuck,
along with State Department representative Steve Pruitt, who
had hidden from me behind a pillar on that curious day in
Palau. Tall, fair, and handsome, Chuck was an easygoing guy,
with an optimism, even naïveté, rarely found in Micronesia.
He said U.S. plans for the Trust Territory (or rather, former
Trust Territory) have progressed well and are "a tribute to the
United States system."

"Three new nations have been created without bloodshed,"
he said. "That is a U.S. achievement." He was proud of the
fact that those three "nations"—the Federated States of Micronesia, the U.S. Commonwealth of the Northern Marianas,
and the Republic of the Marshall Islands—now have a measure of self-government. Once the still pending Republic of
Palau is "independent," the transition away from U.S. rule
will, in his view, be complete. Chuck is looking forward to that
day, because then he will be able to devote all his time to
business dealings on Saipan and elsewhere. He's well connected with the Saipan elite—American, Japanese, Chinese,
and Chamorro—and said he has already struck some real estate deals that are full of promise. The laws on inalienability
of land, apparently, present no great obstacles for him.

■ Mitch Pangelinan suggested we meet at a bar on the water-
front in Garapan, one of Saipan's two towns and the center of
its tourist trade. The bar was an open-air patch of cement next
to a once-prosperous hotel. We had wanted to escape the U.S.
Marines and Mitch figured this would be a good place. The
Marines, thousands of them, were anchored in ships offshore.
They'd come to Saipan for a recreational visit. Brought to the
island in shifts, small groups of them roamed Garapan, casu-

ally dressed, looking like Tom Cruise replicants reconnoiter-
ing an unfamiliar planet. They didn't come near our bar,
which was, in fact, entirely empty.

Mitch told me he was born on Saipan just before the outbreak of World War II. His parents were Japanese. When the
Americans invaded on June 15, 1944, Mitch and his family hid
in a cave. Most of Saipan's 30,000 Japanese defenders died,
either in battle or by suicide. Mitch's family died when a
grenade was thrown into their hiding place. Mitch was pulled
from among the bodies and later adopted into the Pangelinan
family, one of Saipan's most important clans (along with the
Tenorios and Guerreros).

Mitch eventually entered politics, served three times as
head of the local Democratic party, and held various other
offices. He has the manner of a back-room man—tough, impatient, quick to make jokes without necessarily laughing at
them. As a lifelong politician, he is well aware of the commonwealth government's shortcomings. "People come here and
criticize our government. And of course it's too big, a lot of
stupid jobs, people pushing paper around, maybe they don't
even bother to come into the office sometimes. But who did
we learn about government from? We learned everything
from the damn Americans." Mitch spat betel-nut juice, the
distinctive red stain of which can be seen on most Saipan
sidewalks. For years he smoked three packs of cigarettes a day,
but recently he'd switched to betel nut, which can create problems for the mouth but leaves the lungs alone. I chewed some
too. It brings a gentle clarity of mind and a slight physical
stupor, rather like chewing coca leaves, only milder. We
watched helicopters ferrying Marines back and forth between
ship and shore; as night fell a heavy rain dragged down the
palms.

"Politics here is funny. It can destroy you at the last minute," Mitch said, speaking in bursts. "Forget about long term,
it's hit and run. Forget about writing down your blueprint."
Still, the American blueprint had held up pretty well. Most
businesses were controlled by Americans and Japanese (with
Chinese dominating in the garment industry); and govern-

ment employment, as foreseen in the Solomon Report, provided wages for the indigenous people and "a reasonable appearance of self-government." Mitch pointed out that the commonwealth government included both an Office for Carolinian Affairs and an Office for Indigenous Affairs. This was odd for at least two reasons. First, "indigenous" was meant to apply to the Chamorros, while historically the Carolinians are just as indigenous. They arrived on Saipan after the commonwealth's original Chamorro inhabitants were relocated to Guam in 1680. The Saipanese Chamorros remained on Guam for over a century, and in any case were mostly killed by the Spanish or by epidemics. Second, the majority of commonwealth citizens (and government officials) are Chamorro. Why would the majority need an Office for Indigenous Affairs?

Mitch didn't explain this strange circumstance, except to cite it as another example of pointless job creation. But then, job creation was the main activity of Northern Marianas government. As Lydia Romisher discovered, economic development and regulation (for instance) were not priorities. There were no zoning laws or building codes, no foreign-investment board. The various land commissions and boards were about as effective as the Office for Indigenous Affairs—although, because of corruption, positions on them are more coveted. As one businessman put it, "The big game as far as the islanders are concerned is politics."

"I actually think we should be independent," Mitch said as we sat in the darkness (no one bothered to turn on the lights in the bar after nightfall). "But that's not really a popular idea here. Where would our money come from?"

■ One evening I went out to dinner with David Hughes, editor of the *Marianas Variety News and Views,* and Larry Hillblom, owner of DHL Couriers and various other things, including 30 percent of the United Micronesian Development Corporation. Three Filipinas accompanied them—David's fiancée, a friend of hers, and Larry's girlfriend, Josephine, whom he liked to address as *unggoy,* a Tagalog word meaning "little monkey." David, a loud and enthusiastic man, was in a good mood and told me with a flourish that this restaurant had "the best white man's food on the island."

Much of the conversation was about an ongoing trial in which Hillblom was defense attorney for the head of the Republican party, Jesus Mafnes. Mafnes's bank account had been undergoing some strange fluctuations. I wasn't too interested in the case because, despite some impressive evidence against him, Mafnes was clearly going to win. It was all, Hillblom said, a "family melodrama." I was much more interested, from an anthropological point of view, in David and Larry's relationships with these women. The two men dominated the conversation and the eating; between mouthfuls they would tease the women, making suggestive jokes at their expense—about sex, about how silly they were, about how much they love their men. The three Filipinas would giggle and shrink in their seats. They ate very little. American men often travel to the Philippines and bring back girlfriends for one- or two-year stints. I wondered if this was the case with David and Larry but didn't have the nerve to ask. I also wondered if the third woman had been brought along for me.

The only time I remember the women expressing an opinion was when David mentioned a series of articles he'd published on massage parlors. He called it "my slavery series." The articles charged that Filipina prostitutes were kept prisoner in some massage parlors. I recalled a full-page advertisement in his newspaper for the "Folk Pub Disco Restaurant and Massage," where "the sweet smile all-over the faces of our ladies to anyone" guaranteed the club's slogan, "Dull moments is not our business." I asked David's fiancée if the slavery stories were true. She nodded and smiled and her friend said "Yes."

After dinner we went to see the play *Li'l Abner,* sponsored by the Northern Marianas Music Society. Larry said it was a big event—there were only two plays a year, four performances each. The society had also produced *Oklahoma!* and *South Pacific.* The performers were almost all local residents, and almost all white Americans, as was the audience. I hadn't

seen *Li'l Abner* since childhood and had forgotten what it was
about. The plot in brief: Las Vegas has been destroyed by
nuclear fallout, and the U.S. government needs to find a new
site for weapons testing. The town of Dogpatch, "the most
unnecessary place in the whole U.S.A.," is selected by the
Senate. A government representative visits Dogpatch and tells
the residents they are to be evacuated, and that the Senate is
"spending $10 billion just to blow your place off the face of
the earth." Dogpatch's backwoods citizens dance and sing to
celebrate, then realize that if they leave Dogpatch they'll have
to wash themselves and work regular jobs. The play goes on,
at complicated length, from there.

It was, for me, an assault of ironies. The image of the Dog-
patchers was precisely that ascribed to Saipan's Chamorros and
Carolinians—unwashed, lazy, physically powerful. Yet the actors were all affluent white expatriates. Moreover, the central
humor had to do with nuclear testing, which is not a funny
subject in Micronesia. The U.S. did indeed test nuclear bombs
in the Trust Territory, blowing a few islands off the face of the
earth and shortening the lives of more than a few Micronesians. At intermission I chatted with several people and hinted
at the strangeness of performing this play in this place. But no
one seemed to understand what I meant. Days later I mentioned this to Mitch Pangelinan and he said, "If they knew
how strange it was they wouldn't be able to live here."

■ The remainder of my time on Saipan was spent mostly in
the company of expatriates and politicians. As on Guam, the
possibilities for meeting local people, and particularly local
women, were minimal, apart from certain highly structured
exchanges that didn't interest me. I had brought along a book
called *Chamorros and Carolinians of Saipan*, published by Harvard University Press in 1951. It was written by two doctors,
Alice Joseph and Veronica F. Murray, and sponsored by,
among others, the U.S. Navy. "The naval authorities made it
clear that they would welcome factual information about the
inhabitants of our newly acquired Trusteeship area," the au-

thors explained, "which would enable them better to understand and govern the people." U.S. government funding during and after the war paid for the last, great days of American anthropology (in 1943, about 75 percent of American anthropologists were engaged in war-related research). Joseph and Murray, working for the Washington, D.C., Institute of Ethnic Affairs, had subjected Saipan residents to a battery of tests: the Grace Arthur Point Performance Scale, Revised Form II (26) and the Porteus Maze (both intelligence tests), the Rorschach test, and the Bender Gestalt test.

The results are complex, but in general they present an unflattering picture of the Saipanese people, who were found, in most respects, to test below "white norms." For example, "There is a fairly large percentage of children with IQ's or TQ's [Porteus Maze test quotients] which, according to the generally accepted white standards, would indicate borderline intelligence or mental deficiency." The Saipanese were found, variously, to be manic, psychotic, schizophrenic, and depressive. They also suffered from low self-esteem. Other categories included introversive, ambiequal, coarcted, and extratensive. ("Extratensive" children were those with "o $M:x$ sum C and x $M<y$ sum C" on the Rorschach test; the other more technical adjectives had similar definitions.)

I've often wondered whether anthropology is more about its subjects or its practitioners. Toward the end of their book, Joseph and Murray present case studies, including black-and-white photos labeling people as Case 1, Case 2, etc. I was intrigued by Case 4, a forty-five-year-old Carolinian woman who was said "to come of a 'good family.' " After the American victory, Case 4 "was frequently the victim of rape by American soldiers. When her family entered complaints about this, she was apprehended and kept in jail for a few days." By the time Joseph and Murray caught up with her, "Case 4, harmless enough when at large, was kept confined in a small room at her daughter's home because there was no other way to protect her against her propensity for being raped by American soldiers."

To this day I find it hard to get those words, "to protect her against her propensity for being raped," out of my head. They were written by two American women in 1951. I don't know what guidance the U.S. Navy drew from their book.

■ One night I went to the Four Aces, a small and amiably dingy nightclub, to hear Candy Taman. Candy is roughly half Chamorro and half Carolinian and was, as far as I knew, the only active cultural nationalist on Saipan. He has pioneered a music and style he calls "Chamolinian."

The club was dark and lively, the audience mostly Chamorro with a scattering of Filipinos. A Filipina band opened, playing "Blue Bayou," "Go Your Own Way," and other American hits. A Chamorro "sanitation engineer" invited me to his table, where we joined two men and two women and picked at a pile of hot-dog slices pierced with toothpicks. He asked me if I was ashamed to be sitting with a sanitation engineer. I said no. This exchange went into my notes. Later I got up to retrieve some drinks, and when I returned he had written "SURE" next to where I'd written "No." The sanitation engineer baited me in front of his friends. He was convinced I had contempt for him and was concealing it. He invited me to stay at his house, then shouted, "You'll never come!" He kept punching me in the arm, saying the gesture was traditional among Chamorro men. He insisted that I punch him back, so I did. The Filipinas crooned in the background. "I would be insulted if Filipinos came in here and sang in Filipino," he said. "Would you be insulted if everyone at the table spoke in Chamorro?"

"I'd be lonely."

"We're talking about the same thing."

The sanitation engineer bought rounds of straight whisky, which, of course, we were supposed to drink at a toss. His companions were growing skittish. I was reminded of various times I'd been accused of being a CIA agent. It's an accusation that is almost impossible to disprove. And how do you convince someone you don't have contempt for them? Finally I got up to introduce myself to Candy at the bar, and while we talked the engineer and his party left without saying goodbye.

"We're being invaded by other musics," Candy said. A ■
hefty, imposing man with a stern face, Candy looked as if he
could wrestle all those other musics to the ground. He joined
his all-male band on the stage; they wore flowers in their hair.
He sang a slow, pretty tune in Chamorro. I picked out Spanish
words—*bonito, simpático, baila, solamente.* Then he sang a Chamorro version of "Under the Boardwalk," and "Wasted Days
and Wasted Nights" in English and Chamorro. "Yee haw!"
shouted the crowd. The band played a song about marijuana
and everyone laughed and clapped. Candy announced that his
band was Chamolinian, then wound up his set by singing "A
Whiter Shade of Pale," which got an enthusiastic cheer. "It
was my biggest hit," Candy told me. "I recorded it years ago.
People love that song."

A few days later I visited Candy at his house, which was tiny
and very hot as he had no air conditioner. Candy's wife, their
son John-Boy, a sister-in-law, and a baby lounged in the living
room. John-Boy was watching American TV. Candy and I sat
at the kitchen table and had coffee and fruit. He had just
woken up, wore a wraparound skirt that needed constant ad-
justing, and was a little groggy. Candy said authenticity is
impossible for Chamorro culture. "At this point the Chamorros don't have any cultural arts. The so-called genuine Chamorro music is actually very much influenced by Germany."
Germany bought the Marianas (save Guam) from Spain after
the 1898 war, and held them until the Japanese took control
under a League of Nations mandate following World War I.
"When the Spaniards were here there was too much fighting,"
Candy said. "When the Germans were here the living was
more civilized. And I believe that's the reason why the people
had a little more time to adapt music from the Germans rather
than from the Spanish."

Candy gave the Northern Marianas national anthem as an
example. "I grew up with that, and I started believing this was
the genuine Chamorro. But later on I found out it's not. It's
German." The original Chamorro forms were the polka and
the waltz. After 1944 the cha-cha took over, and to some

■   extent the jitterbug. When Candy and others rebelled against imported rock 'n' roll in the late 1960s, they brought back the cha-cha as indigenous music; since then cultural nationalism has been associated with the cha-cha. Today Candy records in various genres—blues, and reggae, but mostly cha-cha. He played a Chamorro song he'd written for the last election called "Fladet i Kemon," which featured a chorus of local children. The children sing of their worries about development and the future, how their island is being taken over and they feel as if they're losing a home. Between choruses, Candy's voice chimes in and he tries to reassure them.

"To tell you the truth, my belief is that us, out here in this part of the world, we are just drifting. And we pick up any kind of influence from all over. To be honest with you we are unfortunate, really." Candy pointed to John-Boy, who was about thirteen and inseparable from the television. "Look at kids like his age. He won't tune to no Chamorro songs. They've got thrown off because of this MTV. Anyone less than twenty, they're all MTV freaks. I know that these kids, they don't really listen to my songs." Many elementary school children don't even understand Chamorro. "It's inevitable you know. Our music will change no matter what. Like I said, we're just drifters. We're always taken by the wind."

The Marshall Islands

■ ■ IIIIIIIIII ■ ■ II IIIIIIIIIIIII ■ ■ II IIIIIIIIIIII ■ ■ ■ IIIIIIII

*Uelip and his wife, the first humans, lived on the island of Ep.
One day a tree started growing from Uelip's skull and eventually split it. From the fracture emerged two boys, Etau and
Djemelut. Etau fought with his father and, believing their
differences irreconcilable, flew away to build a home of his
own, carrying with him a basket of soil. The basket had a hole,
and as Etau flew the soil escaped into the sea, bit by bit,
creating the 1,225 Marshall Islands. Many years later (1946)
U.S. Commodore Ben Wyatt flew across the Marshalls by
plane, landing at Bikini Atoll. It was a Sunday. When the
Bikinians left church that morning Wyatt asked for a meeting.
He compared the Bikinians to the children of Israel, whom
God delivered from the Egyptians and into the Promised
Land. (Two years earlier U.S. forces had taken the Marshalls
from the Japanese.) Wyatt explained that the U.S. needed to
use Bikini to test nuclear weapons, "for the good of mankind*

and to end all world wars," and requested that the Bikinians leave their atoll. The Bikinians were given a few minutes to confer, then their chief, Juda Kessibuki, replied, "If the United States government and the scientists of the world want to use our island and atoll for further development, which with God's blessing will result in kindness and benefit to all mankind, my people will be pleased to go elsewhere."

■ The first time I met Caleb Rantak he was in a restaurant with two white American men. The Americans were drinking beer; Caleb had coffee. I didn't know any of them, but we were staying in the same small hotel and had time to kill. One of the Americans was a bluff, husky pilot (ex-USAF) in his fifties. He'd come to Majuro, the Marshalls' capital, on a World War II fighter plane. An Australian collector had bought the plane and he was supposed to deliver it. Unfortunately part of the cockpit had come off between the U.S. and the Marshalls, so my acquaintance and his crew were temporarily grounded. The other American was a Marine veteran, also in his fifties, who looked as though he'd played most of his cards some time ago. Tall and very thin, with skin that veered dangerously between red and gray, he chain-smoked Marlboros and drank beer at an ominous pace. He lived in Hong Kong now, engaged in some commerce about which he was exceptionally vague. "The doctor ordered me to come here for my health. I've got to put on some weight," he said, a face made blank, through the haze.

The Americans traded war stories from Korea. The thin one had been a Marine sergeant. He said that he'd been ordered once to relieve two Army units pinned down on a hill. He radioed the Air Force and told them to strafe one side of the hill, but the pilot in charge told him he had orders to drop napalm and fragmentation bombs over the entire area. So the planes dropped napalm and fragmentation bombs. No one on the hill survived.

The two Americans told more stories in this vein. They seemed to have an inexhaustible supply of grim anecdotes.

The pilot related them with a sad equanimity, but the thin man was different. He was still inside his stories, and he knew it; he knew he'd swim around in them until his breath was gone. His body seemed like a fragile construction of dried sticks. From various half-hints I got the impression he was involved in intelligence work, one of those agents who are fighting the endless war.

Caleb was a Marshallese, around sixty, in dark glasses. He smiled often at the two men's stories, giving an impression of amiability verging on simplemindedness. The next time I saw him was on the plane to Kwajalein Atoll, the largest coral atoll in the world. The atoll's biggest island, also called Kwajalein (or "Kwaj"), is the site of the U.S.'s most important missile-testing base. Intercontinental ballistic missiles are launched from California's Vandenberg Air Force Base and, with luck, plunk down in the huge lagoon—839 square miles—surrounded by Kwajalein Atoll's ninety-three islands. Missiles are also fired from Kwajalein to knock down missiles from Vandenberg. Kwajalein has been a crucial test site for Star Wars weapons.

Caleb and I landed on Kwajalein in the middle of a nine-hole golf course by the sea. Like all coral atoll islands, Kwajalein is flat, so I imagine the golfing was rather repetitive. But the sportsmen we saw from the plane—solidly built, tanned Americans in bright clothing—looked to be having a good time. Many recreational pursuits are possible on Kwajalein, including bowling, billiards, tennis, handball, basketball, and volleyball, as well as water sports. Such activities require space, but with 900 acres and only 2,000 or so people, Kwajalein feels roomy. Most of the island's residents are private workers, with military supervisors, under contract to the United States. They receive exemplary health care and excellent pay.

Going through the small terminal I held Caleb's hand luggage under one arm and supported him with the other. He had diabetes—hence the sunglasses, as diabetes can make the eyes overly sensitive to light—and circulatory problems that occasionally made his limbs swollen and painful. The Kwajalein security people were not very happy to see me. Months earlier, I had made strenuous efforts to get official permission to visit Kwajalein as a journalist. I even said I'd like to visit on the Fourth of July, hoping that a display of patriotic ardor would move officialdom, but this stratagem did not work. They said Kwajalein was "too crowded" and without accommodations.

So Caleb and I sat on an oily patch of concrete and smoked cigarettes while several military men decided what to do. Eventually they let me pass since I was in transit to Ebeye, a tiny island three miles away. Caleb and I limped down the main street toward the snack bar. White Americans with set faces rode by us on bicycles. "I used to live here before the Americans came," Caleb said. "I remember what it used to be like. It's a good island."

Once upon a time Kwajalein, one of the finest islands in the Marshalls, blessed with space and resources, was inhabited only by Marshallese. Spain asserted nominal control over the Marshalls in the late 1600s. By 1800 foreign traders were making regular visits, often with sanguinary consequences—the Marshallese were a fearsome people. The first Christian mission (Congregationalist) was not established until 1857, and even then the pioneers felt much anxiety; as one of the first missionaries wrote, "the Marshall Islanders have imbrued their hands with the blood of many strangers." Germany bought sovereignty from Spain in 1899 and established modest trading posts, mostly for copra (dried coconut meat). As elsewhere, Japan seized the islands at the outbreak of World War I, founding large Japanese communities and pouring in development funds; by 1938, over half the population was Japanese. In early 1944, U.S. soldiers invaded Kwajalein, the second stop of America's island-hopping strategy (the first was Tarawa, in the Gilbert Islands, now independent Kiribati). They've been there ever since.

Caleb and I eventually reached the snack bar. Marshallese are allowed to use the Kwaj snack bar; most of the other facilities, notably the well-stocked food and dry-goods stores with their low prices, remain forbidden. "The food here is fresh and good," Caleb said. "Enjoy it, because the food on Ebeye is not like this." We had a big meal of chef's salads and pie. Ebeye is where the Marshallese now live. At low tide it is a mile long, about one-tenth of a mile wide or, at sixty-six acres, roughly one-fourteenth the size of Kwajalein; Ebeye shelters 10,000 people. Some 400 of them are ferried to Kwajalein in the morning and returned in the evening. They aren't allowed to live on Kwajalein or to remain there over-night. During the day they can be seen mowing lawns, sweep-ing buildings, or cleaning the swimming pool.

After lunch we caught the ferry to Ebeye. It was full of Marshallese, most of them asleep. Twenty minutes later we docked and walked into the crowded shacks, unpaved roads, and endless din of Ebeye. We went to Mon La Mike, a private gambling and dancing club near the dock, and Caleb talked about nuclear testing. He grew up on Ujae, a small atoll due west of Kwajalein. He could remember the 1946 Crossroads test series, the first postwar nuclear explosions: "The glass on my kerosene lantern broke." More than sixty nuclear tests would follow until August 1958, when the U.S. ended its program; the next year, missile-testing facilities were con-structed on Kwajalein.

"I had no education. I started by sweeping floors in Majuro and worked my way up. Eventually I went to the outer islands as a paramedic. In the early sixties I went to Brookhaven. There was a federal program then to train field-workers to identify symptoms of radiation-related sickness. But the pro-gram was cancelled." The Brookhaven (New York) National Laboratory, contracted by the U.S. government, monitors the health of some Marshallese exposed to radiation.

"I remember that when I was doing fieldwork—after the bombs the women didn't have kids. They were all aborted. Two of my sisters got pregnant and the babies came out early and were dead. After that, I knew something was wrong." Caleb was looking at me steadily through his dark glasses and I tried to meet his gaze but ended up staring at the floor. The club was cool and airy. There were a few people there having a buffet, and a young Marshallese man was tinkling away on a synthesizer against one wall. Caleb told a story I'd heard before. It was about the people of Rongelap, a large atoll north of Kwajalein and eighty miles east of Bikini. At 6:45 A.M., March 1, 1954, the U.S. exploded Bravo above Bikini's lagoon. At fifteen megatons, Bravo was the largest bomb ever detonated by the United States government. A few hours after the blast, eighty-two Rongelapese were showered with a snowlike ash. Two days later, suffering from severe burns, vomiting, and diarrhea, the Rongelapese were evacuated to Kwajalein for testing and treatment. Three years later they were returned to Rongelap, along with 200 Rongelapese not on the atoll during Bravo. "[Even though] the radioactive contamination of Rongelap Island is considered perfectly safe for human habitation, the levels of activity are higher than those found in other inhabited locations in the world," a Brookhaven report explained. "The habitation of these people on the island will afford most valuable ecological radiation data on human beings." The 200 unexposed Rongelapese would provide "an ideal comparison group for the studies."

Soon after the Rongelapese returned, Caleb said, they threw a big picnic for the scientists. The centerpiece was a feast of coconut crabs, the premier delicacy of Marshallese cuisine. The Rongelapese hosts noticed that the scientists didn't like coconut crabs, or at least they refused to eat them. Over a year later, a Brookhaven team told the islanders not to eat coconut crabs, because radiation concentrates in the crabs' bodies.

Caleb told this story, in a passionless voice, while bent uncomfortably over a picnic table. Women around us were wrapping up the buffet leftovers in aluminum foil. "The Rongelap people and other people here are still having bad babies. A lot of the kids are retarded. There's one who walks around and can't help himself from bumping into things. You should see him. That's the very terrible thing. The new generation, it will be terrible. That will be the end of Rongelap."

■ One afternoon I went for a walk around Ebeye, strolling up the ocean side. Tropical storm Roy had hit the Marshalls a year earlier and Ebeye's residents were still rebuilding. Just beyond the small guesthouse where I stayed were two graveyards. Thanks to the efforts of missionaries most Marshallese are Christian, so their dead are buried in the shallow ground (the island is at most a meter high) with a slab of stone over them. Tropical storm Roy had tossed the stone slabs and crosses, jumbled them, and they still lay like monumental piles of jetsam. Bodies were wrenched from the earth but had been quickly reburied.

I watched children playing on the beach beneath the graveyards. They were extremely friendly to me. The majority of Ebeye's population are under nineteen. Marshallese children are well loved by their parents; they have an easy assurance, and at times Ebeye felt like a huge playground blessed with an unusual tolerance for adults. At puberty, a kind of cultural hammer comes down, especially on the girls, who tend to withdraw indoors and take over much of the responsibility for raising children. The boys play sports, organize into gangs, and in their teens usually begin to drink beer (and vodka, and bourbon). During two weeks on Ebeye I wasn't able to have a single sustained conversation with a teenaged Marshallese. This was not surprising. Most American men who visit Ebeye come from Kwajalein to party and have sex with the local women, often after a small payment. There were many children on Ebeye with unusually light skin.

At the northern end of Ebeye I came upon an orderly settlement of wooden barracks built to accommodate those Marshallese whose homes had been destroyed by Roy. The density was as high as twelve people per room. Beyond the barracks was a garbage dump where fires burned and kids played. One rode a bicycle, and I was mesmerized by the sight of him pedaling back and forth among the flames. At the tip of the island three older men fished with poles. A boy sat atop the wreck of a red car and cleaned a large green fish.

Dusk settled as I walked down the lagoon side. I stopped in at a grimy restaurant-nightclub and met the owner, a tall, excessively muscular Filipino named Bobby. He encouraged me to come back that night when the place got hot. "Ebeye has a great spirit," he said, "much better than Kwaj. Everyone there has a clique. The bachelors come over here on weekends." (A Kwajalein bachelor I met explained that "if you wanna get a bit of leg you gotta come over here.") I passed a ramshackle video arcade packed with kids. The unpaved roads were jammed, children playing and laughing. Sometimes they would giggle, point, and cry out *"Ribelli! Ribelli!"* when they saw me. *Ribelli* is the Marshallese word for white people.

That evening at Mon La Mike I met a Marshallese who works on Kwajalein. He and his wife live in a twelve-foot-square room with their five children. "When we want to make love we have to go outside!" he said, laughing.

■ A few nights later I had dinner with Julian Riklon. Julian was well into his thirties and had been among the leaders of Operation Homecoming, during which several hundred Marshallese reoccupied Kwajalein and ten other islands on the atoll from June to October 1982. They lived in tents and even built houses, went fishing, wove mats, harvested pandanus and breadfruit and coconuts. The U.S. military closed Kwajalein to reporters and did their best to discomfit the protesters—cutting off water and food from time to time, conducting searches, limiting travel, denying them access to telephones and the bank, and firing a quarter of the Marshallese work force on Kwajalein. Julian was beaten during one peaceful protest. Rolls of concertina wire, a watchtower, and searchlights were erected on the Kwajalein shore facing Ebeye, from which most of the Marshallese had come. The Marshall Islands government, led by President Amata Kabua, tried to dissuade the protesters but failed. Eventually, the U.S. agreed to reduce the term of its missile-test rights from fifty years to thirty, and an Interim Use Agreement was negotiated that contained promises to improve conditions on Ebeye. A Community Relations Council was formed to ease relations between Kwajalein and Ebeye.

The first time I saw Julian was at his house, which had a

ragged sign on the door saying "Bible Translation." Julian had worked for years translating the Bible into Marshallese. He was watching TV with his kids—a movie set in Australia and featuring Rachel Ward. He showed me photos of the damage from tropical storm Roy. "The Marshallese love to sing," he said, "though it's dying out now, with TV, videos, and imported music. On the outer islands people still sing to greet visitors." We watched the movie for a while, then I asked about Bible translation. He said it had been difficult. For example, in Marshallese the throat takes the symbolic place that elsewhere is reserved for the heart. So that Jesus's famous remark to the rich man would be "Love your God with all your throat."

Over dinner Julian said with a smile, "Tell our friends back in New York that I'm not a radical anymore." The leaders of Operation Homecoming are now immersed in local government and the flow of money that comes with it. Radical agitation and cultural nationalism have lost much of their appeal. "Americanization is coming. The children are bored with traditional life. People are beginning not to share things with their family." Julian said he had three children—seventeen, eleven, and six. The oldest was at a high school in Miami, Oklahoma. "She likes it there. She probably won't come back."

One aspect of traditional life that has survived is the power structure. Marshallese society is hierarchical, with the *iroij* (supreme chiefs) at the top, followed by the *alabs* and *dri jerbals*, beneath whom are the *kajur,* or serf class. The sphere of the *iroij* is divided into *bwij*, or clans. Perhaps the most radical action of the Operation Homecoming protesters was to reject the authority of President Amata Kabua, who is also the highest Marshallese *iroij.* In fact much of the protesters' succeeding quietude can be blamed on a resurgence of traditional authority. From 1979 to 1986, half of the U.S. land-use payments for Kwajalein were distributed on a per capita basis to Kwajalein landowners. After 1986, *iroij* Kabua and other leaders managed to name themselves distributors of the money, roughly $6 million a year. About seventy-eight traditional chiefs were now free to disburse the money as they pleased; some one-third of it goes to the four highest *iroij*, and about half of that goes to President/*iroij* Kabua and his immediate family.

These maneuvers were accomplished through both traditional means and lawsuits. In 1983, 400 *dri jerbals* brought a class-action suit against the Kwajalein Atoll Corporation charging that "per capita distribution is not in accordance with Marshallese customary practice and traditional rights." Because of the direct distribution of money to non-elite Marshallese, "the customary and traditional relationship with [the serf class's] leaders and peers within their respective Bwijs and with the Kajur as a whole are being subjected to an insidious and irreversible process of social erosion." The suit was eventually dropped, but a manner of argument had been established: the claim of Marshallese aristocrats on any land payments. Most of the 400 *dri jerbals* would lose out when the seventy-eight *iroij*, *alabs*, and senior *dri jerbals* made their move and began to enrich themselves. The highest-ranking Marshallese had transformed themselves from chiefs into landlords, a type of modernization that further impoverished their own people. In 1985, Julian said, 300 Marshallese, mostly women and children, occupied two houses on Kwajalein for four weeks. The Kwajalein authorities flew in police officers from Majuro and Honolulu, who put the protesters on a boat and took them back to Ebeye. An angry crowd at the Ebeye pier wouldn't let them dock, so the police took the Marshallese to a tiny island just beyond the garbage dump and threw them off the boat. This protest, Julian said, resulted in little publicity and no change.

In the course of my stay on Ebeye Julian introduced me to many people, including Imata Kabua, a relative of the president and the senior *iroij* on Ebeye. Imata frequented the two tennis courts that are next to both the Ebeye government buildings and Imata's spacious home. Imata and other high-ranking Marshallese, many of whom had been active in Operation Homecoming—Imata himself was a firebrand at the time—had formed a private tennis club. Beer flowed and the food was piled high. They tended to disport themselves in the quiet hour before dusk. I wasn't a member, but because I knew Imata and some other officials I could sit inside the high fence surrounding the courts and even get the occasional beer or plate of food. Imata cut a dashing figure in his polo shirts and dark blue tennis shorts—dashing, but morose; he seemed weighed down with a certain sadness. When we traded stories of being drunk in foreign places he perked up, but usually his attitude was remote. "It's hard being a chief," he said at one point.

One evening I went to his house. I removed my shoes and padded into the ample living room. At its center Imata sat in an easy chair watching baseball on TV. The room was unlit and bathed in television's blue glow. An ancient man sat at Imata's feet, massaging them. I approached deferentially and asked Imata if he might like to play tennis. I'm a poor tennis player, and was hoping that a victory over me would give him such a feeling of well-being that I might extract some personal favors. Specifically, I needed a boat to get to Mejato, where the Rongelap people were relocated after they got tired of being poisoned on their home island. Imata was an *iroij* and could get a boat (in fact he owned a boat, a nice one, but it was in Hawaii). "I'm not feeling well," he said. He had been at Mon La Mike the previous night and that morning, gambling and drinking. He didn't invite me to watch the game so I padded back out.

Getting a boat to Mejato proved to be extremely difficult. I began to realize that a certain resentment affected people's impressions of the Rongelapese, who, because of their being irradiated, receive money and food that they don't like to share. So I sought out Caleb Rantak once more and we hatched various plans. We went to see Mike Kabua, Imata's brother. It was nearly noon and Mike was still in bed; he'd been out late the night before. We waited outside at a picnic table with two women and a young man. Caleb said that two children had died of leukemia on his own home island, and he wondered, now that irradiated people were mixing with nonirradiated people, how quickly the disease would spread.

Caleb whispered to me that Imata was planning to sue the Rongelapese on Mejato because they weren't giving him enough of their radiation money. "The Marshallese are arguing over pennies!" he shouted. "The radiation-claims tribunal is a diversion! USDA [U.S. Department of Agriculture] food is destroying our culture! Ah! Sit under a coconut tree, play the ukulele, eat USDA food!"

The two women collapsed with laughter. "You always ate it!" one of them said. Caleb grinned painfully and went silent. He had eaten it, for most of his life, and now he had diabetes and circulatory problems. "Divide and conquer," Caleb muttered. "Divide and conquer."

■ After days of influence-peddling, negotiation, and the odd misrepresentation of fact, Caleb, Julian Riklon, and I managed to persuade an American commercial fisherman to sail to Mejato. Early one morning we loaded sugar and flour, five teenage boys, two women, three girls, an elderly man named John Anjain, and his adopted grandson onto the fishing boat. An uneventful five-hour passage followed. John had come along as my guide. He'd been the magistrate of Rongelap when Bravo exploded in 1954. Like many survivors of that time—including his wife and three sons—he had a scar on his throat, marking the removal of his thyroid. Radiation tends to create tumors in the thyroid. I was to meet many people with these scars; they began to seem like a subgroup of the population. John also wore dark glasses because of astigmatism (which, once again, may be caused by radiation). He'd been among a group of Rongelapese flown to Honolulu after the Bravo test for examination. I'd seen an official U.S. film of him and his companions, who were outfitted with overcoats and other Western clothes for the examinations and, the film's commentary pointed out, allowed to keep them. The film presented this trip as a lark for the "natives."

Eighteen years later John would travel as far as Bethesda, Maryland, to be with his son Lekoj, who died at the National Cancer Institute there of myelogenous leukemia. Lekoj had been one year old when Bravo dropped. On the boat, John and I crouched in the prow together to get out of the sun. I considered asking him about his experiences but his English was very poor. Also I felt a kind of prohibition inside myself. Somehow I didn't want to lure his memories. Maybe the pain of thinking about such things had, for the moment, reached a surfeit within me. I watched John and his grandson, a silent boy who clung to him, then closed my eyes and felt the rocking of the boat as we motored toward Mejato. John began singing in Marshallese.

At Mejato about half the population of two hundred had gathered on the beach. A tiny open launch putted out to collect us. The Marshallese passengers clambered into the launch while the skipper, his American mate, and I unloaded the hold. On the beach the teenage boys helped offload the food and other supplies, though they left me to carry the heavier items. John, his grandson, and I went to look for someone who could speak English. We walked along footpaths that meandered faintly through the undergrowth, linking shacks of plywood and corrugated iron. We'd stop and John would talk with this or that person, but apparently there was no one around who knew English; the mayor, school principal, and senator were all off-island. After nightfall we settled around a fire with several Rongelapese and drank weak tea with heaps of sugar. I asked a few questions and John tried to translate, but I was tired and no one seemed in the mood for interviews. Pigs and dogs milled about. After gallons of sweet tea we went to a treehouse to sleep. The Mejato treehouse is something of a joke. It is eight feet square and reserved for guests. The tree itself is only about fifteen feet high. Our ascension occasioned amusement among onlookers. This was, John explained with resigned embarrassment, the only treehouse in the Marshall Islands. Its name meant "Sun-Goes-Down House."

John, his grandson, and I lay down together on pandanus mats. I woke often during the night and could hear the surf. I hadn't slept with anyone for months so it was odd to awake with John and the boy sprawled across me. Several times I got up and wandered around beneath the treehouse. Mejato shone in the light of a full moon. There was just enough breeze to rattle the palm, pandanus, and *uti lomar* ("jungle flower") leaves. By early morning I was exhausted and put my arms around John and the child and we slept until dawn.

The previous day John had arranged for an island meeting. Soon after daybreak we went to a large, one-room building with a tin roof. About thirty people, young and old, male and female, sat against the slat walls. In the center were two chairs—one for me, and one for a translator, who turned out to be a man in his late twenties with a basic grasp of English. He told me he'd studied English in high school. Three years ago he'd had a mental breakdown and was only now recovering his stability. He was very nervous and apologetic and seemed about to spin away.

I explained my questions to the translator, who would then broadcast them generally. Most of the responses came from an old woman—a stocky, agitated figure with thinning gray hair. Several older men also spoke; sometimes all the older people would debate among themselves before offering a collective answer, usually through the old woman. She painted a general picture which I received, in fragments, from the translator: they had left Rongelap in 1985 because they felt they were being poisoned in order to provide information for the United States. Independent medical studies confirmed that they had extremely high levels of radiation in their bodies and in their food. "We are guinea pigs," the woman said.

U.S. scientists come to Mejato every six months to take blood and urine samples. Children are often born retarded or dead. Sometimes they are "jellyfish babies," dead infants who emerge from the womb as unformed collections of organs and fluid wrapped in skin. Mejato itself was not irradiated, but it is much smaller than Rongelap and has little food, either on land or in the sea (that's why it was previously uninhabited). The children suffer from malnutrition. Food shipments from the U.S. and various charities are inadequate, and consist only of rice and corned beef. I was urged to tell the American people that the people of Mejato are not receiving enough food.

I asked about the young people: Do they want to live on Mejato? A debate followed, and then I was told that young Rongelapese are as eager to live on Mejato as old Rongelapese. I asked about the Rongelapese living on Ebeye and Majuro. The old woman replied that they live there because they have jobs, not because they want money or dislike Mejato. An ancient man in one corner started to laugh uncontrollably. Two young men near him smiled uneasily then absented themselves from the room. The old woman watched them leave and said none of the teenagers on Ebeye are from Rongelap. The man laughed even louder. I asked other questions concerning Rongelapese teenagers, and the translator began to smile as he traced the logic of these questions. I ended up by smiling too. Because they knew what I wanted and weren't going to say it—that the next generation was drifting away and, except for the poison in their veins, would no longer be, in any powerful sense, Rongelapese. I knew what they wanted me to say—that they were honorable people, ruthlessly victimized and continuously neglected. The problem was that this terrible and obvious truth was *all* they wanted me to take away from the interview. They knew that generous people overseas wanted them, the objects of their generosity, to be pure, and for their victimhood to be pure as well. This put the Rongelapese in the grotesque position of having to dissemble in order to assure their supply of food.

We all smiled to save each other's honor. They didn't want to be victims but they were. *Love your God with all your throat.* They had scars on their throats and they needed food. But they also needed pride, and the spectacle of their children fleeing at the first opportunity, standing transfixed at the Ebeye video arcades, drinking, forgetting, even joining the U.S. military to escape altogether—it was too cruel. It was a victimhood without any practical benefit or compensation, a tragedy which they had no choice but to mourn alone. When the laughter had subsided the old woman spoke with restrained anger: "She says to tell your readers we'd like them to remember us in their prayers and to send best wishes of Mejato people."

On the trip back to Ebeye we had nine passengers, six of them boys. They had expensive high-top sneakers which they stowed away carefully for the trip. By this time, unfortunately, the captain and his mate had realized that they were being taken advantage of—I was the only paying passenger, and I wasn't paying much. The weather turned bad. Winds had reached twenty-five miles per hour and brought with them a heavy rain. The captain wouldn't allow us to shelter in the cabin so we huddled on deck. On occasion the waves were higher than our boat. It's unnerving to stare into the trough of a wave and know that the entire thing is about to pour over your head. The ink of a love letter I kept in my passport ran, covering the visas with tender, illegible phrases. One of the passengers, an infant, threw up on the deck. After five hours the storm passed and we motored along quietly as the sun went down. We put out two fixed fishing lines and caught a forty-five-pound yellowfin, a twenty-five-pound skipjack, and a thirty-five-pound *al.* I'd never fished like this before and hadn't realized that you club the fish to death. The goal is to strike them just behind the head and break the spine. Fish that big are quite strong; we had to wrestle one of them to the deck and hold it before getting in a good blow. Their skin glistened in the dwindling light, glints of yellow, blue, green, and gold against the white of the deck and the red of their blood spreading.

■ Back on Ebeye I met Caleb Rantak and Mike Kabua and told them about my trip. "People should work," Mike said with irritation. "The old way, in outriggers on the open ocean." "The Marshallese are a very tough people," Caleb added. I mentioned the rough weather and they let me know that it was a trifle, barely a storm at all. "That area is called the 'Dead Sea' because there are so many sharks," Mike said. "Sometimes you could walk from shark to shark, like on a bridge. Many people died out there. Many people." I thought: So who wouldn't prefer to eat corned beef and rice on shore?

I passed another week on Ebeye interviewing people, going for walks, hanging around the tennis courts, and waiting for money to be cabled from home. One afternoon I met Lijon Eknilang at Mon La Mike, where she worked part-time as a security guard. She was a large, attractive woman with a suggestive smile. The Marshallese men I knew spoke of her with an intriguing mixture of awe, lust, and disapproval; Marshallese women don't usually project such sexual assurance or power. I found her company a great relief since, during two months in Micronesia, I'd enjoyed only a handful of substantive conversations with women.

When Lijon was seven she and her family were staying on Ailingnae, a small atoll near Rongelap. On the morning that Bravo exploded they were all asleep. "There was bright lightning in the back of my eyes. When I woke up I was really scared. Outside my grandmother was fighting with her cousin over the bright lightning. We never understood where the bright lightning was from. When we looked around we saw there was no fire. But there was the big round thing. It was like the sun. I was really scared. I was just running around in a circle. When it explodes, it's just a big loud noise, you know, the earth's moving, it's just shaking. And all of a sudden we see the big cloud. You know, it's just a big cloud. When you see a big cloud you think it's raining. But no rain, just a sunny day. So we all sit together and sit with each other. I remember they think, It's a war started."

Lijon spoke in a pleasant, gentle voice. Sometimes she took sips from a can of soda. "Then we had something in the eyes. My grandmother tried to look in our eyes. Two hours later we got very thirsty. Others came and said they were thirsty. An old man said the water was changing colors. We didn't eat much, but drank a lot. Later that night everyone started to get a fever, itching their skin or something. And the eyes were— like sunburnt. The next day we went about our work as usual, planting copra. That evening a ship came to take everyone away. They told us not to take anything except the clothes we wore." Lijon and her relatives were then put on a larger ship. "The people from Rongelap were already there. They were really crying. They were itching all over. Their skin was turning black and you know their hair was all falling out." The ship took everyone to Kwajalein. "They made everyone wash up very clean. We got really hurt when we used that soap. That's pain! It was Ivory soap, and some yellow soap in blocks like you use for laundry. They never gave us any medicine. Just the soap."

In the succeeding years Lijon traveled often—around the Marshalls, plus two trips to the U.S. She wandered through America for several years. I imagined she must have been a fairly wild young woman. Hitchhiking in a foreign country is not the normal fate for a Marshallese woman. She said she'd been her father's favorite. He had been out sailing when the first ship came, so he wasn't quarantined. He died three months later of a high fever "and I don't know what else."

When Lijon finally settled on Ebeye she tried to have children. "I had seven miscarriages. Seven for which I went to the doctor. Maybe I had more than that. But those I don't really count. I just count those seven." Some of her sisters have borne children. "The kids have developed problems—physical problems." Two of her sisters have had their thyroids removed, as has Lijon. When I met her she was caring for several adopted children. Often in the following days I'd see her around Ebeye shepherding her family.

Coincidentally, the day I met Lijon was the Fourth of July. As far as I knew there were no formal plans to celebrate my country's national holiday on Ebeye. I wandered around the shacks at dusk and was happy to watch the children play. When night fell I went to the home of Tommy Milne, perhaps the only Marshallese entrepreneur on Ebeye outside the traditional ruling class. We sat on his living-room couch, drank beer, and watched the stateside celebrations on television. I told him about my trip to Mejato and Tommy, a handsome and energetic young man, explained that many people resent the Rongelapese because of their wealth. "The radiation victims and the Kwajalein landowners are envied because of their

payments. When they go to Majuro they are expected to spend
a lot of money. You even hear people telling stories about
radiation victims faking it so they can get more money."

On the screen we saw a succession of second-rate American
celebrities. The Fourth of July broadcast featured segments
from almost every American city. Each segment began with
panoramic shots of St. Louis or Cincinnati, a narration about
the city's historical interest, then a song or comedy act. America looked like a foreign country to me that evening. Tommy
said the Kili people—that is, the Bikini Atoll people, who
were relocated to desolate Kili after their home was irradiated—were once considered "country cousins. They were
looked down on. But with their [radiation-victim and reloca-
tion] payments they became admired. They put up a big
Christmas tree at the church, and they even compete with
Ebeye in giving the church money." As we talked I tried to
recognize the people on the TV screen but didn't have much
luck. Clearly they were well known, because the crowds were
cheering. I do remember Glen Campbell singing "Wichita
Lineman."

I asked Tommy how the Marshallese chiefs fit into this
pattern of backbiting, resentment, and struggle over money.
He mentioned the lawsuit *iroij* Kabua Kabua brought in 1984
against Imata and President Amata Kabua. Kabua contended
that Amata's father was Japanese, therefore Amata could not
really be the supreme *iroij.* How Imata fit into this I couldn't
quite tell. But the idea was that Kabua Kabua would, if he won
the suit, become supreme chief and be able to enjoy Amata's
income (and, perhaps, the presidency of the Marshalls as
well). At the turn of the century, the Marshalls were ruled by
a single chief, Kabua the Great, who in his old age divided the
realm between two sons. That was when the trouble started.

What I found most fascinating was that this conflict was
being argued in court, with lawyers, expert witnesses, and all
the paraphernalia of modern jurisprudence. The case was still
dragging on; apparently the key witness was Leonard Mason,
an American anthropologist who had many years' experience
in the Marshalls, much of it funded by the U.S. government.

■ I found it incredible that the Marshallese were turning to an American anthropologist and, in all likelihood, a non-Marshallese judge to decide this key question of Marshallese custom. Tommy thought it was grimly hilarious. "It used to be these things were sorted out by war. Then the Germans stopped wars, and decided custom power struggles by force. Now—ha!—they go to court." The Independence Day show culminated with actress-vocalist Pia Zadora singing "The Star-Spangled Banner."

■ After subtle and extended negotiations I got a reservation to fly from Kwajalein back to Majuro. I joined early-morning commuters on the Ebeye–Kwajalein ferry. The ferry's crew were well-fed Americans of a type I hadn't seen for nearly two weeks. They had the healthy look of people who staff resorts, and talked among themselves about parties and alcoholic excess. Their clothes were bright and clean.

On Kwajalein there were problems with the flight so I had a day to kill. I went to the ocean side and sat on the beach, which ran the length of Kwajalein. It was entirely empty and utterly clean. After the crush and hubbub of Ebeye such solitude gave relief. Dark clouds gathered, moistening the breeze. Over the preceding weeks something in me had loosened, so that the strictures of national and ethnic origins felt quite intangible and I found it difficult, in a radical sense, to say exactly where I was. This shouldn't have been surprising, since Kwajalein isn't really a place; it's more like a symptom. I prepared to curl up next to the sea for a long rest when I heard the voice of a little girl. "Hi," it said from somewhere, then shouted, "Monica, come here! I found a man!"

Monica and Diana were sisters, about twelve and eight years old, respectively. They joined me and talked about sticks, hermit crabs, the "forts" they'd built, and life on Kwaj. They thought life on Kwaj was okay, much better than on Ebeye, which they'd visited once. They complained that people on Ebeye throw their garbage in the ocean and that it floats

to Kwaj and dirties things. Rain began to fall. They took me
to one of their forts but it was too small, so we ran to a shelter
by the swimming pool. Two Marshallese men were cleaning
the pool; around it were molded plastic chairs decorated with
characters from the television series *The Flintstones*. Monica
suggested we go to the shark pit and watch the feeding (a
popular diversion for Kwaj children). But the rain was so hard
that she phoned for a shuttle bus instead. The bus came in
minutes. The Marshallese driver called me "sir." He drove
through the downpour, stopping frequently, and various
white Americans boarded. They were adults and regarded me
with suspicion. They spoke with Monica and Diana but not
with me. Eventually we arrived at Monica and Diana's house,
a comfortable, cluttered bungalow. Inside might have been
anywhere in America. Draped over the couch was a towel-like
rug with portraits of Robert Kennedy and Martin Luther
King. Monica introduced her father as "Sergeant." Sergeant
had his tools spread out and was putting up window curtains.
Monica took me to their backyard to see the family's bicycles,
each of which had a history, then back inside to play a game
I've always liked—we stood around hitting and kicking a balloon, trying to keep it in the air as long as possible. When I
was a kid we called this game "balloon." The three of us
played happily for ten minutes or so. Gradually it dawned on
me that I was an adult and a stranger, and that playing balloon
with two little girls was a breach of American custom. I asked
Monica to call the shuttle and we went to the phone book to
find the number. On top of the Kwaj directory was a warning
against discussing classified information by telephone. The
shuttle came quickly. From the door I shouted, "Thank you,
Sergeant," and heard Sergeant say, "Take it easy now."

The rain broke and I rambled around Kwajalein taking
photographs, mainly because I'd been told not to. I saw a
woman bicycling toward me with a fixed smile on her face.
Behind her in a tiny seat was a girl, her head bowed and face
hidden. As they passed, the girl looked up for an instant. It was
Diana. I waved and Diana stared at me as if I were from
another planet or had betrayed her, then hid her face again.

■ Majuro is a crowded, dirty, and depressing place. When Robert Louis Stevenson visited in 1889 he called it "the pearl of the Pacific," a phrase that still appears on tourist brochures. In the stretch of land between town and the airport you could almost imagine what it had been like: small homes tucked among the palms, plenty of open space. But most people—most Marshallese, anyway—live in cramped, collapsing houses or low-rise apartment buildings in town. The American elite, the businessmen and government advisers, have nicer homes.

I stayed at a modest hotel near the airport. The clientele were American and Japanese, with a few better-off Marshallese. I made friends with two young Americans from Hawaii. They were here on an environmental research project, so they had access to a lot of distressing information. A coral atoll is a fragile thing, and Majuro was being destroyed by pollution and landfill. One of the two scientists, Tahl, was despondent. "All this garbage!" Tahl said. "People can't take care of themselves." She'd been visiting a friend and noticed a Marshallese man nearby whose foot was bandaged. The friend told her that the Marshallese man had been sleeping when a rat came and chewed off the soles of his feet. The man's child also had an infected foot, and Tahl's friend had urged him to take her to the hospital. Finally the friend took her there herself. The doctors operated immediately and managed to halt the spreading gangrene.

Tahl was outraged. "Six kids have died of malnutrition so far this year. *Six kids.* And it's not like they're not eating, it's because they're eating junk food. And they *die.* People don't work, they just wait for handouts. The radiation victims play on U.S. guilt to get money, then go and buy condos in Hawaii. Majuro is disgusting." Tahl thought the U.S. should cut off the money, forcing the Marshallese to go back to the outer islands and fish and eat coconuts as they'd done for centuries. They could keep some medical care and education, even start some light industry. But basically the only way out of the horror was to return to a traditional life. And the only way to make that happen was to pull the financial plug.

We were joined by a middle-aged American who'd spent his adult life in Micronesia. Tahl was asking, "What if we just cut off the money? What would the Marshallese do if the Americans left?" The American grinned and laughed. "They'd find someone else to take them over. Probably the Japanese. Or the Russians. Who knows?"

Majuro *is* disgusting, though one day I was walking the dusty streets and saw Marshallese picking up rubbish. I asked what was going on and they said that all government employees had been given a day off to clean the streets. U.S. Secretary of State George Shultz was coming for a five-hour visit, and the government wanted to make a good showing. Shultz would be the highest-level U.S. official ever to visit the Marshalls.

I asked around and secured an interview with Louis Polichetti, who headed the United States Information Agency's Pacific programs. Polichetti was in town as part of a large advance team, most of whom spent their time lounging around my motel. I met him at the U.S. mission's chancery, an imposing and attractive former residence set in a lovely park of lawn and palm trees. The Soviets, Polichetti explained, were expanding their "blue-water port" at Camranh Bay, Vietnam, adding six docks to the existing three. He reminded me that the Soviets also have an air base at Da Nang. These two facilities give the Soviets "strike capability" against "sea lanes of communication." Polichetti said the Soviets were expanding their Pacific fleet, though, for the moment, only within the 200-mile zone near Vladivostok. He suggested that there were many other signs of increased Soviet (and Libyan) activity in the Pacific, including a fishing treaty with neighboring Kiribati, but was unable to give many specifics. He also said that the U.S. State Department would, "in two or three years," have a "coherent and forceful" Pacific islands policy. George Shultz, of course, wouldn't be around to see that happy day. Some clever people in his entourage had already been selling "George Shultz—Farewell Tour" T-shirts in the style of rock-concert promotion shirts, complete with a list of gigs: Seoul, Tokyo, Majuro. Shultz's tenure was almost over. But everyone knew that the next administration would be much the same as its predecessor, so any agitation or insecurity was minimized.

On July 20 I went to the Marshalls airport to await the secretary of state. Photographers from the Kwajalein Authority milled around, tending a mountain of fabulously expensive equipment. They said they were taking pictures "for the Command." The Marshallese police force arranged itself in two short lines, everyone wearing dark glasses. A group of local women stood expectantly in red dresses, bearing flower wreaths. The U.S. representative, his wife, and Marshallese officials were closeted in a VIP lounge built for the occasion. About 500 Marshallese gathered behind barriers; U.S. Secret Service men, pale functionaries dressed incongruously in dark suits and ties, roamed the area with their walkie-talkies.

An uninformed observer wouldn't have had any trouble recognizing Shultz's plane. It was larger than the airport and entirely white except for "United States of America" painted on each side. The Boeing 707 had doors front and rear. The rear doorway disgorged a platoon of dark-suited men with briefcases, most of whom crossed the tarmac at a slow run. From the front door emerged Shultz, his wife, more security people, and aides. Eventually some journalists debarked, immediately recognizable by their modest clothing.

Shultz mounted a platform across from the VIP lounge and speeches were made, brief statements touching on the long and deep friendship between the Marshall Islands and the United States. Shultz ended his remarks by saying, "We look forward to the next several hours, to seeing Majuro and to getting to know the Marshallese people." He and his wife danced momentarily with the flower-bearing women, then everyone except the 500 spectators, the policemen, and the greeters piled into cars for a quick ride to the U.S. chancery. In the press van my colleagues were fatigued; the Farewell Tour had been exhausting. A few showed some mild interest in the Marshalls, asking questions of me and Giff Johnson, the best of Majuro's few journalists. Questions like: "Is this an independent country?" and "What's the major industry around here?" Only two of the seventeen journalists filed stories, and these simply stated that Shultz had landed and given a speech about friendship. At the chancery a photo opportunity occurred—Shultz posed with local Peace Corps volunteers—then a meeting between Shultz and the U.S. representative, Samuel Thomsen, a career diplomat with long experience in Vietnam, Laos, and several African countries.

After a half hour at the chancery we were taken to a dock. Several ranks of elderly men stood stiffly along a high fence. They had been "scouts" during the American invasion of the Marshalls in 1944. As dusk fell the secretary of state arrived to give another speech. "Join me in looking across the Majuro lagoon and remembering a late January day in 1944," Shultz said, his voice barely audible and his face obscured in darkness. There weren't enough lights. "A small bank of American forces came ashore here to liberate Majuro Atoll from imperial Japanese forces. Like many other Pacific islands, these islands were removed from the hands of the aggressor and came again into the possession of the sovereign Marshallese people." Shultz pointed out that the taking of Majuro had been bloodless, while the battle for Kwajalein was severe. "That day saw some of the most brutal hand-to-hand fighting of the Pacific campaign. These Americans fought and died to return to you what has always been yours—these islands, these waters, this country." Shultz and a Marshallese politician, Oscar de Brum, threw flowers into the lagoon.

We then sped to a restaurant. American expatriates I'd never seen before came out of the woodwork for this party. So did the Marshallese matriarchs, unsmiling women occupying their own tables against one wall. After a few quick drinks Shultz's entourage loosened up. James Berg, a young State Department official and one of three bureaucrats largely responsible for Micronesia policy, was answering questions about the Soviet and Libyan threats. Shultz and President Kabua arrived. Kabua spoke briefly about peace; Shultz said more words about friendship; then we all attacked a splendid

buffet of Marshallese food. As Shultz and Kabua ate, old Marshallese women in grass skirts and muumuus danced a war
dance before them. I noticed Imata Kabua propping up the
bar and went over for a chat. He said he'd been talking earlier
with a Marshallese government minister about how Shultz was
only talking to white people and not to Marshallese. Imata
seemed sluggish and challenged by the effort of conversation.

After rushing through dinner we were herded back to the
press van. My colleagues had become noticeably more animated. The ABC News correspondent, Jeanne Merserve,
started singing an operetta. No one else knew the words, so
we switched over to songs from the Rodgers and Hammerstein musical *South Pacific.* Jeanne led with "I'm Gonna Wash
That Man Right Outta My Hair." Too soon—I'd wanted to
try "Some Enchanted Evening"—we arrived at the airport.
Everyone trotted aboard and the great white plane took off.
Night still hadn't fallen, not completely.

I rode back to the hotel with Louis Polichetti and compli-
mented him on how well the five-hour visit had gone. "All
these people really want," he said in a bored, tired voice, "is
for the U.S. to act like we know they're there."

■ Before leaving the Marshalls I went to meet the queen, or
leiroij, of Majuro, Atma Zedkaia. Generally speaking, each
bwij, or clan, has a single matriarch, and land is inherited
through the female line. According to Marshallese custom, a
family's or clan's wealth is administered by men on behalf of
the female leader. The matriarch is supposed to be consulted
on all decisions, but for the woman to do the work herself
would give her a bad name. This is changing somewhat: a few
women now prefer to rule by themselves, and some men have
tried to rule without deferring to the matriarchs.

Despite this erosion, the *leiroij* maintained that "in
Marshallese custom the woman is the power." We met in a
dank cafe across from the government buildings. Her English
wasn't good so a local journalist had come along to translate.
The *leiroij* was a small woman with an aggressive manner; her

sentences came in bursts, followed by long pauses during
which she chain-smoked Benson and Hedges. She sits on the
Council of Iroij, an "advisory" body of six *iroij* and six *leiroij*.
The council, she said, has thrown legislation back to the
elected parliament when the legislation was unacceptable. She
said it would be "unfair" for her to contest an elected office
because everyone would have to vote for her.

I asked whether she was troubled by the increasing emphasis on money and the apparent unruliness of young Marshallese. "We're trying to find a way of going back," she said. Then
came a rush of English and Marshallese mixed together. The
journalist translated: "She says the matriarchs are trying to
control monetization by squeezing on rents." I thought of all
the Marshallese I'd met or seen who were barely able to
survive. The children dying of malnutrition; the teenagers
committing suicide, usually by hanging. "Everyone's paying
in," the *leiroij* said. I asked about the president and supreme
iroij, Amata Kabua. "He's a good man," she said. "If he gets
money he gives it to me."

I returned to my hotel and watched American sitcoms on
TV, but their narcotic hold wasn't adequate to the task. My
room was in the center of Majuro and overlooked the back-
yards of various rusting shacks. That week's *Marshall Islands
Journal* brought the news that global warming would cause a
rise in the sea level. "Some scientists are predicting that the
sea level in the Pacific will rise by nearly five feet over the next
40 years," the article said, quoting a New Zealand report.
This would mean that the Marshall Islands have only a few
decades left. It seemed eerily appropriate that the Marshalls'
eulogy should be delivered by mysterious, selfish actors living
far away—people dedicated to the use of aerosol spray cans,
attached to the convenience of private automobiles. Brazilian
loggers profiting from the sale of rain-forest timber. Hasn't
postwar Micronesian life been a tale of slow destruction
wrought by enigmatic foreign desires? Radiation commits its
many little murders, minor episodes in the construction of
what used to be called the "postwar order" (it was also called
the "American Century"). Now rising seas, seemingly a force

104

■

of nature (but isn't radiation also, in some sense, a "force of nature"?), are added to the arsenal. And of course money, captivating the *iroij* and *leiroij*, winning hearts and minds, setting *alab* against *dri jerbal* against *kajur*—a universal solvent, also of foreign provenance.

ANNALS OF
SELF-DETERMINATION

■ *Most colonial powers, at least in principle, have enter-tained the idea of independence for territories they control. The patterns of self-determination in the Pacific are probably more complicated than in any other region on earth. Ger-many, Spain, France, the Netherlands, Japan, Indonesia, the United States, Britain, Australia, and New Zealand, to men-tion only the most important players (also Portugal, Chile, Russia), have all claimed possession of various Pacific islands. Most have since given them up, the key exceptions being the United States and France.*

The fortunes of small, independent Pacific countries have not been great. They rarely possess valuable resources, and even more rarely the means to exploit them. Many countries retain traditional political structures that graft awkwardly onto more European systems, and vice versa. The phenomena of a money economy and heightened consumer desires further strain the legitimacy of social institutions, whether new or ancient. Under such pressures, "modern independence" takes on almost as many forms as there are nations: monarchy in Tonga; a delirious mix of aristocratic, parliamentary, and military rule in Fiji; dispersed traditional systems combined with representative central government in Vanuatu. Each independent country seems to be finding its own way, as if foreign rule were a long but passing storm. And I was very glad to be visiting, at last, other people's ex-colonies.

Kiribati

"These countries are not going to disappear overnight and hopefully they're not going to disappear at all," Australian Prime Minister Robert Hawke said during a 1989 visit to Kiribati. He was referring to the possibility of rising seas inundating Kiribati (population 67,000) and other low-lying island countries. Hawke mentioned the possibility of relocating islanders to high ground in Australia. Such an action would, as Cook Islands Prime Minister Geoffrey Henry noted at a South Pacific Forum meeting, raise "questions of sovereignty," since no precedent exists for governing a country whose entire territory is underwater.

■ Originally I'd planned to go from Majuro to Fiji via Nauru. Nauru, known previously as Pleasant Island, is at once the envy and nightmare of its neighbors. The Nauruans are fabulously rich, with probably the world's highest per capita in-

110 come. Countless birds over millennia defecated upon the eight
■ square miles of Nauru. The feces of ages hardened into phosphate, and are now the source of enormous and entirely coin-
cidental wealth.

A joint British-German concern, the Pacific Phosphate
Company, began mining in 1905. Australia kicked out the
Germans in 1914. After World War I, Australia formally became administrator of the island, sharing the mining profits
with Britain and New Zealand under the corporate heading
of British Phosphate Commissioners. Nauruans received no
money at all, save for a minuscule royalty, but they did acquire
foreign diseases, and by 1920 there were only 1,210 Nauruans left (the pre-contact population was probably somewhat
more than 1,500). Japan took the island in 1942. After World
War II, the Nauruan population had dwindled to less than a
thousand. Back came the British Phosphate Commissioners,
who continued to make vigorous profits until 1967, when they
sold the Nauruans' remaining phosphates back to the Nauruans for twenty million Australian dollars.

After independence in 1968, Nauruans discovered prosperity. They bought cars and stereos and junk food and alcohol. A
combination of poor diet and sloth has left Nauruans with one
of the highest diabetes rates in the world, and one of the lowest
life expectancies—39.5 years for men, 48.5 for women. Driving accidents are the second leading cause of death for men.
Nauru has one road, ten miles long, which circles the island.
Few people stray from the road because nearly 80 percent of
Nauru consists of played-out mining fields—impassable
stretches of coral pinnacles from around which the phosphate
has been removed. In a sense, Nauru is part of the developed
world. It has industry, people who live off the labor of others, a
high level of consumerism, and a class of workers who are
relentlessly exploited (mostly imported Chinese, Filipinos, and
less fortunate Pacific islanders). Current estimates suggest that
the phosphate will be gone by the year 2000. The government
has set up a national trust fund, which would make Nauru the
first country to subsist entirely on interest payments.

I was very eager to visit such a place, but unfortunately

there were no flights. The only airline that served Nauru was Air Nauru. Air Nauru's pilots were Australians, and while I was in the Marshalls these pilots were carrying on a financial dispute with the Nauruan government. The pilots got fed up, emptied their bank accounts, and flew Air Nauru to Sydney, where they abandoned their planes. This may be the first instance of an airline hijacking itself.

With the demise of Air Nauru the only way to reach Fiji from Majuro, without taking a long detour through Hawaii, Hong Kong, or Manila, was by Air Marshall Islands (AMI) via Kiribati (in the Kiribati language, *ti* is pronounced either as *s* or *si*; Kiribati is *keer-i-bas*) and Tuvalu. One reason there's precious little contact between Micronesia and the South Pacific is the lack of transport. It's child's play to fly from Reykjavik to Fiji, but to get there from the Marshall Islands is nearly impossible.

When I finally got an AMI flight to Fiji I was surprised to find that it stopped for the night on Tarawa, the largest and most densely populated atoll in Kiribati and the seat of its government. Kiribati incorporates the Gilbert Islands, formerly a British colony, and various other tiny atolls. Both Kiribati and the Republic of Tuvalu, to the south, are grab bags, vast entities that control most of the vague space between American Micronesia and the South Sea Islands. They possess huge maritime resources thanks to the international law of the sea, which gives every nation economic sovereignty over the marine area within 200 miles of its shores (the Exclusive Economic Zone). Neither country, however, has the capital necessary to exploit these resources. Instead they lease the waters to wealthier nations—usually the U.S. and Japan, whose ships fish for tuna. Kiribati briefly came to the attention of the U.S. State Department when, in 1985, it signed a one-year fishing treaty with the Soviet Union. The next year, Kiribati demanded more money from the Soviets to renew the treaty. But the Soviets hadn't found the fishing particularly good so they said no, and the Soviet threat retreated. (When I was in Majuro, both Louis Polichetti and the U.S. State Department's James Berg had mentioned Kiribati as an exam-

ple of Soviet expansionism; neither expert seemed to know
that the treaty had been cancelled several years earlier.)

Apart from its rare appearances in the literature of East-
West paranoia, Kiribati is a forgotten corner of the world. It
found brief fame in World War II because Japanese and Americans died there, mainly during the horrific fighting on Tarawa
in November 1943 (990 Americans killed, 4,690 Japanese;
only seventeen Japanese were taken prisoner). There are still
guns, planes, and other military detritus scattered about the
islands, but no one pays them any attention. They're like
grounded meteors that have become familiar with time. The
command bunker of the great Japanese admiral Keiji
Shibasaki is used as a toilet by locals.

There were no hotel rooms available near the airport. It
turned out that earlier flights had abandoned passengers on
Tarawa, and so accommodations were scarce. A man at a
so-called hotel at the other end of the atoll said by telephone
that he had space, so I hopped on the local bus. There is one
road that links most of Tarawa. Few people own cars, so the
buses go very fast. Tarawa itself has a reputation for ugliness,
but it was paradise compared to Majuro or Koror. Here the
houses were well spaced, with taro patches and gardens. The
coconut trees looked cared for, making Tarawa seem much
different from most of the places I'd visited in American Micronesia; you felt that people were actually *living* there, not
just camping out. They walked the streets and paths to socialize instead of holing up with their TV's to watch martial-arts
videos or *Miami Vice*. Kiribati is money-poor; what cash exists
comes mainly from foreign aid (British, New Zealand, Australian), which funds the government and sometimes trickles
down. Most of Tarawa's residents are people from other
Kiribati islands who've immigrated to live with relatives who
have government jobs. It was explained to me that if relations,
however distant, appear at your doorstep you have no choice
but to shelter and feed them indefinitely. Among other things,
this puts a brake on financial ambition: the richer you become,
the more demands will be made on your wealth.

After forty minutes I arrived at the hotel, which consisted

of several rooms behind a restaurant. The innkeeper's optimistic notion was that I could sleep in spare beds in rooms that were already occupied. Sadly, the occupants didn't agree. I grew depressed and cast despairing glances toward passersby. Finally the hotelkeeper's accountant, a gentle man with many earrings, invited me to his house.

His name was Wirama. Together we walked to the street—it was dark by now—and waited for a bus. The street was full of i-Kiribati (people of Kiribati), strolling and lounging. The people nearby seemed happy to watch us and laugh. Why they were laughing I didn't know.

Wirama's house was actually his brother's wife's, or so he said. Kiribati remains, in many ways, "the old Pacific." Wage-paying work is still scarce; weekends are not much different from weekdays; education is derisory; people can be found wandering about the island at any hour; and family means everything. Wirama made it clear that a person might sleep here one night, elsewhere another, but always at a home that was dimly connected to one's family. The schedules and notions of privacy that make Western life orderly are largely missing. When I told Kiribati stories to other Pacific islanders they would often sigh and say, "Yes, it used to be like that here, too."

Across from Wirama's house, which had walls and a solid roof, unusual luxuries in Kiribati, a group of people—the Butiraoin Nei Kaueke troupe—were dancing. Wirama happened to be the group's director, so we went and sat down among the spectators in a small open space between two buildings, under fluorescent light. The dancers were close together in three parallel lines of eight each. They were led by a stocky man whose appearance and manner reminded me of a cinema samurai. He was dancing in the center of the group, and his gestures were sharp, truncated, and powerful. Most of the other dancers were young girls and boys, gifted with a confident lightness. The samurai would call out in song and the other dancers would respond as a chorus.

After a few dances Wirama chatted with the samurai. I couldn't follow the conversation because it was in Kiribati

(Gilbertese). I asked Wirama about one of the dancers, who was very pretty and danced more suggestively than the others. Wirama laughed and explained in his gentle, slightly melancholic voice, "She is a boy. Do you like him?" A good deal of murmuring and laughter ensued. The young boy scurried into a side room, then reemerged with a shy smile and wearing a fake grass skirt. A cassette was popped into a portable player and the boy performed a Rarotongan dance, fighting back his smile. At the end everyone clapped and he hurried back into the side room.

The samurai jumped up and again organized the dancers into three lines. Three young boys sat in front. The standing dancers sang while the boys made delicate, highly stylized gestures with their hands and arms. Kiribati is famous for this type of dance. "There are some dances that are only done by . . . by . . . pooftahs," Wirama said. "Do you use the ass?"

Wirama asked me many questions about the sexual habits of white people. He was particularly interested in homosexuality. I said that homosexuality in white culture varies greatly from place to place. In some areas one could be homosexual without too much trouble, in other areas one could be beaten or imprisoned for it. Certainly homosexuality *existed* everywhere.

"In secondary school, St. Joseph's, I was just like a girl," Wirama said. "On my home island I played very often. When I go back there I still play. But not here on Tarawa. I don't know why." Wirama didn't look much like a girl anymore. He was around thirty and, by Western standards, overweight, his skin puffy and pockmarked. He had a wonderful, humorous alertness, and was fond of smoking the Kiribati cigarette—about eight inches long, tapered, black tobacco wrapped in dried pandanus leaf, bound with fibers. We watched the dancing and smoked and talked. Wirama occasionally pointed out a boy or girl and asked if I wanted to take him or her to the house. He made these offers in a friendly, slightly conspiratorial way. He also said that it wasn't right for me to be alone. An older man sitting next to us offered to marry me. "In English you have a word, 'shame.' We don't have that word," Wirama said. "Here anyone can play with anyone." Behind us, outside the pool of fluorescent light, people sat or stood, wandered past. There always seemed to be laughter, here and there in the darkness. Fifty yards down the road another group was dancing and singing in their own pool of light. I quite lost track of time.

After a series of dances, Wirama's group rested. Then a cassette with Western pop was put on and one or two couples rose and jumped around to Michael Jackson and Madonna. They danced something like the twist (*te tuiti*). They often looked at the ground while dancing, as if searching for marks that would show where their feet should go. They almost never looked at each other.

The samurai asked through Wirama if I would show them some dances from my country. I became very confused. I love to dance, and wanted to be a good guest, but several considerations intervened. Clearly the i-Kiribati dance according to a pattern, and I don't know any patterns. So I said, "We don't really have *dances*. We just dance." Wirama stared at me as if to say: that doesn't make any sense at all.

Fortunately, he gave me another opportunity to reciprocate. "After the dancing you should give a speech." Wirama said I should give my name and country, my parents' names and their current whereabouts, my level of education, and my profession, then express my admiration for the dancing and Kiribati in general.

Once the cassette had stopped Wirama announced my speech. The dancers sat on the ground and looked toward me expectantly. I stood up and covered all the topics, with Wirama translating after each sentence. At the end everyone applauded. I had no idea what my speech meant or why I had to give it. Wirama said I'd done well. I liked to think that this was a society in which one could be applauded simply for being oneself.

Everyone drank a few cups of weak, sugary coffee, then

Wirama and I returned to the house. Wirama put me in his brother's bed, while he took the floor. I woke up three times during the night: to the feeling of a rat crawling up my leg, to the agitated rustle of Wirama groping through an erotic dream, to the sound of a couple making love nearby.

Fiji

"*O ira ga na turaga era tabaki keda sobu tiko,*" *the saying goes in Fijian.* "Only the chiefs are pressing us down." After independence in 1970, Fiji was presented as a model South Pacific democracy, one which had somehow succeeded in blending its various ethnic traditions with parliamentary government and a cash economy. The sudden arrival of military rule in 1987 changed all that and begged long-dormant cultural questions. As Fijian administrator Rusiate R. Nayacakalou wrote in 1975, with impressive foresight, "It seems to me that one of the greatest obstacles facing the Fijians*

---

*A note on pronunciation: Several letters in Fijian are pronounced as if other letters precede them. *G,* for example, is pronounced *ng*; thus *turaga* is "turanga." Additionally, *b* is *mb* (Bau—Mbau); *d* is *nd* (Nadi—Nandi); *q* is *ng* (*yaqona*—yangona). *C* is pronounced like the *th* in "there" (*maca*—matha). The *r* is trilled, as in Spanish; generally, vowels are also pronounced as in Spanish. Emphasis usually falls on the penultimate syllable.

■   *today is the failure to recognize that there is a contradiction;
      they must now make the momentous choice between preserving
      and changing their 'way of life.' The belief that they can do
      both is a monstrous nonsense with which they have been sad-
      dled for so many years now that its eradication may be very
      difficult to achieve."*

■ Getting out of the airport at Nadi proved to be difficult. I
told the humorless immigration agent that I was a journalist.
There had been two military coups in Fiji the year before
(May 14 and September 25, 1987), and foreign coverage of
the events hadn't been flattering. In fact, when I arrived there
was an informal ban on foreign journalists. A *New York Times*
reporter had snuck in a few weeks earlier; the fact that he'd
been traveling incognito made his article particularly impressive.

I did not feel very impressive myself, sitting alone for hours
in the transit lounge. The immigration officer came by from
time to time to continue negotiations. He wasn't remotely
optimistic about my chances of entering Fiji, but as the hours
went by it appeared that I did have one strong card to play:
namely, the home phone number of Ratu Jone Radrodro.
Radrodro was, first of all, a *ratu*, or Fijian chief, and, secondly,
he was the permanent secretary for home affairs. As such, he
was in charge of immigration, an important figure in the state
intelligence apparatus, and the immediate underling to Brigadier General Sitiveni Rabuka, who'd staged both coups and
named himself minister for home affairs (and head of the
armed forces). Though I didn't know Radrodro, I began to
refer to him familiarly as Ratu Jone, and hinted to the officer
that he was awaiting my arrival with the keenest anticipation.
The immigration officer phoned Ratu Jone repeatedly at his
home in the capital, Suva, but the chief was out at a party.
After five hours, I was given a two-day visa and told to report
to Ratu Jone at the first opportunity.

Nadi is on the opposite side of the country's largest island,
Viti Levu, from Suva and surrounded by fields given over to

sugarcane, Figi's most important export. The town itself is a drab collection of two-story duty-free shops and travel agencies. Tourists plied the main drag sniffing at watches and jewelry; hustlers followed them offering guided tours. Tourism had dropped by some 26 percent after the coups, and many of the town's storefronts were boarded up.

So it was a relief to leave Nadi on a tourist bus bound for Suva. The bus meandered along a narrow highway surrounded by cane fields. Indian women wrapped in saris shepherded children through the fields, down unpaved side roads, or into the rough shacks where they lived; Indian men and women stooped here and there gathering cane. Sugarcane is harvested by hand and piled onto a narrow-gauge train that dates from the last century. More than three-quarters of the cane cutters are Indian, descendants of indentured laborers imported by the British between 1879 and 1916. Under colonial policy and—after independence in 1970—under the Fijian constitution, over 80 percent of Fiji's land has been controlled by ethnic Fijians. The intent and effect of this policy have been to keep Fijians in their villages and Indians in the cane fields. Rents accrue to the government (25 percent), high Fijian chiefs (30 percent), and male Fijian heads of households (45 percent). Land ownership is thus a scheme to ensure the solvency of Fiji's customary rulers while sparing them the necessity of working. It's been 116 years since the British annexation of Fiji in 1874. Yet many Fijian chiefs cannot read or write in English, and many Indian families remain in the same fields that their indentured ancestors worked during the period they called *narak*, or "hell."

The road eventually ascended from the light green cane fields into steep, forested hills whose peaks gestured toward the southern coast of Viti Levu, the "Coral Coast." Along the coast we stopped at each resort. The resorts were very pleasant, with gardens, golf courses, and calm verandas under thatch roofs. Australian accents filtered through the placid hallways and restaurants. Every resort seemed to have a platoon of insanely friendly Fijians. Fijian friendliness is a key component of the country's tourist image, an image whose plausibility was damaged by the two military coups. So local cheeriness had been turned up a notch. Everywhere our tourist bus was greeted with cries of *"Bula! Bula!"*—Fijian for "hello." Another key tourist draw is the opportunity to meet "natives." No one comes to Fiji to eat *dahl* or hear about the accomplishments of Mogul civilization, even though a bare majority of Fiji's citizens are of Indian descent. So the hotel staffs are heavily weighted toward ethnic Fijians.

After a dozen or so resorts we left behind the din of *Bula!* and finally arrived in Suva. My first appointment, naturally, was with Ratu Jone Radrodro at his third-floor office in the Ministry of Home Affairs. He turned out to be a large, phlegmatic man who was trying hard to quit smoking. I offered him a cigarette but he pulled out one of his own. We chatted in a leisurely fashion about cigarettes, cigars, his difficulties in raising a family, the joys of children, beer, and New York. I struggled to be ingratiating yet confident and brought up Marxism. Americans abroad are generally perceived to be anticommunist, and the Rabuka regime took anticommunism as a basic tenet. Ratu Jone singled out Suva's University of the South Pacific, a regional institution funded by Pacific governments, saying, "There are too many Marxists there." The military government often sends its troops to the university to arrest or beat students and professors. "I believe other developing countries have found it useful to intervene in their universities." I signaled my sympathy, we talked a bit more, then Ratu Jone gave me a month's visa. Back on the ground floor I paid my respects to a meek and nervous part-European who directed the state information office. On the wall was a poster: "Security Is an Open and Shut Case—Eyes Open, Mouth Shut."

■ The immediate purpose of the first coup, on May 14, 1987, was to oust the month-old government of Dr. Timoci Bavadra. Bavadra and his Coalition party had defeated the Alliance party. The Alliance was led by Ratu Sir Kamisese Mara, Fiji's fourth-highest chief, and supported by the traditional Fijian hierarchy, ethnic Fijians, and businesspeople; the Coalition drew its support from workers, intellectuals, and, above all, Fiji's Indians. Though Bavadra was himself Fijian, a minor chief, and the husband of a high-ranking chief, Adi Kuini Bavadra (*adi* is an aristocratic term similar to "lady"), just over half his cabinet were Fiji Indians. The feeling of some Fijians that they were being taken over by Indians went very far in legitimizing the coup.

The group most responsible for stirring anti-Indian sentiment before the coup was the Taukei, an informal clique whose venerable name means "People of the Land." The Taukei went about erecting roadblocks, holding rallies, and intimidating people. After Bavadra's victory they built a *lovo*, or earth oven, in front of the Parliament buildings and proposed putting their enemies in it, a nostalgic reference to the cannibalism widely practiced before the arrival of Methodist missionaries (though the most famous cannibalizing was of a missionary, the Reverend Thomas Baker, in 1867). Various Taukei members met with then Lieutenant Colonel Rabuka prior to the coup, as well as with Ratu Mara's son, Ratu Finau, and a son of Fiji's paramount chief, Ratu Sir George Cakobau. The meeting took place over a bowl of *yaqona*, the traditional Fijian intoxicant made by infusing the crushed roots of the kava pepper (*Piper methysticum*). They covered various possibilities for destabilizing Bavadra's government and ended with a prayer linking Fijians to the Israelites, "whose land was taken from them by foreigners."

Among the small group of Taukei who had paraded around the *lovo* was Ratu Meli Vesikula, a powerfully built, bullet-headed man who returned to Fiji in 1982 after twenty-one years in the British Army. I met him one afternoon at the informal Taukei headquarters—a few unadorned rooms in a miniature, unadorned shopping mall in downtown Suva. The rooms were crowded because a lottery was under way, but Ratu Meli and I found quiet in his dirty, glass-walled office. Ratu Meli pounded himself in the head. "The Fijian people are confused!" he shouted. "How did a happy race of people living in paradise with a big smile on their faces—they lived on their land and worked hard, no Fijians begging on the streets, no Fijian unemployment, no Fijian prostitutes—go from a race of winners to a race of no-hopers . . . what the *hell* have they done to my race? I was fortunate in that I was picked up from Fiji in 1961, to a different society. But up here"—Ratu Meli pointed to his head—"I always had that Fijian society, unpolluted by anything. When I came back, into chaos, I could handle it, I could see it clearly."

"Seeing clearly" meant rising against the Bavadra government and Fiji Indians in general. The belief was that Indians were succeeding in commerce at the expense of Fijians and, with the new government, were taking over politics as well. In fact, Indians, Europeans, and Chinese do dominate Fijian business. The reasons for this are complicated. Fiji's Indians, prohibited by law from owning most land, invested their meager earnings in capital and education. Capital and education are useful for commerce, and those who were able to leave the cane fields, often after decades of backbreaking labor, became merchants. Second, many of Fiji's biggest Indian merchants are Gujaratis, from the western Indian state of Gujarat, who emigrated to Fiji in the 1920s and later. They never cut cane; they were businesspeople when they arrived, and many made fortunes. (Many Gujaratis also supported the Alliance party with their money, a fact often overlooked in ethnic analyses of Fiji.) On the Fijian side, moneymaking was culturally frowned upon, and hobbled by the fact that custom requires Fijians to give money to relatives and fellow clan members, not to mention chiefs. The chiefs themselves were unlikely to seek careers in accounting or management. Culturally, they were obliged to distribute wealth more than accumulate it; their power and prestige were based on lineage, not money; and, of course, they had a permanent sinecure in the form of rents paid by Indian cane cutters.

But these factors, and many others—like the wealth of European and Chinese businesspeople—were far too complex for the Taukei, Rabuka, the Fijian chiefs, and the many Fijians who supported the coups. They felt they were being taken over by non-Fijians, non-Christians, and so Bavadra's government was overthrown on behalf of, in Rabuka's terms, "the Fijian way of life," "the chiefly system," "the interests of RFMF" (the Royal Fijian Military Forces), anticommunism, and the Methodist God.

Ratu Meli supported these goals, for he felt there was no other way out of the chaos he had found on returning to his native land. At the root of that chaos, he believed, was democracy. "Historically, Fijians were governed autocratically. In 1970 democracy was introduced, but Fijians were not ready for it. The solution is to educate Fijians in democracy." In the meantime, Ratu Meli advocates a legislative council: "Leave democracy to our great-grandchildren." On Ratu Meli's desk were a Bible, a hefty volume called *World Christianity*, and a videotape titled *Forbes in Fiji*. (The American billionaire and free-market propagandist Malcolm Forbes owned a small Fijian island. He was also pals with Ratu Ganilau, Ratu Mara, and other Fijian leaders.)

As time went by Ratu Meli's reflections became a little contradictory. On one hand, he saw democracy as a desirable goal; on the other, "In a democratic system, you can never be free, never be equal." He didn't show any enthusiasm for Indian culture, yet he felt that the Indian race in Fiji was "advanced," while the ethnic Fijians were "backward." And while he prized the Fijian way of life, he believed that the chiefs were, in effect, profiteering from the coups.

The second coup, on September 25, came on the heels of an agreement between the Coalition and the Alliance to form a caretaker government. This arrangement offered nothing to Rabuka and his military allies and threatened the Great Council of Chiefs, whose blood-and-soil enthusiasm was by now quite high. The Great Council welcomed Rabuka's second coup, which resulted in Fiji's leaving the Commonwealth of Nations (formerly the British Commonwealth) and becoming a republic. The more worldly chiefs of the Alliance party had many reservations about the second coup, but their party refused to condemn it; eventually the Alliance's two scions, Ratu Sir Penaia Ganilau (ex–governor general) and Ratu Mara (ex–

prime minister), agreed to become president and prime minister, respectively. The assertion of Fijian primacy was complete. "The chiefs are living in the best of both worlds," Ratu Meli said. "They are chiefs in an autocratic system, and the heads of a democratic system." After the second coup, Rabuka removed Ratu Meli and several other Taukei veterans from their government posts. The Taukei had split into two factions, and Rabuka decided to exploit the division. Since then, Ratu Meli had realized that the coups were not intended to protect the Fijian people, but rather to protect the interests of the Alliance party, the chiefs, and their Gujarati, Chinese, and European financers. Ratu Mara, he said, had known about the first coup beforehand, and Rabuka overthrew the Bavadra government on behalf of Mara and the Alliance. "Some were in the Taukei movement solely to see Ratu Mara and Ratu Penaia back in power, particularly Ratu Mara."

Ratu Meli gave me a crushing handshake and I pushed my way outside through the crowd of Fijian lottery players. Suva's intricate, slouching streets were quiet. Some storefronts were still boarded up; others displayed copies of Rabuka's as-told-to book, *No Other Way* (Suva, 1988), posters of the handsome, mustachioed, beefy general, and T-shirts celebrating the one-year anniversary of his first coup. I strolled up Victoria Parade, past the dreary government buildings—a bilious pile of gray, streaked cement—to the Grand Pacific Hotel. The Grand Pacific and the governor-general's residence (now the president's residence) are the remaining splendors of high-colonial architecture. The Grand Pacific has two wings: the Colonial Wing and the New Wing. I wondered why they didn't call the addition the Postcolonial Wing. Maybe management lacked the nerve, or maybe they thought it would have been premature.

I stayed in the Colonial Wing: louvered doors, ceiling fan, porcelain washstand. At dusk I usually sat at a table by the swimming pool. A uniformed Fijian waiter would serve cold quarts of Fiji's excellent beer, called Fiji Bitter (made from an Australian recipe). The poolside terrace gave onto Suva Harbor. A Cyclone fence topped with barbed wire guarded the

bulkhead. Rats cavorted at the fence's base; across the harbor
forested mountains brooded during the day, reflecting a show
of colors at sunset.

The Grand Pacific was a congenial place to reflect on Fiji's
history. I'd heard much about the Fijian chiefly system as the
guardian of a Fijian way of life. So I was surprised to find
that, judging from the few scholarly works on the subject,
the chiefly system didn't exist in any national sense until ces-
sion to Britain in 1874. Prior to 1800, according to historian
David Routledge, Fijian society was typically organized in
"small, localized kin-units having a clearly defined corporate
entity, each working to build up advantage against neigh-
bours or to maintain hard-won prestige." The remnants of
village architecture, still visible today, suggest that warfare
was constant, though more oriented toward fearsome display
than large-scale slaughter. In the late eighteenth century, an
"empire" was established in Verata, just north of Suva.
Verata was the first sizable political unit known to have existed in Fiji. By the early 1800s, four other centers of power
with roughly similar customs fought over the declining
Verata empire: Bau, Rewa, Cakaudrove, and Lakeba. These
four were all located in what is now called eastern Fiji. Bau
and Rewa are near Suva; Cakaudrove is based on Vanua
Levu, a large island 120 miles northeast of Suva; Lakeba is a
tiny island of the Lau group, about 200 miles due east of
Suva across the Koro Sea.

Their intricate struggles went on for decades, subject by
mid-century to three simplifying factors: guns, Tongans, and
Europeans. As elsewhere, firearms, readily available by 1830,
had a kind of leveling effect. As an English observer noted at
the time, "The fact that bullets are so promiscuous in their
work, striking chief as well as commoner, makes the people
less disposed than ever to come to fighting, while their faith
in the diviner qualities of their commanders is much shaken."
Fighting nevertheless proceeded, under conditions that favored the Tongans. They possessed a highly stratified society,
formidable war canoes, and imperial ambition. The Tongans
established themselves in the Lau islands, of which Lakeba is

the capital. Under Taufa'ahau and, later, Ma'afu, Tongan power grew steadily.

Ma'afu became king of Lau in 1853. The Fijians continued to battle among themselves, the key rivalry being between the neighboring regions of Bau and Rewa. In January 1855, they came together in the decisive battle of Kaba. The Tongans sent an unprecedented force (over thirty war canoes) to aid Bau, which quickly won.

As for the Europeans, they were in no way united until the 1870s. But Protestant missionaries did have ties to the Tongans, who were Wesleyan Methodists. It was the Tongans who forced Cakobau, the king of Bau, to accept the *lotu toga,* or Tongan Church, as Wesleyan Methodism was called in Fijian. (What would John Wesley have thought?) As Europeans expanded their economic interests in Fiji, particularly cotton, they sometimes played the Fijians off against the Tongans. The 1860s was a decade of jostling, with Ma'afu and Cakobau competing for advantage with the Europeans and their own people. Fiji's eastern chiefs, fearful of settlers, Tongans, and the western Fijians (who were subject neither to Methodism nor eastern chiefs), asked Britain to take sovereignty, but their request and subsequent reiterations were denied.

Britain was reluctant because colonies can cost a lot of money. There were serious profits to be made growing cotton, but they were temporary. Fiji's cotton boom, which began when American exports were interrupted during the Civil War, ended with Union victory. In 1870, their cotton dreams having collapsed, Fiji's Europeans were scrambling nervously. Local efforts at government, usually involving Cakobau as the putative king of Fiji, came to little. The British consulate sometimes aided and sometimes obstructed these efforts. More important, many settlers opposed Cakobau's government because it had the nerve to attempt taxation; some formed a British Subjects' Mutual Protection Society, which came to be known familiarly as the "Ku Klux Klan" (Fiji branch). The mercantile stronghold of Levuka was notorious. One emissary of Cakobau hesitated even to land there: "A row was going on and bullets were being slapped about with an

abandon anything but attractive to married people of quiet
taste and regular habits." Slaves were traded through Levuka,
as were, in the words of a British consul, "attractive girls
verging on womanhood."

On March 20, 1874, Cakobau and other chiefs once again
offered to cede Fiji to Britain. This time Britain accepted,
thanks largely to the towering self-assurance of a visiting naval
captain, J. G. Goodenough, who liked the idea of playing a
visible part in history. Britain, however, didn't want one more
far-flung drain on the exchequer, and in 1879 the first Indians
arrived as laborers to build a sugar-plantation economy. The
Fijian population had been decimated by a measles epidemic.
Moreover, Britain felt the Fijians weren't much use as genera-
tors of colonial revenue; they were thought, on the basis of
social Darwinist theory, to be a dying race, one to be protected
up until its inevitable demise; and in any case the Fijians were
too strong in their own country to be reduced easily to peon-
age.

They were encouraged by the British to govern themselves.
As an early British official put it, "Through them it might be
possible to govern, against them it was impossible." In practice, indirect rule extended the power of a few eastern chiefs
and ex-Tongans over all of Fiji. The "chiefly system" was
born. Fijian provincial administrators became chiefs (*ratu* is a
late-nineteenth-century term), acting essentially as colonial en-
forcers; the traditional *bete* ("priest") was replaced by the
talatala ("minister"). With time, these arrangements were
recast as immemorial tradition and crucial to "the Fijian way
of life." And, over a century later, an elected government
would be overthrown in their name. Its replacement would
have at its head two eastern chiefs, Ratu Mara of Lakeba (*tui*,
or "king," of Lau) and Ratu Penaia Ganilau, king of Cakaudrove. As Brigadier Rabuka, a member of the traditional war-
rior caste, told the U.S. ambassador, "I will always kneel
before my chief"—who was, it turned out, none other than
Ratu Penaia.

• • •

128 ■ The past would probably have no hold on the present if it
■ didn't conform to our imaginations and needs. The past is
retrieved through remembrance, but its most valuable gifts—
meaning, a sense of identity—seem always to lie just beyond
memory. Their origins, and their power, are inaccessible.
Even if you could name the origins of feeling you would never
have more than a genealogy; and even if you could name the
first birth there would still be another one before it, unname-
able. I thought often of Ratu Meli Vesikula while staying in
Suva. During twenty-one years abroad, Ratu Meli said, he'd
kept Fijian society in his head, "unpolluted." Which is why,
when he returned, he could see clearly. He saw that Fijian
society was threatened, and the obvious culprit was the Indians. Though Indians had been a demographic majority since
1945, they had never gained substantial political power—that
lay with the British and, after independence, the ethnic Fijians.
In fact, the British had excluded Indians from the franchise
until 1929. And Fiji's constitution, written under British influence, had elaborate safeguards for ethnic Fijian hegemony.
The "inalienability" of 80 percent of the land was one; legal
recognition of the Great Council of Chiefs, also a colonial
invention, was another; and, finally, a voting system that divided the electorate along explicitly racial lines and favored
ethnic Fijians. (People often criticize democracies for dis-
criminating against minorities; Fiji's democracy discriminated
against the majority.)

What Ratu Meli discovered after the first coup was that the
threat to Fijian society was much greater than that posed by
a part-Indian government. Fijian society, as he imagined it,
was not simply a creature of feeling and tradition. It was also
a product of British administrative needs, economics, chiefly
ambition, the affective requirements of modern nationalism,
and a host of other influences. In the exercise of power, Fijian
society had lost its timelessness—which had itself been born
in the exercise of power, namely that of the eastern chiefs and
European colonials, a century before. Ratu Meli was confused
because the Fijian society in his head was forever gone, and

contemporary Fiji was not, really, a place where one could hope to see clearly.

I went to visit Apisai Tora, Taukei firebrand and veteran of the *lovo* incident, at the office he'd acquired as minister of public works after the first coup. A bodyguard searched my notebook for explosives, or at least that's what he said he was looking for. After the search he asked, "Do you have any explosives?" I gave it a moment's thought, hoping he'd see the humor in our situation, but he didn't. Also his two front teeth were missing.

Apisai Tora appeared and took me to his office. He wore a fierce expression, smoked a cigar, and pounded frequently on his desk when making a point. "You have to be born here and understand our cultures and traditions to understand what has taken place," he said. On his wall were pictures of Queen Elizabeth and the Duke of Edinburgh. "It's all very well for Indians, for non-Fijians, to talk about democracy. But democracy was used to steal land from the Maoris, the [Australian] aborigines. You can't satisfy [the Indians]. The more they get, the more they want. They wanted to own the whole country. And we said, 'No way!' "

Our conversation was interrupted by a phone call from Australia. The caller was a business friend in Sydney. "This place is ripe for carpetbaggers," Tora shouted into the phone. "You better get your guys in here if you want a slice of the action, as it were. Where else have you heard of thirteen years tax-free, man!" Tora was referring to tax-free economic zones, the major economic initiative of his government. The coups had inspired an enormous flight of both expertise and money. "This government has got the gall and the balls to ensure stability," Tora told his foreign friend, "political or otherwise."

After the phone call we returned to discussing Fijian tradition. In the event of a dispute, Tora said, "we have something to fall back on. There's whales' teeth [*tabua*, a kind of symbolic political currency], *yaqona*, we talk, and everything's fine and dandy. Countries that lose their traditions are unstable.

Our system has stood the test of time. We must have the will, we must have the strength!" He stood up and pounded on the desk. "Rabuka is one of the greatest heroes in the world! He has coconuts for balls!"

Back outside the Ministry of Public Works I encountered a young Fijian. "All this has nothing to do with Indians," he said. "They're just a scapegoat. The young people want jobs, not whales' teeth. Our leaders are very confused."

■ The Fijian way of life is said to be found in the villages, so I set out to visit a friend in Lutu, a tiny hamlet far in the interior of Viti Levu. The bus passed handsome houses on a ridge overlooking Suva. An elderly Fijian man sitting next to me said they belonged to "the commissioners." Many of the homes had Indian names displayed on brass plates. Suddenly we came upon the village of Tacirua, a collection of corrugated tin boxes. "This is where Fijians live," he said.

The bus ascended the dirt road with difficulty, entered into a lush forest of mahogany and pine, then collapsed in the mud. We all climbed out through the windows, stood in the muck, and waited. I chatted with a Fijian policeman, who said crime is worsening in Suva, expecially drug use, and that people in this area support Rabuka. After an hour the bus was repaired and I returned to my seat next to the old man. We descended into a broad river valley given over to cattle. "Fiji is a beautiful place," the man said, pointing out various sites, "but the Indians have spoiled it." I looked around me. There were a few Indians. They spoke Fijian and appeared every bit as poor as their compatriots.

Eventually we left the last Indian settlement and entered the purely Fijian interior. The old man had disembarked, so I struck up a conversation with a young farmer from Lutu named Ropate. He said things were going well in Lutu, partly because it was an ideal location for growing *yaqona* plants. Both Fijians and Indians had shown an increasing thirst for *yaqona* lately (there was even talk of "*kava* addicts"; *kava* is the Tongan word for *yaqona*, and is used widely in Fiji and elsewhere). So the traditional village of Lutu, population 200, was prospering. Ropate said he'd already bought 300 head of cattle with his profits.

As we talked, a group of young Fijian men in the back of the bus began singing. They were drinking some Fiji Bitter they'd bought at the last Indian shop. Ropate was furious. "They shouldn't be singing. There are elders on the bus. In Fijian custom we show respect for our elders. They shouldn't be singing. It's not the Naitasiri way!" Naitasiri was the province we were in. At the stop just before Lutu a dozen people were standing in the darkness and rain. A tiny boy sat atop a horse looking stunned. "They've come from villages ten, fifteen miles away," Ropate said. "They will return there tonight, barefoot along the path. No flashlights." The jungle weighed heavily around us, drenched in torrential rain.

My friend Luke Talaiyasi met the bus in Lutu, gave my bag to his wife, Ateca, and led the way across a muddy playing field to his house. It was a *bure*, the traditional Fijian home: thatched roof, walls made of vertical wooden poles covered with leaves, mats of woven pandanus on the floor. Luke was Lutu's headmaster, and his *bure* adjoined the schoolhouse. I thought how nice it was for the village headmaster to have a traditional house. Luke explained that the village didn't have enough money to build a modern one for him. A *bure*, made of local materials, can be erected in a week. Luke's *bure* was fifteen feet by twenty-five, with a table and chairs, a small gas range, and a big color TV complete with VCR. Once we had settled in, Luke went outside to turn on the generator so we'd have electric light.

Soon some of Luke's friends came by with two cases of Fiji Bitter. They turned out to be the back-of-the-bus singers. They were schoolteachers; an exam had just been administered that day, so Lutu's educators were ready to party. Also in attendance were Ropate, the *yaqona* farmer, another farmer, and an ex-policeman. There was much joking and singing of the kind you get with beer. Everyone spoke in Fijian, so I couldn't follow it, though one teacher, Manoa, did talk to me in English for a while. I told him about Ropate's

■ earlier remark, that Lutu's parents weren't sending their kids
to Suva anymore because they felt the city was a corrupting
place. "If they're keeping their kids at home," Manoa said,
"that just means they can't afford to send them away."

I had brought a *sevusevu*, or ritual gift, of *yaqona* roots for
Lutu's chief, so after the beer was gone we all trooped over
to visit the chief—actually the acting chief, since Lutu's chief
was traveling. The chief sat with other old men, some women,
and children in a tiny tin-roofed house. The house was divided
by a log into sleeping and reception areas, both covered with
mats. The women and children sat or reclined on the sleeping
mats; the men sat apart, the chief at their head. Opposite him
was the *tanoa*, a wide, shallow, spiritually charged wooden
bowl from which *yaqona* is served. My gift was presented by
a *matanivanua*, or spokesman, whom I didn't know. The offering of a *sevusevu* is the necessary precursor to conversation
with a chief. A sperm-whale tooth, or *tabua*, would have been
required if I were asking a favor or seeking the chief's support.
As it was I just wanted a night's hospitality and some company,
and for that a *sevusevu* sufficed.

My *matanivanua*'s speech, I gathered, was a combined introduction and entreaty of a highly ritualized sort. I recognized
only the words "New York" and "America." When he was
finished, the chief's *matanivanua* responded. Manoa said the
matanivanua was telling me that the chief appreciated my gift
and welcomed me to stay in Lutu for as long as I wished. The
yaqona roots were pounded then steeped in water; the infusion
was strained through muslin into the *tanoa*. Different stages of
the process were marked by desultory clapping, after which
we drank—the spokesmen first, then the chief and I. I received
a half-coconut shell of *yaqona*, turned to the chief, and said
bula while facing him. I clapped once, then drained the shell.
As I drank others clapped three times; once I had finished, all
the men clapped and I said *maca*, which means "empty" or
"dry." The chief went through the same steps. Things quickly
loosened up once the rituals were over and we each had a few
shells of *yaqona* holding down our bellies. Someone brought
out a guitar and the young men began singing wildly out of

tune. I was enjoying this. Fijian *yaqona* isn't particularly
strong, but several cups induces a sense of ease and general
cheeriness. The songs (or maybe it was the singing) were
apparently very amusing, as everyone laughed often and
loudly. Three women lounged on the sleeping mats, watching
the men, sometimes laughing along. They played cards with
the kids, but they didn't sing. I saw the chief's wife mouthing
words soundlessly with a faint smile.

Ropate came over to keep me company and gestured
proudly at the gathering. "Fiji is unlike any other place in the
world because what you have belongs to everybody. If I have
something you need, then I give it to you. If you need something to eat or a place to stay, I give you food, you can stay
with me. Nobody goes hungry in Fiji." Ropate seemed deeply
agitated by something, but I couldn't tell what it was. He did
mention that he was related to the people who ate the Reverend Baker. He also said that soldiers had instructed the chief
of Lutu to question any Indians who passed through the village, a policy Ropate appeared to support. "We don't believe
that one should be rich and another poor," Ropate continued,
with conviction. "We shall all be rich, or we shall all be poor.
That is why Fiji is not like any other place in the world."

Eventually cups of *yaqona* were passed to the women. The
old men took over the guitar and started to sing. "Old tunes,"
the young men grumbled. I couldn't tell the difference. Luke
suggested I go home. He was worried that quarts of beer
followed by *yaqona* might cause me some digestive upset. So,
after I said my goodbyes and thanks, Luke's wife, Ateca,
helped me through the low doorway and into the night. The
rain had let up; we walked through chill, moist darkness, our
feet squishing in mud. The ground was populated with toads.
I asked Ateca about life in the village, and she said it was
separated into women's work and men's work, along fairly
predictable lines. She asked if it was different in New York.
I said it was sort of different and sort of the same. I remembered that, back in Suva, I was told there'd been an increase
in domestic violence and desertion by husbands since the
coups, in part due to economic hardship. The long-term trends

are toward more education and wage-paying employment for
women, both Fijian and Indian, as well as an increasing urban
orientation toward nuclear rather than extended families. In
the villages, the trend has been outmigration by women to the
towns.

Back home we slept with the children on the floor. Luke and
the others straggled home later. By 3 A.M. we were all in a
pile. Several large rats played on the mats; rain fell on the
thatch, sounding like a distant brook. As Luke said, "It's good
you can spend the night in a real Fijian house."

In the morning clouds of mist rose slowly through tropical
mountain gorges. I sat in the *bure* doorway watching the dark
green hills and the Wainimala river. It was a Saturday morning
and wonderfully peaceful, the rain came and went. Luke and
Ateca's guests gradually stirred themselves, stumbling outside
with difficulty. Over a breakfast of lemon-leaf tea and *rourou*
(cooked taro leaves) Luke offered some opinions on the Lutu
scene. He said Rabuka was very popular. People had been
worried that Indians wanted to take over their land; Bavadra,
they felt, was the Indians' stooge. Fijians believe that "the
government is supposed to protect and take care of them," and
Bavadra didn't seem interested in doing that. Luke said respect
for the chiefs is breaking down among young people. "They
think chiefs should farm for themselves. They're tired of supporting them." They still honor their chiefs, but not like they
once did. "In Fiji now the thing that gets respect is money. It
doesn't matter if you're not a chief, if you have the most money
then people will respect you and seek your advice."

After breakfast Luke went back to sleep. I wrote notes and
helped his and Ateca's kids with their homework. *D* for Dog;
E for Elephant; *F* for Fox. Matthew sang "We Are the
World"; his sister chimed in with Bruce Springsteen's solo,
the one that sounds as if Bruce is strangling. Eventually, after
prayer, we ate lunch: more *rourou*, cassava, and hot pepper in
vinegar as a condiment. Luke apologized for not having fish.
Ateca glanced at the *rourou*. "Green fish," she said. We
laughed and drank more lemon-leaf tea, heavily sweetened
with sugar.

I wandered out toward the Wainimala and met up with Tevita, a farmer. We chatted about crops—*yaqona*, taro. Tevita pointed to the mountainsides and described his days spent cultivating *yaqona* here and there, or hunting wild pigs. He showed me one of his taro patches nearby. I asked if I could take a picture. He insisted on hiding himself among the taro leaves while I snapped away. We walked to the river, where boys were washing clothes on the stony bank. A horse broke loose and ran crazily among the marshy humps that lined the river. Boys and men chased after it with switches, shouting. I looked toward the mountains and imagined Tevita sweating his way among them, pushing through the wet leaves, hunting for a wild pig to give as a gift to his chief and his people.

■ Back in Suva I spent a week talking to anyone who seemed willing: politicians, merchants, tourists, diplomats, waitresses, journalists, barflies, laborers, priests. A few months earlier, Rabuka had declared an Internal Security Decree modeled on Singapore's (which, like Fiji's constitution, was also influenced by British advisers). Some weapons caches had been discovered by the military and, though their destination was unknown, the government announced its suspicion that they were intended for Indian and other opponents of the regime. Rabuka felt emergency legislation was necessary to strengthen the hand of his security forces. The decree is a study in legalist thoroughness, including phrases like "prohibition of organisations and associations of a political or quasi-military character and uniforms, etc." and "Every document purporting to be a subversive document shall be presumed to be a subversive document until the contrary is proved." (Better yet: "Where the officer responsible for holding a death inquiry upon the body of any person is satisfied that such person has been killed in a security area as a result of operations by the police or by the security forces for the purpose of suppressing organised violence, the officer may dispense with the holding of a death inquiry on the body of such a person.")

Since the decree went into effect there had been dozens of
arrests and many rumors of beatings, though the elaborate
tortures and killings one finds elsewhere didn't seem yet to
exist in Fiji. The decree did have a subduing effect, particularly on the press. Fiji once had an independent press, but now
most journalists had decided to toe the line. While I was in
Suva one editor at the *Fiji Times* was arrested for what turned
out to be a typographical error. Since arrests of journalists
were fairly rare, this seemed to prove that more serious of-
fenses—more serious than a typo—no longer appeared in Fiji
publications.

In conversation, people in Suva didn't appear to be censor-
ing themselves, though most requested anonymity. There was
so much to talk about. The Fijian world had turned upside
down. The most basic questions—What is a Fijian? an Indian?
What is the past?—lay about with no convincing answers. In
such a situation, and in the absence of severe repression, emotions tended to overwhelm discretion. A senior government
minister who'd helped overthrow Bavadra was worried about
chiefly credibility. The average Fijian, he said, expected the
chiefs to deliver economic advancement, but the chiefs were
doing quite the opposite; they were obstructing the government, hobbling development, and fighting among themselves.
"Fijians are expecting a lot," he said. "This is supposed to be
their chance to get a leg up on the modern world, and if the
chiefs let them down there'll be trouble."

Once, in the Grand Pacific bar, I met a young, very drunk
Indian man. By day he sold T-shirts in a shop that had been
torched by rioting Fijians after the second coup, then rebuilt;
by night, at least in recent days, he drank. "As an Indian—you
can see my straight hair—I can tell you this situation is a
national disaster. We, the Indian people, we have worked for
these people and we have built this country. If you look at the
other countries here—Papua New Guinea, Vanuatu, Tonga,
Nauru—they are not like Fiji. Fiji is the most prosperous
country, and it is the Indians who have built this prosperity,
we have made Fiji a golden island. It is Indo-Fijian *nationalists*
who have built this country." He braced himself against the

back of a chair, stared at nothing, and spoke thickly about the greatness of Hinduism and his desire to emigrate. I wondered what it must be like not to have a country, even an adopted one, not even to have a homeland, really—just a big world and nowhere that will welcome you.

The uncontrollability of emotions, the sheer confusion, had even reached into the heart and mind of the coup maker himself, Brigadier Sitiveni ("Steve," "Rambo") Rabuka. I went to see the general at his office in the Ministry of Home Affairs. He was two hours late, so I had a chance to lounge around the ministry. An aide refreshed me with *yaqona* from the ministry's tearoom, a small kitchen papered with magazine photos of bodybuilders. *Yaqona* is drunk from morning till night in the halls of the Rabuka government. I'd never met a coup maker before, let alone the leader of two coups, and was a bit nervous. *Yaqona* is good for nervousness, which may account for its increasing popularity in Fiji.

Rabuka arrived in an armored sedan and walked briskly past his personal guards with their M-16s and the ministry's own security man, who had L-O-V-E tattooed on his right fist (maybe he'd seen *The Night of the Hunter*). Rabuka ascended to the third floor and into his spacious office, where we shook hands and exchanged pleasantries. The shades were drawn and Rabuka looked tired—less fit than in photos I'd seen of him from the first coup, and with flecks of gray in his hair.

No one has ever accused Sitiveni Rabuka of being a profoundly reflective man. Yet, sitting there in his uniform, he appeared to be weighed down by introspection. "In the past we have been labeled 'the way the world should be' [a precoup tourist slogan], or we have labeled ourselves that, and we have sort of believed it. And, you know, when something like a coup takes place we are ourselves hurt that we can no longer be the way the world should be." I mentioned his Internal Security Decree. "I can understand why people are worried," he said in a deep, slow voice. "Everybody uses the old cry of 'fundamental freedoms' et cetera. But I've always believed that fundamental freedoms should be subordinated in the national interest, in particular the national security interest. Peo-

ple that have nothing to hide have nothing to worry about at
all."

One widely accepted fundamental freedom is the right to
worship. That, too, Rabuka had subordinated. He'd declared
a number of sabbatarian rules loosely modeled on Tonga's,
including compulsory rest on Sundays. Rabuka believes that
God inspired his first coup; on the day he took power, Rabuka
prayed to God for rain, and it rained. He told me he remains
committed to converting Indians, whom he has called "hea-
thens." "A lot of people think that it's a fanatical view of the
whole thing. But for Christians, they have to do it [prosely-
tize]. If they really love their fellow human beings they tell
them about the truth of the gospel, the truth about God, not
just sit back and say, 'Okay, you have your freedom of choice
of religion, and go to hell'—literally!" He didn't think conver-
sion should be forced, but that Indian evangelists should be
imported "to get across to them. It [conversion] was done by
force on us, but the time was right for it to be done by force,
because it was a time when things were done by force."
Rabuka is a Methodist lay preacher; about 80 percent of ethnic
Fijians are Methodist, and most of Fiji's Methodist Church
hierarchy backed the coup. In Fijian, *lotu* ("church") is a verb
as well as a noun.

Like everyone else, it seemed, Rabuka was worried about
the chiefs. He showed great respect for senior chiefs, particularly Ratu Mara, Ratu Penaia Ganilau, and his supreme chief,
the enfeebled Ratu Sir George Cakobau, a direct descendant
of the Cakobau who ceded Fiji to Britain. But even high chiefs
don't live forever, and Rabuka was preoccupied by the possible unsuitability of their successors. "I hope their children and
grandchildren will live up to the reputations of their fathers
and grandfathers. From the constitution point of view, there
will be due recognition for their status. It's up to them to be
worthy of this respect." Rabuka's tone was not exactly one of
uncluttered fealty. He may kneel before his chief, but there's
more to politics than gestures. The Great Council of Chiefs
played a crucial role in supporting Rabuka's takeover, though
not without reservations. Rabuka and many in the Taukei

spoke of founding a republic, while the chiefs professed loyalty to Queen Elizabeth and the Commonwealth, a natural enough attitude for aristocrats. In any case, Rabuka's main problem was not chiefly royalism but chiefly ineptness; most chiefs are poorly educated and preoccupied with issues like the relative strengths of the Tovata Confederacy (led by Mara and Ganilau), the Kubuna Confederacy (led by Cakobau), and the Burebasaga Confederacy, based south of Suva. These three confederacies are the basic units of Fiji's chiefly system, and their struggles are vitally important to many Fijians. But lengthy Great Council wranglings over such issues hardly move Rabuka's government closer to, say, creating employment.

In his book *No Other Way*, Rabuka talks a lot about social discipline and submission to the chiefs. When we met, he spoke more about discipline *tout court*, and about a concept new to both his regime and Fijian institutions generally: the importance of work. "I believe the Fijian race is a disciplined race. It's part of our culture. . . . We are used to being led, or we're used to being leaders." Rabuka emphasized that discipline will be achieved by educating the young to be proud of their culture. I couldn't quite see how that would transform them into productive laborers, particularly when jobs were so scarce. But Rabuka was confident. "Perhaps the dirty four-letter word in there is work. That's what we want. To instill in them [Fijians] a sense of discipline that will make them work, and be proud to work."

I asked Rabuka what he thought his legacy would be. He guessed that in fifty years Fijians would contemplate him and say, " 'Oh, we had a mad guy fifty years ago who did this, that's why we're here, so better off than we would have been without him,' or, 'We're very poor because of this stupid guy fifty years ago who did that.' " Rabuka laughed and smiled winningly. It was easy to imagine him on his post-coup victory tours, kissing babies, drinking *yaqona*, a big, not very complicated favorite son.

Rabuka left and I wandered off into the streets of Suva. I wondered why he was so concerned about work. He seemed

140 like a man in search of a metaphor, or maybe several. "The
Fijian way of life" and "the chiefly system" had sufficed for
years, and I suppose Rabuka and the Taukei had thought, in
May 1987, that they'd work again. Since then, there appears
to have been a crisis of cultural faith. As the government
minister had said, if the chiefs don't deliver economic advancement and education their people are going to get very
angry. But why should anyone expect the chiefs to deliver?
Apparently Rabuka had skipped this stage and moved on to
a purer abstraction: the people simply must work. But work
for what? Even soldiers get wages.

Besides, it was precisely the Indians who'd been working
for the last century or so. That's why they owned the shops and
filled the prescriptions. And one big reason they'd been able
to do it was that their indentured forebears abandoned the
caste system upon arrival in Fiji (for many Hindus, crossing
the seas is believed to lead to loss of caste; the system was, in
any event, unsustainable under the conditions of indentured-
labor plantations). Unlike Fijians, the Indians had no choice
but to embrace the spirit of capitalism. Also unlike Fijians,
they gained experience in the psychological traumas of alien-
ated wage labor and entrepreneurism. What will happen if the
Fijians' struggle between economic desire and cultural integ-
rity becomes too intense? Perhaps, if Rabuka and other Fijians
find that the Fijian way of life no longer coheres adequately,
the military way of life will seem to be the only metaphor left.

■ Soon after the interview with Rabuka I left Suva and returned to Nadi. I stayed at a small Indian-run motel surrounded by cane fields. The cane cutters were under official
suspicion; the crates of weapons that were Rabuka's proximate
cause for the security decree had been found in this area.
Armed soldiers had set up roadblocks and were searching
Indians' cars. Whites and Fijians were let pass; Indians had
adopted the strategy of picking up Fijian hitchhikers to help
get through the roadblocks. So Fijian farmers hardly needed
to use their cars, as long as they were willing to sit next to

Indians. Many, of course, were not; they foresaw an opportunity to take over the Indians' land, and often informed on their neighbors. All this made it difficult to talk with Indian farmers. They anticipated paying a high price for speaking to a journalist, or at least for speaking frankly—and why bother at all if you would only be able to lie?

After tortuous negotiations through third parties, I met, under cover of darkness, an Indian farmer I'll call Vijay. A soft-spoken, reflective man in his mid-fifties, Vijay quit school at eleven to support his family—three brothers, two grandparents, and his mother. His father had died. Vijay's grandparents, like many Fiji Indians, had come from Uttar Pradesh as indentured laborers on a standard five-year contract with the Colonial Sugar Refining Company of Australia. They were from the *lonia* caste, whose responsibility is making ceramic ware.

When his father died Vijay was left to support the family by himself. His grandfather was too old to work, his brothers too young. The farm where I first met him was the same farm his parents had worked. "I work then, from my age eleven, until now. We are very poor at that time. Only we got a *bure* house. When the rain come, all the rain come in the house, and we want to see, 'On whose bed tonight the rain will come?' That life, I never forget it." As they grew, Vijay's brothers were able to join him in working the fields. Eventually Vijay sent them off to school, one in Fiji, two in New Zealand. "Before, there was so much interest to make a house—work hard, and save money, and make a house. And properties for my children, and I want to go *up,* like that. From that time when this thing happened, when the coup came and this last election, everybody suddenly they don't want to do anything. The building industry is dead in Fiji. You can't see any improvement in the standard level. Everybody, on his tongue nowadays, 'How can you go out?' Everybody is trying to go out."

Vijay himself doesn't plan to go abroad. "I have seen these other places. And I have seen that Fiji is a very idle place, very idle means a slow place. You can sit anywhere, talk anywhere, don't worry about anybody." This was obviously untrue, but

142 I could imagine, perhaps, what Fiji had been like when it was
■ "the way the world should be." Vijay was well disposed toward Fijians. In fact, he didn't think they were all that different
from Indians, except for the question of earning money. "Fijians, they are not much hardworking people. Indians, they only
want to make money, very hardworking people Indians. But
if Fijians go to another person's place they can say *kerekere*
["request"]. Say '*Kerekere*, fifty cents,' then nobody can say no.
Very popular word, *kerekere*.

"This is the *kerekere* system, for Fijians, and it's very bad.
That's why they're not going ahead. If you got money, more
things to have and cultivate the farm, then they come and say
kerekere. In Fijian that is very easy word, *kerekere*." I remembered what Ropate had said, back in Lutu: "We shall all be
rich or we shall all be poor."

■ How do a people decide their origins? Viseisei is a breath-
takingly lovely village, a quick drive from Nadi. It lies on level
ground next to the sea. Viseisei appears almost to be a theme
park. Large, well-maintained wooden houses sit on ample
grassy plots; the many trees are each bordered by a ring of
stones, painted white. At the village's center stands a solid
Methodist church.

According to one tradition, the first Fijians arrived at Vuda
Point, next to Viseisei, led by the chief Lutunasobasoba. His
brother, Degei, then took an expedition overland to the
Nakauvadra Mountains, from which the rest of Fiji was settled. In a 1966 *Journal of Pacific History* article, Peter France
investigated this story and found it wanting. He traced the tale
to two European schoolteachers in the 1880s. The pair, influenced by anthropological fashion, believed that the Fijians
were originally Africans taken captive by Egyptians; after es-
caping from Egypt, they sailed the seas until landing at Vuda.
The schoolteachers' views were put in a book used by missionary educators. In 1892, a Fijian-language newspaper sponsored a contest to determine the origins of Fiji, and the
Lutunasobasoba/Degei story won. It went on to gain wide

currency, including publication in R. A. Derrick's classic *History of Fiji* (1946).

Nevertheless, as historian David Routledge says, "France's was a fine piece of literary detection, but it did not go far enough, failing to consider the possibility of some authentic foundation for later elaborations." So much depends on that word "authentic," in Fiji as in most places. At least one Degei story existed prior to the arrival of European anthropological conceits, and I doubt that two foreign schoolteachers could have manufactured such an important myth out of whole cloth—that, too, would be a European conceit.

In any case, authenticity is only one criterion in judging stories of ethnic origin. Utility is another. In the second decade of this century a Fijian commoner, Apolosi Nawai, began to attract a following among Fijians. He preached the Degei story, emphasizing that Viseisei was the Fijians' place of origin, not the mountains of Nakauvadra, as claimed by Cakobau and the people of Bau. Nawai's point was to argue the authenticity of western Fijians against that of the eastern chiefs, whom he derided as Tongans. This in itself was a substantial threat, but Nawai made matters worse by urging Fijians to be independent entrepreneurs and quit funding their chiefs. He even founded a corporation, Viti Kabani, in 1913 to encourage Fijian capitalism. This was too much. European merchants, missionaries, and chiefs alike united to crush Nawai and his company. Nawai was exiled three times; by the 1940s he had gone mad.

When I visited Viseisei one afternoon the most impressive structure was a brand-new immense *bure.* It was said to be the finest *bure* in Fiji, even finer than Cakobau's. In this *bure* lived Dr. Timoci Bavadra, his wife, Kuini, and the family.

"This is quite a *bure*," I said as Bavadra greeted me, and I couldn't help but laugh. Here was a man portrayed as the tool of grasping Indian infidels living in the most chiefly *bure* imaginable. Bavadra smiled modestly. "It's part of a deliberate strategy." After the first coup, Bavadra was able to travel with relative freedom around Fiji. His wife, who is a prominent chief from eastern Viti Levu, suggested building a *bure* to mark his importance as prime minister, but he declined. After the second coup, Rabuka's government restricted Bavadra's movements, so he agreed to have the *bure* built. It was constructed by his wife's subjects, other Fijians, and Indians. All the laborers were volunteers. To have Indians working on a *bure*—what a message that must have sent to the eastern chiefs. "It provides a place for people to meet us according to custom, to bring tribute to us, to discuss our positions. My opponents often live in apartments." Bavadra grinned happily. A career public servant who specialized in family planning—though he'd had eleven children himself, by three wives—Bavadra exuded an avuncular pleasantness, its effect enhanced by his round, pudgy face.

Bavadra ran on a platform that, at least in its ideal form, emphasized the rights of workers, anticorruption, economic growth, and nonalignment in foreign affairs, including the rescinding of permission for U.S. nuclear warships to dock in Fiji. The extent to which this platform would have found expression in policy is highly debatable. During his brief tenure in office, Bavadra had already begun to backtrack from the campaign's official antinuclear position, and his labor and economic policies depended on support from the trade unions, whose interests were not necessarily those of their workers.

The Coalition party also stressed that it was multiracial, democratic, and "modern." This helped engender support from Indians and a crucial percentage of ethnic Fijians who were tired of chiefly rule and economic stagnation. Yet such apparent modernism was hardly pure. Coalition workers in western Fiji often invoked Apolosi Nawai, who can't be described as modern. Early on, Bavadra acquired permission in the customary way from Cakobau to campaign in Fijian villages; a week after the coup Bavadra said in a statement from Honolulu, "I have always been and am now still loyal to the Vunivalu, Ratu Sir George Cakobau, the highest-ranking traditional chief in Fiji."

In addition, Bavadra and his Coalition supported the idea of a "fourth confederacy." The three existing chiefly confederacies—Tovata, Kubuna, and Burebasaga—are based in the east. Chiefs (and average Fijians) from the interior and west of Viti Levu are distinctly second-class; they have been since the first flowering of eastern imperialism in the nineteenth century. "The Fourth Confederacy is part of an urge for freedom among people in the west," Bavadra said. "They have always been kept down by people in the east. The Fourth Confederacy has always been a Coalition position. The Alliance has always fought against the west. And by the way, the western chiefs have been very removed from their people for seventeen years [since independence]. They have been busy being pawns of the east."

We talked on about Rabuka and the coups, but Bavadra's heart was clearly with his new *bure* and what it represented. I was struck by how much Fijian history interested Bavadra, and by how malleable that history still seemed to be. What might have been an interview about democracy versus military rule turned into a chat about the Fourth Confederacy, here in this village where the Fijian way of life may, or may not, have begun in the unreachable past.

Bavadra's *bure* was already bringing political benefits. The night before, Ratu Meli Vesikula had visited, the same Ratu Meli who less than a year earlier had proposed putting Bavadra in the *lovo*. He presented Bavadra with a whale's tooth and they talked. "He wanted to confess," Bavadra said gently. They drank *yaqona* together into the wee hours. I looked over at the mats that took up one-half of Bavadra's reception room—the other half, where he received me, had sofas and chairs—and imagined Ratu Meli sitting there, with his military posture and face like weathered stone, tipping back cups of *yaqona*, pounding himself in the head no more.

■ Shortly before leaving Fiji I went with two European friends, Georges and Caroline, to visit an Indian friend of Georges's. He was a Muslim who lived in a poor house in the cane fields. He mixed *yaqona* in a metal bowl and we all drank heartily. We made a play at imitating Fijian custom, just for fun, but none of us really knew the rituals and besides it was too much trouble. Georges and I told stories about North Africa, and our host was pleased that we knew something, however little, of Islam. His wife provided a stream of appetizers: roasted peas with chilis, puri, mangoes dipped in red pepper and salt, a pastry of rolled taro leaves stuffed with bean mash. Finally we went inside the tiny kitchen for supper. The table was set only for the three of us, but Caroline forced the farmer and his wife to join in. Then Caroline noticed their daughter, a thin and reticent fourteen-year-old. She had prepared the food: goat, *dahl*, rice, more puri. Caroline insisted that the daughter eat with us at the table. She was terribly shy; she pushed at her food but hardly tasted it. Her mother said she was an excellent student, second in her class. She hoped to send her to Sydney. She had a male relative there who thought he would be able to find her daughter a husband.

After too much *yaqona,* we staggered back along a dirt road to our motel. *That, too, is tradition,* I told myself, thinking of the daughter and listening to the whisper of wind among the cane. I left Georges and Caroline at the motel and went for a walk on the beach. The sun took an hour to set, coloring the horizon an ever deeper orange. And then it was night, the surf glistening from the faint light of a crescent moon and the sky crowded with stars. A post-harvest fire in one of the fields sent great billowing clouds of smoke into the darkness over the sea, its orange glow silhouetted the palm trees. A slight, cool breeze carried the smell of burning cane.

In November 1989, Dr. Timoci Bavadra died of spinal cancer. Dr. Bavadra's wife, Adi Kuini Bavadra, agreed to become head of the Coalition. Ratu Sir George Cakobau, Fiji's highest chief, died after a long illness, only three weeks after Bavadra. Several versions of a new constitution were presented in January 1990—all of them proposing, in varying degrees, the further institutionalization of ethnic-Fijian power—but the death of Cakobau left traditional Fijian politics in extreme disarray. Chiefly confusion has reached new heights.

The Internal Security Decree was repealed in late 1988;
Brigadier Rabuka left civilian government, though he stayed
on as head of the armed forces and is an influential figure. Fiji
remains under the rule of an interim government headed by
Ratu Mara and Ratu Penaia Ganilau, and including mem-
bers of the Taukei.

Due largely to emigration, Fiji's Indian population has
dropped below that of ethnic Fijians. Tourism has returned
to pre-coup levels.

Vanuatu

Vanuatu, jointly administered by Britain and France as the New Hebrides/Nouvelles-Hébrides until independence in 1980, has 143,000 inhabitants, about 105 indigenous languages (plus English, French, and the pidgin lingua franca, Bislama), sixty-two inhabited islands, maybe twenty-one established religions of foreign origin as well as a multiplicity of pre-colonial religious traditions, several political parties, and an international reputation as the most left-leaning country in the Pacific. Vanuatu's prime minister is an Anglican priest, and a socialist, and a middle-rank participant in the "pig-killing system" of his home island (named, of all things, Pentecost). Vanuatu, 500 miles due west of Fiji and 1,400 miles northeast of Sydney, is surely the most culturally chaotic nation on earth. Or, as a friend in the capital, Port Vila, said, "It's the way the world should be."

150 ■ From a small grandstand at the uphill edge of Port Vila's
■ only cricket pitch the entire harbor could be seen, a deep and
undulating blue enclosed on three sides by low hills. Tropical
verdure everywhere, a pleasant breeze. It was a Sunday morning. On the downhill side of the pitch—now called Independence Park—ni-Vanuatu (people of Vanuatu) hurried to ser-
vices at the Presbyterian church, an odd structure rather like
the A-frame vacation homes called, in the U.S., "Swiss-chalet
style." Vila was quiet save for a few sidewalk cafes catering to
tourists, local white expatriates, and other atheists. (Why is it
that the religions introduced at such cost by colonizing white
people are now so neglected by their descendants?)

The ni-Vanuatu men wore dark slacks and white or colored
shirts; the women wore Mother Hubbards, long, lightweight,
brightly colored dresses with short, puffed sleeves. Mother
Hubbards were recommended by missionaries in the last century as an alternative to female nakedness and the customary
garments of bark and other materials. Today the Mother Hub-
bard is in some quarters a symbol of cultural nationalism. In
others it is a symbol of colonial repression, against which
women rebel by wearing more modern, Western clothes.
Most of the worshippers were clutching Bibles, and most were
female. I could just make out the words "Praise Him above
ye heavenly hosts," sung very slowly and in gorgeous har-
mony, as a lone boat scudded across the harbor, a sloop before
the wind, its mainsail billowing.

Port Vila, on the island of Efate, is a combination of squat
colonial and low-budget contemporary buildings that spills
down a steep hillside into the main street, Rue Higginson,
named for an Irish entrepreneur who sided with the French
around 1870. Stories about the French-British "administration"—the word deserves quotes—of Vanuatu make it sound
very much like an interminable dinner party at which the
guests are uniformly rude. Colonial regimes inevitably have a
parodic quality. The New Hebrides "condominium," as it was
called, was more parodic than most. One senses that in the
early days neither side wanted Vanuatu all that much, that it
was more a matter of "strategic denial," to use today's jargon.

The point was not to acquire a colony, but rather to prevent
the adversary from doing so. France and Britain, two countries
not noted for their mutual respect, agreed to share the islands,
establishing a joint naval commission in 1874 and later founding the historically unique condominium in 1906. The French
and British flags were raised simultaneously in the morning,
and lowered simultaneously at sunset. Some ni-Vanuatu attended lycées, learning about Charlemagne's empire and
when to use *tu* instead of *vous*; others attended British schools
and studied the Long Parliament and the difference between
"who" and "whom." The ni-Vanuatu had to reckon with both
the King's (or Queen's) Birthday and *le 14 juillet.* The New
Hebrides probably suffered more national holidays than any
political entity on earth. For a century the French and British
made crude gestures at each other across the Rue Higginson.
According to several sources this behavior continued right up
to independence on July 30, 1980.

Apart from the chance falling of geopolitical chips, European interest in Vanuatu was commercial and religious. Certain Australians, concerned about their nation's balance of
payments with China, began in the 1800s to harvest Vanuatu's
abundant sandalwood; the sticks were burned for incense by
Chinese Buddhists. A second trade grew up in bêche de mer
(trepang, sea cucumber, sea slug), a saltwater holothurian that
resembles a huge worm. Dried sea slug was coveted by the
Chinese as an aphrodisiac. Ni-Vanuatu labored in both trades,
as well as being subject to "blackbirding"—a marginally pret-
tier version of slavery, in which ni-Vanuatu were more or less
forcibly shipped to Australia (and Fiji) as agricultural workers.
Many died in the fields of Queensland, where conditions were
grim. Blackbirding also occurred in the Melanesian Solomon
Islands to the north, and to a much lesser extent in Fiji and
elsewhere. I wonder how many Australian schoolchildren
learn about this peculiar institution in their history classes.

While in Vanuatu I tried many times to wrap my mind
around the idea of bêche-de-mer commerce. Here you
have unpleasant pale people of mysterious origins (Australia
mostly) expressing great interest in a previously humble crea-

ture (the sea slug) which they prepare, with some effort, and sell to even more mysterious people far away (the Chinese) for strange purposes. All the while, other foreigners (the French and British) are arguing over what must have seemed a completely obscure issue, namely the government of a country (the New Hebrides) that didn't exist outside their own imperial imaginations. The only word that provided me any solace was *tuturani*: the people who appeared one day and never went away.

> ■ DEAREST HOME-FRIENDS, AND OTHERS,—In the end of March last, we were greeted with awful tidings—poor [the Reverend J. D.] Gordon, killed on Erromanga! . . . Sad to say, dear Gordon was tomahawked by a superstitious Native, who regarded him as bringing disease amongst them, though they were indebted to a trading vessel for that. . . .
> —letter of M. Whitecross Paton, wife of the missionary John Paton, Aniwa, New Hebrides, 1872

In the early days, the other white people with whom ni-Vanuatu had contact were missionaries. The letters of Mrs. Paton, a Scottish Presbyterian, reveal their main goals: to make the ni-Vanuatu behave like orderly petit-bourgeois Europeans and to rescue their souls from eternal torment after death. The two intentions were mixed together and, as in the case of the Reverend Gordon, not always well received (the published version of Mrs. Paton's letter includes a photo of Gordon's murderer leaning against a wooden post, looking confident). There was some missionary-killing throughout the islands, and even some missionary-eating. The ni-Vanuatu had their own ideas about death and proper behavior.

The most trying aspect of proselytization, for the missionaries, was probably the unfamiliar style of life. But it must also have been difficult simply to preach the Word, so far removed from the cultures and languages of its origin. Mrs. Paton quotes from one of her husband's sermons: "Jehovah very good. He love Black Man all same White Man. He send Son

belonga Him. He die for all Man." With some spelling
changes to account for modern Bislama, this message could be
delivered today. And, in fact, it is.

One of the twenty-one-odd nonindigenous religions now
being purveyed in Vanuatu is Seventh Day Adventism. The
SDA Church believes in, among other things, the second coming of Christ, capitalism, and, in Vanuatu, the absolute importance of eradicating any trace of indigenous culture. The latter
two beliefs are shared, to varying degrees, by most of the
Western denominations in Vanuatu; but they are carried to an
extreme by the SDA, which has engendered most of the few
successful ni-Vanuatu entrepreneurs.

On a beautiful Sunday morning I went with Hilda Lini, a
sister of Prime Minister Father Walter Lini and the only female member of Vanuatu's Parliament, to an SDA celebration
in Pango village, a hamlet outside Port Vila. As Hilda's com-
panion, I was ushered past semi-uniformed SDA guards into
the tent for "bigmen," about half of whom were women. The
celebration was being thrown by a women's auxiliary group,
the Dorcas Society, which makes handicrafts and performs
good works (the SDA men, by contrast, run businesses and
perform good works). We attended a meeting where Dorcas
leaders, all ni-Vanuatu women, gave reports on the group's
finances and activities—prompted now and then by a white
man who was apparently their adviser. Then the group elected
new leaders for the coming year. Hilda and I sat in a VIP
section and wore plastic VIP leis. On the stage, behind the
speakers, were large, complicated charts explaining the na-
tures of God, Christ, the Devil, and their disciples, and the
relative positions of each. Afterward an exclusive and delicious buffet was set out for the bigmen.

The bigmen tent looked upon a broad grassy playing field
that sloped downward to a narrow band of palms bordering
the sea. After lunch I wandered along the beach—where
young people snuck cigarettes and children played barefoot
on the sharp coral—then went to sit among the ni-Vanuatu
crowd that sprawled around the playing field. I had felt ridiculous sitting with the bigmen, and once the buffet was gone

there wasn't much point to remaining with them. People began giving speeches. Hilda praised the church's encouragement of enterprise and said it was good that women were learning to do modern tasks for themselves. Hilda is in her thirties, which, in a country with an average female life expectancy of 53.7 (56.2 for men), makes her middle-aged. Before her marriage a few years ago, she was famous for her independence, beauty, education, and family connections. The Linis are like the royal family of post-colonial Vanuatu; Hilda's and Father Walter's father, Harper, was a respected musician, storyteller, and builder of Anglican churches. My frequent contact with Hilda provided entrée into the upper echelons of Vanuatu government; it also compromised my standing with Father Lini's opponents. In Port Vila, as in any small town, whom you're seen with greatly determines who you are. While the speeches proceeded, a woman named Valerie, who was running the event, asked if I was the Australian high commissioner. Like me, the Australian high commissioner is tall, male, and white. I said I wasn't, but that if he never showed up I'd be glad to impersonate him at the podium. Valerie didn't smile.

After the speeches there was marching. A four-piece rhythm section played minimalist Sousa, a man blew a whistle to signal the turns. Two white church officials weaved among the marchers with a video camera. Each sub-unit of the Dorcas Society performed its own march—there were at least ten groups—though the choreography varied little. Mostly it consisted of single-file marching up and down and around, with a lot of saluting toward the bigmen tent. Each group had a slightly different outfit (shoes, no shoes; blue skirt, red skirt), but the basic look was: simple, below-the-knee skirts and white T-shirts with "Community Service—Seventh Day Adventist Church" printed over a medallion design and topped by a torch. The overall effect was somewhere between a McDonald's training camp and a pared-down country fair.

After an hour or so of marches I fled backstage and ran into the SDA president for Vanuatu, a tall, extremely thin Australian with ravaged, reddish-yellow skin. The SDA Church, he said, came to Vanuatu in 1912, when most of the missionaries were Presbyterian or Anglican with a scattering of Catholics. The SDA pioneers were allowed to go to Malekula. "Malekula was a very black island, with heathenism, headhunting, cannibalism. The Adventists were allowed to go there because they [the condominium government] figured they'd all be eaten!" He laughed. I later heard that the first Adventist had actually arrived on Malekula in 1911, but he died quickly of malaria and so was airbrushed from SDA history. Succeeding Adventists established a beachhead on the tiny island of Atchin, off Malekula, which has since become a lonely outpost of entrepreneurial ideology. The endless marching and martial music had put me in a pretty bad humor so I somehow imagined Atchin as a treeless island with people walking back and forth in single file, an archway over the quay, *Arbeit Macht Frei*. It seemed fitting that Atchin is shadowed by the forested mountains of northern Malekula, where the fearsome Big Nambas live relatively undisturbed by modernity. A *nambas* is a penis sheath; the Small Nambas, who are reputedly even fiercer, live on southern Malekula.

The SDA president said that this day's celebration was poor compared to the previous year's, in which the ni-Vanuatu Adventists performed a historical drama about the church. It began, he said, with a traditional dance, near-naked performers stomping their feet and singing. Other Adventists, dressed as missionaries, would try to take people from the dance and over to a structure representing the church. Some would go, then run back to the traditional dance. Gradually more and more were pulled away. The drama ended when all the characters reappeared in outfits like the ones people were wearing today and marched to oom-pah music.

During that same fête, the president said, there was another drama involving a dancer whose elaborate headdress included a boat complete with functioning smokestack. The hat represented the ship that brought the first missionaries. The dancer paraded about the field—this same field—with smoke belching from his hat. Then the hat caught fire. "People had to rush out and douse him with buckets of water so he could put the hat back on. They [the ni-Vanuatu] were all laughing. If you break your leg here, they'll laugh. They think it's funny." The president pointed toward a young man who was a grandson of the first SDA convert. "It took six years to get a single convert." Next to the boy was a group of men in their twenties, all decked out in stylish polo shirts and trousers. They were a cappella singers. They'd performed earlier, doing "He Is So Wonderful" among other tunes. Two of them were on their way to Australia, where they were to perform "a cannibalism-to-Christianity drama. Initially, they'll appear as cannibals." The young men smiled graciously in our direction when they realized they were being discussed. "They can stand up anywhere," the president said proudly.

They can stand up anywhere. What a strange thing to say. He may have been translating from Bislama. "Stand up" is literally "stannap," which connotes strength and pride. The national slogan is "Long God Yumi Stannap," that is, "In God We Stand." *They can stand up anywhere.* I wondered what people did before they stood up. Certainly the a cappella singers could stand up anywhere; in fact, at that moment, they seemed to be standing up as if it were simply coincidence that they were in Vanuatu and not Prague or Harare or Newcastle. On the playing field, the marching groups got younger and younger until tiny uniformed girls who could barely walk were struggling to maintain their single-file line. The white men with their video cameras were particularly keen to get these children on tape, intending to send the footage back home as evidence of the church's good works and the worth of investing in missionary enterprise. The SDA president was watching the girls too, smiling broadly. "It keeps them out of mischief," he said.

■ The best place to escape the worker-bee world of Adventism, if you're male, is a *nakamal.* They are quiet places, devoted to conversation and the drinking of *kava. Nakamals* are usually men's clubhouses. As Vanuatu has over a hundred distinct cultures, the *nakamals* vary greatly from region to region. On some islands there are women's *nakamals*; on other islands, until recently, women could be killed for entering a *nakamal*. In Port Vila, the *nakamals* are streamlined, more like bars, though each is tied to a particular clan somewhere outside Vila. Women are virtually absent, except for the occasional European. But for men, *nakamals* are the only places where blacks and whites can meet on a nearly equal footing. So over three weeks in Vila I drank a lot of *kava*.

Vanuatu *kava* is to Fiji *yaqona* as whisky is to sarsaparilla. It is drunk at a toss from half-coconut shells. Five shells was, for me, an upper limit, the intoxicating equivalent of perhaps seven shots of whisky. As you might imagine, ni-Vanuatu men like to pass time comparing how many shells each of them can drink. The Christian churches don't approve of *kava*. The government, however, does, and after independence it introduced a pro-*kava* scheme encouraging production and consumption. Its slogan was "Plantem wan Kava, wan Richest Plant blong World" (Plant Kava, the Richest Plant in the World). The idea was to wean urban ni-Vanuatu from imported alcohol—keeping the profits of intoxication in domestic hands rather than exporting them to Seagram's—and to give Vanuatu farmers a cash crop. Also, ni-Vanuatu men often beat ni-Vanuatu women, something that *kava*, unlike alcohol, makes difficult if you drink enough; while I was in Vila there were two rumored instances of wives beating their *kava*-drinking husbands because the drink was making them "too slack." One heard of "*kava* widows."

Kava does indeed make you slack in most every sense. Part of *nakamal* etiquette is to speak very softly. One concentrates carefully on the words; they come slowly, more so as the drinking progresses. The lighting is always dim and there is no music or other avoidable noise. "Time to get into my shell," a friend used to say cheerfully as the *kava* hour approached. At its precious best, a *nakamal* evening acquires a fragile intimacy, everyone whispering and laughing softly with no particular awareness of time.

One evening I met Godrington, a ni-Vanuatu friend, and his cousin Reith Bule at Binini *nakamal*, a hangout for people

1 5 8 from the northern part of Pentecost Island. After a few days
in Vila it was clear that the only way to get anywhere in
Vanuatu was to ally oneself with a specific clan/linguistic
group. Clan and family ties are determining in Vanuatu, and
if one isn't linked to a clan or family one is of very little value
or interest. As a white person I was, by default, a member of
the white clan and expected to be satisfied with the company
of other whites. Many whites in Vila, some of long residence,
complained of being shut out from the ni-Vanuatu world. This
can be partly explained by anti-white sentiment, but the primary reason seemed to be that whites aren't especially relevant to those aspects of ni-Vanuatu life that matter most—
family, clan, and traditional hierarchies. When white people
get together they talk a lot about the ni-Vanuatu, usually
referring to them as "they" without further explanation;
among whites the third-person plural is reserved for the black
people who surround them. Among the ni-Vanuatu, in my
experience, one rarely speaks of white people at all. So I
frequented the North Pentecost *nakamals* and tried to make
friends, accepting that, for ni-Vanuatu from other regions, I
would be doubly a stranger.

"In the village it is very hard work. You have to work very
hard to get the pigs," Reith Bule said. A big, alternately
overbearing and considerate man, Reith is chairman of the
National Housing Corporation. "You pay your father with
pigs in order to reach his grade. You go up the ladder step by
step. To surpass your father you start paying pigs to other men
who are higher than him. It is very, very complicated. You
borrow pigs and then they are put on your account. The
village is very small, so everyone knows how many pigs you
own. To go up the ladder you must work very hard. It is a way
of proving your manhood. That is the world.

"If a man from Ifira [an island off Port Vila] goes to North
Pentecost, it doesn't matter if he's president, he is just another
man if he has no rank. He has to kill pigs; he has to earn it.
The main things in custom society are obedience, respect, and
responsibility." I was struck that the chairman of Vanuatu's
National Housing Corporation was more interested in talking

about the "pig-killing system"—which exists, with wide varia-
tions, in most ni-Vanuatu cultures—than about housing. But
this proved to be typical. Anthropologist Kirk Huffman, the
Anglo-American head of Vanuatu's Cultural Centre, once told
me about bringing a high chief down from Malekula to Port
Vila. He was the first person from his tribe to visit the capital.
This was in the 1970s. The chief spent several days in Vila.
Eventually Huffman asked him his impressions. The chief said:
"Everyone told me stories of how wealthy Port Vila is. But I
have been here five days and haven't seen a single pig." The
following day the chief went back to Malekula.

I was also struck that Godrington, who is a waiter, and Reith
Bule treated each other as virtual equals. In a (democratic,
secular, modern, etc.) town like Cleveland or Strasbourg
you're unlikely to find a high government official and a waiter
engaged in respectful, public conversation, even if they're
cousins. But, as Reith said, you can be president but if you
haven't killed pigs you're just an ordinary guy. And neither
Reith nor Godrington had killed any pigs. "In the village you
have to work all the time, planting, getting pigs," Godrington
said with a trace of regret. Young and handsome, with a trim
mustache and a charming smile, he had decided in his teens
to leave North Pentecost for Vila. "Here it's easier. You just
go to work for a while during the day, and the work is easy.
In the evenings you can go out." We drank another shell and
chatted some more about pigs. I wondered if both Reith and
Godrington didn't feel that they had failed somehow.

In another *nakamal* one night I talked with Willy, the son
of a prominent chief on Ambrym, an island feared by many
ni-Vanuatu because of its strong magic. Willy, a small, intense
twenty-two-year-old, had left Ambrym when he was seventeen
and never went back. "When my father was alive I sent some
money back to the island for pigs, but since he died I don't
send it. There's nobody I trust now back in the village. I left
because, back home, it's too much hard work. Planting, killing
pigs. There's no job on the island, no way to make money so
you can buy things and have a good time. Yes, you can make
copra, but it's very hard work." The night was warm and the

160 *nakamal* almost empty. Willy and I bought each other rounds
of *kava*. With time our bodies became numb. Nothing much
existed except the dim *nakamal*, the night air, the other men
sitting on low benches and spitting on the dirt floor, and the
conversation. "Here in Vila, you come, you get a job, you
work from eight to four-thirty, and then there's money in your
pocket. You can go out and have a good time, go to a club,
have a drink or go dancing. Also, there are so many girls here,
and girls in Vila! I think that's the main reason people come
to Vila—there are so many boys and girls."

Willy was slowly growing agitated, or as agitated as you can
get drinking *kava*. We sat hunched over on the wooden
bench; Willy seemed worried that others might hear what he
was saying. "Some people in Vila, they'll come and stay here
forty or fifty years. They spend and spend, they have a good
time, they drive around in cars. Then maybe one day they try
to go back to their villages, and it's no good. They don't know
anyone, they don't trust anyone, and they have to work hard.
Starting from nothing like they're just a baby. Black people
are not very smart. They can't go home."

■ I spent nearly three weeks in Port Vila, doing many of the
things Western journalists are expected to do: reading reports
and histories, interviewing government officials, and going to
parties with locals who were, by a rough standard, the same
color as me. The first two activities were by choice, the last
somewhat less so. As a decently mannered emissary from the
(vaguely defined) Outside World, I was in demand. But isola-
tion among tribal fellows quickly weighed on me, as it clearly
weighed on them. The *nakamals* seemed to be the only places
of solace. And it was in the *nakamals*, through conversations
with people like Godrington, Reith, and Willy, that I realized
why Vanuatu felt like such a profoundly destabilizing country.
The modern world—perceived, rightly or wrongly, as
white—came very close to being irrelevant. Its rules, its categories, its ways of understanding just didn't pertain, or at least
they didn't pertain in the ways one might think.

For example, journalistically Vanuatu has two key issues:
money and politics. Vanuatu is supposed to be a socialist country. Right-wing journalists and commentators, particularly
from Australia, consider it a trouble spot. I heard many tales
about journalists arriving in Vila and asking where the Cuban
missile silos were, or scouring the streets for Libyans. Father
Lini had a brief period of enthusiasm for Qaddafi's Libya, and
has been paying for it ever since. The main results have been
nineteen Libya-trained "journalists," who now work as bodyguards, bad press overseas, and the enmity of the U.S. State
Department.

But Vanuatu socialism is a complex thing. The country is an
international tax haven, providing discreet shelter for the sur-
pluses of capitalists from all over the world. The majority of
its private businesses are owned by foreigners. Its economy
greatly depends on tourism—that is, the expenditure of
money generated by capitalist economies (though one Soviet
cruise ship, the *Alexander Pushkin*, often calls at Vila, freighted
with Australian tourists). The import and export of basic com-
modities is controlled by a half dozen Chinese and (pre-com-
munist) Vietnamese merchants under license from the government. The government's technocrat advisers are almost all
nonsocialist Westerners. Vanuatu receives consistently good
marks from the International Monetary Fund, and actively
courts foreign investment, particularly from Japan.

Somehow it wasn't surprising that Vanuatu's Red tenden-
cies were highly overrated. This is a country whose first experience of Western priorities took the forms of incense,
aphrodisiacs, and slavery. Later the ni-Vanuatu were exposed
to Presbyterian and Anglican housekeeping combined with
speeches about some bearded white figure who "die for all
man"—and, later still, to Western ideas of government as
conveyed by one of the most bizarre political arrangements in
colonial history. Now Vanuatu is tossed about by the ignorant
tides of "East-West relations," "Libyan-Cuban influence,"
"Soviet expansionism," even "terrorism." And in the *nakamals* we talk of pigs. What do white people want? Sitting
around with friends in Vila, I read aloud a *New York Times*

162 article about "the Cuban and Vietnamese presence" and how
■ Father Lini's effort to unite Melanesian heads of state was "a
role not unlike the one Fidel Castro played" in the Caribbean
and Latin America. It provoked a kind of visceral, absurdist
laughter.

There are many sides to that laughter. While I was in
Vanuatu, the government and its opponents were having their
worst feud since independence. ("Vila Strife May Have Libya
Link: Island Terror for Tourists," a Sydney paper headlined
with factless brio.) There had been rioting four months
before, in the spring. I spent much of my time trying to find
out why. In essence, it was part of a power struggle between
Father Lini and his onetime comrade Barak Sope. Together
they had been the chief architects of the independence struggle. As a university student in Fiji, Sope had written poems
about socialism. Returning to Vanuatu in 1973, he showed
enormous talent for political organizing and the sort of public
gestures that captured the ni-Vanuatu imagination. Sope also
did pioneering research on land tenure, a key issue in Vanuatu
as throughout the Pacific, and helped write the land policies
that distinguished his—his and Father Lini's—Vanua'aku
party (Vanua'aku means "our land").

After independence Sope gave every sign of enjoying
power. He also, from humble beginnings, began to accumulate wealth, a wealth that had no clear provenance. He gained
weight, he bought nice clothes. Eventually he opened an office
to advise foreign investors interested in Vanuatu. His partner
was Dinh Van Tan, a rich and quite shadowy Vietnamese
businessman who would later receive several import-export
monopolies from the government. Sope traveled with an intimidating entourage of Libyan-trained ni-Vanuatu "journalists" sometimes called the "Red-Eye Brigade."

Barak Sope is from Ifira, an island in Vila's harbor where
one goes only by invitation. The Ifira, or Fila, islanders claim
to be the rightful landowners of Port Vila. Naturally Sope
involved himself in the Vila Urban Land Corporation (VUL-
CAN), the government body that, upon independence, administered Vila property. Most of Port Vila's valuable land is

leased by foreigners; their payments went to VULCAN, which
was supposed to hold the money in trust until the vague day
when competing traditional claims to the land could be sorted
out. (Several villages claim part or whole title; one even claims
proprietary rights to that part of Vila which was created with
landfill, because the soil came from their village.) By the late
1980s, a large portion of VULCAN's money had been "pissed
up a tree," as one ni-Vanuatu put it; much of the spending was
accounted for as "expenses." The government closed the land
corporation and seized its files. There was a demonstration
followed by street fighting in Vila (with the Red-Eye Brigade
pitching in), and eventually a parliamentary crisis after which
most of Sope's allies, and Father Lini's opponents, were
ejected from office.

The situation when I arrived was exceedingly complicated,
involving innumerable court cases (with imported judges),
broken friendships, corruption in virtually every quarter, clan
and family rivalries. What preoccupied me were the languages
used to make sense of it. I went to talk with Morrison Tangarasi, an official of the Union of Moderate Parties. The UMP
has been, since before independence, the leading opposition
to Father Lini's Vanua'aku party. We met at the UMP's spare
headquarters in Vila; on the conference table were copies of
Asian Outlook, a publication of the Asian Pacific Anti-Commu-
nist League, and *You Can Trust the Communists (To Be Communists)*, a book by Dr. Fred Schwartz. Anticommunism and
defense of the French language—the UMP is largely francophone—have always been the party's main political products.
During the spring demonstration a few people had shouted
"Father Lini wants communism." Tangarasi, self-effacing and
unsure of himself, said his party, by contrast, would encourage
free enterprise. "The usual policies that would be used by any
center-right party anywhere. And law and order—the rule of
law in Vanuatu. The present government is controlled by the
party, just like any totalitarian state. Our country is on a course
typical of any dictatorship. It's crazy. We thought we were
going to have a great future, with independence and all that."

I kept asking Tangarasi to explain how the government was

communist and how the UMP wasn't. His answers both made sense—"We want to open the country to foreign investment," "Socialism just hasn't delivered the goods"—and didn't make any sense at all. In this they reminded me of the Western press. The "Cuban and Vietnamese presence" mentioned by *The New York Times* certainly existed, but the Cubans (two of them, and their two kids) were doctors, while the Vietnamese were businessmen. When an Australian journalist wrote of "Libyan influence" he was correct, but only insofar as Libya had trained a few young men in how to look menacing. Both the journalists and Tangarasi were floating words in a way that made the very idea of language rather suspect. The words were hardly meaningless, but the rhetoric they were rooted in was. It was a rhetoric that could stand up anywhere, as the Seventh Day Adventists' president would say. It could stand up anywhere; it was standing up nowhere in particular; it certainly wasn't standing up in Vanuatu, which is as socialist as Luxembourg and already has as much per capita foreign investment as, say, Grenada. It wasn't surprising, then, to find that "free enterprise" as perceived by the UMP and Barak Sope (they formed an antigovernment alliance after being expelled from Parliament) would mean easier leases for foreigners, more incentives for foreign investors, less red tape, and more promotion of tourism. That Sope's rhetoric concentrated on giving ni-Vanuatu control over land while his intentions were precisely the opposite was, after a few weeks, the kind of contradiction I would have been surprised not to find. His slogan, by the way, was "Freedom and Justice."

I left Tangarasi's office and walked a few blocks to Reflections, a restaurant owned by a tall Australian named Jim. The European-style cafe—Jim had studied at the Sorbonne, among other places—was frequented by tourists, expatriates, and better-off ni-Vanuatu. I was there a lot because the coffee was good and Jim let me run a tab; in exchange, he assailed me with stories of perfidious journalists, who usually stay at the hotel above his restaurant when an "event" occurs in Vanuatu. My favorite tale concerned several Australians who paid a young ni-Vanuatu man to hold a gun and stand in front of a wall to be photographed. Jim didn't have a copy of the published photo, so I never found out what the young man was meant to illustrate—probably just generalized violence by dark-skinned people. Anyway, after seeing Tangarasi, I sat at Jim's cafe and thought about Bislama. The common language of Vanuatu has exactly two prepositions, "blong" and "long." "Blong" is connective; "long" is directional. "Hand blong leg" means "foot," "tabu blong smok" is "no smoking." "Lukaot long dog" means "look out for the dog (beware of dog)." Bislama has taken on foreign words with the arbitrariness typical of most languages. Many expressions use nineteenth-century words that are now all but forgotten in their countries of origin: here guns are muskets, and a spearfishing gun is a "musket blong saltwater"; to know is to "savvy." Words continue to be adopted as the need arises, usually without much attention to their social origins. "Basket blong titties" means a bra, and "i singsing long microphone" describes fellatio. This last phrase comes from watching female singers on music videos; according to my sources fellatio is a relatively new act in Vanuatu, post-dating the arrival of VCR's. Bislama verbs have no tenses. The future is indicated by "bambae" ("by and by") at the beginning of a sentence, the past by "finis" ("finish") placed after a verb.

Sitting at Jim's restaurant drinking coffee, I wondered if Bislama wasn't the perfect language for Vanuatu. Bislama is equally "inadequate" for both abstractions and specifics; the idea, popular in current Western literary theory, that words, things, and meanings are three very different phenomena happens to be the guiding principle of Bislama. The established Western notion of language, closely tied to the historical emergence of law and centralized government (not to mention printing), strives toward a communication that can never be lost in translation. It is the language of Civilization, a language whose meanings are not supposed to be tied to the identity of the speaker; it prizes sentences that can mean the same thing to many people. This is almost impossible in Bislama. Meanings in Bislama are created much more by who is speaking, how they're speaking, and what comes before and

166 after a given sentence or remark. It is not a "rich" language,
yet the relations between people are as rich in Vanuatu as
anywhere else. Bislama, in a way, subverts the idea of precise
meaning; it places the burden of truth firmly in the mind of
the listener or reader, and doesn't pretend that it might inhere
in the words themselves. All this, of course, in the context of
a tiny but dispersed country with 105 primary languages and
two tertiary ones, French and English.

It took me quite a while to appreciate this aspect of Vanuatu
life. Journalists, after all, make their living by putting things
into words and then selling them. This can be done with
greater or lesser confidence. Every day, journalists fly to countries and describe them in terms that will be readily under-
standable to readers at home. "El Salvador is becoming more
democratic" or "Iran is gripped by fundamentalist fervor";
"Indian traditions in Guatemala are slowly being eroded" or
"The yen remains a strong currency despite softness in manu-
facturing." Such sentences are considered by their writers and
readers to be comprehensible. Journalistic language is en-
coded well enough that even undefinable words like "terrorism" and "freedom" sometimes acquire the ring of truth. In
Bislama, words as such lack this power to convince. The difference is one of degree and pretension. The Western pretension (speaking generally) seems to be that once you name
something you have understood it—and much of journalistic
activity, especially overseas, involves naming things. Vanuatu
is a place where things cannot be named in a way that is
reasonably truthful; it makes sense, then, that Vanuatu's lingua
franca has so few names, that all cars, buses, trucks, tractors,
etc. are "troks," that pistols, rifles, machine guns, spear guns,
shotguns, and bazookas are "muskets." Some would consider
this lack of "precise" communication primitive. Yet it is remarkably similar to the theories of communication and linguis-
tics lately arrived at by hypercivilized, extremely well educated academics in Europe and America. Who's primitive
now?

• • •

■ At the same time, the Vanuatu government, more than any other Pacific island regime, has imbibed the rhetoric of Western progressive thought. Father Lini speaks of Melanesian socialism, a combination of respecting indigenous traditions and developing the country economically without creating the income disparities typical of free-market models. His country is by far the most militantly antinuclear in the Pacific. These were the Vanua'aku party's principles at independence and still are, though current practice is a long way from earlier idealism.

The party is also committed to equality for women. I went to see Grace Molisa, special secretary to the prime minister, in her office at government headquarters. The plain, one-story, horseshoe-shaped building overlooks Vila Harbor, and is distinguished only by a flagpole out front on a grassy knoll. Molisa's tiny office was decorated with two "Nuclear Free Pacific" posters, pictures of her children, a "Pacific Women—Partners in Development" calendar, a pro-*kava* advertisement, and a large poster of Malcolm X. Molisa was a strapping, attractive, forceful woman, alternately charming and defensive. She made it clear at the beginning that she doesn't like foreign journalists (there aren't any ni-Vanuatu journalists except those working for the government). She once wrote a poem describing us as dedicated to "sniffing the farts of transient scavengers," a reference to expatriates. Molisa studied as a child in New Zealand, where she was, among other things, the first ni-Vanuatu to have a debutante coming-out party. She went on to become the most active ni-Vanuatu feminist and the highest female government official, a distinction she retains (all top government posts, apart from hers, are held by men).

"The colonial era didn't have any role models for women," she said. "People in visible positions were men." Molisa has helped change that; two women have been elected to Parliament, a bureaucracy has been set up to promote women's interests, and, she said, there had just been a mechanics' workshop for women. "There is much room for improvement. But at least there has been a change in mentality. Though, as far as male and female roles go, some things don't change."

168   As we talked, Molisa's strong feeling for traditional social
■   arrangements began to surface. She grew up on Ambae—
allegedly the model for James Michener's Bali Ha'i, at least in
its scenery—where women, unlike on many other islands, can
acquire rank and titles. "In life crises, the decisions must be
controlled by women, even though in the ceremony it may
well be the men who are prancing around and singing, while
the wife may be gossiping under a tree and not appear to be
involved. The present government has a lack of voice for
considering what women may consider is important. I'm in-
clined to believe that in the traditional setting there are ways
for ensuring that everybody's views are expressed. The democratic process we are adopting doesn't quite have a place for
women. Whereas in the traditional system there were ways by
which the views of women were taken into account." Outside
Ambae, on the other hand, societies existed where women
were killed for such infringements of the social order as entering a *nakamal.* In some systems, when a chief had killed a
specific number of pigs he was then obliged to kill a woman
to cap off his progression up the chiefly ladder. In the British
police files on one island, there were three main categories of
conflict—arguments over land, arguments over pigs, and arguments over women, in that order. Most ni-Vanuatu wives are
purchased by their husbands' families (the National Council
of Chiefs is trying to fix uniform bride prices; the cash economy has made some islands rich enough that their women are
unaffordable). In parts of Malekula, women wore head-
dresses, and when a man of a certain kinship category approached they were required to cover themselves with the
headdress and kneel by the side of the road. The man would
greet the woman by placing his foot on her head and saying,
"Good." A male friend, not from Malekula, told me once how
strange it was to walk along a path and suddenly come across
a bundle of fabric heaped to one side. It's worth remembering
that Vanuatu, unlike most places in the world, records a sub-
stantially lower life expectancy for women than for men. Ni-
Vanuatu women generally do more manual labor than men,
as well as bearing and raising children.

Things are different in Vila. There women can get wage-earning employment, which upsets the traditional order of things. Molisa sees this as a precursor of larger problems, namely education and urban drift. "With the old [pre-independence] educational system, you learn to expect running water, you expect roofs like this"—she pointed upward—"and naturally you are drawn toward development and urbanization, and with that you would then have urban drift. No matter how far people are educated, they should still be at home in their home environment [the village]. People learn to want things they may never see. We want to educate people to be at home at home, rather than misfits the other way around."

I remembered what Willy had said that night at the *naka-mal*: "Black people are not very smart. They can't go home." Where is home? Or maybe, *what* is home? I wondered whether Grace Molisa felt at home. She emphasized education, but an education that encouraged contentment rather than aspiration. She emphasized women's rights, but rights that should be exercised within traditions that might or might not be oppressive. And she emphasized economic development, but a development that could generate cash for the national economy while keeping ni-Vanuatu on the farm. "The ni-Vanuatu are not sufficiently active in the economy. There is too much dependence on the government. In the old days, people made copra so they could pay school fees. Now the government gives primary education for free. So people don't work the plantations. And that's not good for the country. So you have to have things that make people work so that the country develops, land is developed, and that helps everybody in the nation."

Molisa seemed very much to be speaking in code—a code that came from elsewhere. She was grafting foreign words onto local goals and they didn't really fit. How do you have education without dissatisfaction? How do you motivate people to work harder than they otherwise would when the only goal is "national development"? How do you convince women that their traditional position is unjust when you don't necessarily believe that yourself? Molisa admitted that many ni-Vanuatu women might not agree with her position. "I have the advantage of being exposed to what is international and what is local, whereas a woman who has never been exposed to anything outside the home would not share my views." She has experienced resentment from women over her success, as had other women in Vila who have achieved some prominence. "For women staying at home, not knowing what others do, not having seen the other things we have seen, maybe it's a sore point."

Once I spoke to a woman in Vila who had been a community worker. She used to visit villages to explain the new policies, and "sometimes I wouldn't talk because literally the men wouldn't listen." She was there to organize the rural bureaucracy for women, setting up classes in sewing, business management, home improvement, gardening, etc. "On most islands there have been problems. Men have usually treated women as third-class people [after men and pigs]. If you're talking about custom, women were always at the bottom. To get this feeling from men, that we are just nothing, is gradually changing, but I would still say it is there in every level of development. Most women don't want to be in high positions. They think those positions should be held by men." This woman, around thirty, with a quick and brilliant smile, said that traveling abroad had helped her gain confidence. She had been involved in an up-and-down romance with a white man who was now overseas. She was torn; she couldn't decide whether to go and join him.

■ From the windows of a biprop Otter, flying low over the ocean, the islands were a deep warm green. We headed north from Vila airport, over copra plantations on the west coast of Efate. As with many Vanuatu copra plantations, the coconut palms were too tall, old, and barren. Here and there were trees whose tops had been blown off during the last tropical storm. They looked pretty pathetic, forty-foot stalks waiting for time to push them over. The plantations' decline began during the 1930s depression and has worsened since independence; the uses for dried coconut meat become fewer as the years go by, and copra buyers become more demanding about quality. Buyers these days prefer hot-air-dried copra to Vanuatu's sun-dried variety. Hot-air drying requires machinery, which requires investment capital, something hard to find in Vanuatu.

The twelve-seat Otter droned with the incessancy of a long dream. We drifted among the clouds, sometimes seeing the sea below, sometimes an island—Efate, Emae, Ambrym, Malekula. Most of Vanuatu's islands are steep and mountainous, with tiny villages scattered along the coastlines and even tinier villages inland. There are very few roads, and most everyone travels by boat or on footpaths. Between islands one usually goes by plane; planes in Vanuatu are, if you have the money, like buses, making all local stops. The flights are scheduled, though in an informal way. Airports are usually strips of grass cut from the jungle. Accidents are not uncommon.

The airstrip at Lolowai, on Ambae, sloped upward from a cliff. We approached from the ocean side. Coming into a sloping airstrip can be quite dramatic. The feeling is one of flying straight into the ground. I had been placed in the co-pilot's seat (no co-pilots in Vanuatu) so I could better appreciate the drama. The landing pattern was a sort of steeply angled U. The Australian pilot headed down into the end of the strip then, once we were able to count the blades of grass and observe the insects and dew, pulled the nose up. He then flew bumpily to the uphill end, though technically our wheels were on the ground.

I was on Ambae as part of an elaborate and ultimately doomed effort to reach another island where a pig-killing was due to take place. The notorious airstrip on that island had been closed because heavy rain had mucked up the field. Fortunately, that day on Ambae was set for the final celebration of the Vanuatu Interregional Games at a new school near Lolowai. When I arrived at the games, after hitching two rides then walking for about an hour through the jungle, it was

raining gently. The field had a grandstand on one side, concession shacks on the other, and tropical hills all around. I didn't
know anyone there. I attempted to socialize with several ni-
Vanuatu but was greeted with a combination of politeness,
distrust, and incomprehension. Eventually I hooked up with
two Canadian aid workers living on Ambae. We sat in the
grandstand and watched the soccer final. The level of play was
very low. Afterward all the teams lined up, facing the grandstand, to hear speeches and receive their awards. There was
a great deal of booing, cheering, and catcalling by the athletes
during the awards ceremony. At one end was the Port Vila
team. They wore flashy, matching uniforms; the young
women even wore shorts, a daring impropriety. At the other
end were the Malekula athletes, who seemed to be wearing
whatever they could find. There were, as I recall, no women
on their team.

The awards presenter tried to be decorous, but the athletes
refused to make the ceremony a decorous event. First of all,
the Malekulans had gotten angry the day before when they
lost in Ping-Pong. They had brought the Ping-Pong table
from Malekula themselves so, the night after their defeat, they
cut off the table's legs. The next morning the table was found
on the ground, and the rest of the Ping-Pong competition was
cancelled. There was also a contretemps involving the relay
race, which the Malekulans claimed to have won though the
prize was given to the Vila team. When the presenter tried to
give a second-place award to the Malekulans they refused to
approach the podium and accept it. A protracted stand-off
ensued. The Malekulans sat down on the field and looked
away, the rain came and went. Most of the other athletes sided
with the protesters; the Port Vila athletes were generally seen
as overfed, arrogant, and too urbanized to be real ni-Vanuatu.
The Malekulans never did take their award.

After the ceremony Father Lini gave a harsh speech. It
wasn't so much the athletes' behavior that angered him as the
government's having had to pay for the games—and to solicit
financial help from neighboring countries to do so. I had
trouble following his Bislama, but I did hear something like

"I hope next time you'll be able to pay for yourselves." He made this point several times. Father Lini looked worn out. He'd always had a tendency toward overworking; while a student in New Zealand, Lini habitually pushed himself to exhaustion. In 1987 he suffered a stroke in Washington, D.C., and has been partially paralyzed since—an infirmity capitalized on by his political opponents. He walks with a cane and must rest frequently. He looked older than forty-six. I wondered what was going through his mind on that rainy day, addressing a crowd of young people who would outlive him. Essentially he was telling them to work harder and earn more money, not least because the government needed it. It was the same problem that Grace Molisa had chewed over: After eight years of independence, the government found itself in the position of overseer, exhorting the people to work for cash, knowing that such wage-labor was precisely the solvent that could undo traditional ni-Vanuatu ways of life . . . which the government sincerely wanted to respect. Honoring the complex uniqueness of ni-Vanuatu life was one of the main reasons for ejecting the British and French in the first place. But ni-Vanuatu cultures don't fit well into national democratic government, or cash economies, or even interregional games.

After the speeches, it was announced that the following year's games would be held on Malekula. The Ambae team handed over the official banner to the Malekulans. The master of ceremonies then requested that the teams march in orderly fashion around the field, with the Malekulans leading. There was a great cheer as the teams paraded off. The Malekulans, however, once halfway around the track, began chanting and marching in a more customary fashion. Some of the other islanders started their own chants. In an instant the Malekulans were tearing around the playing field, swinging their banner. The Vila athletes in their pricey outfits edged nervously toward the concession stands. Being from everywhere and nowhere, they had no chant to take up except the national anthem, which isn't exactly a danceable tune. An old Malekulan chief, in torn clothes and unshod, hobbled from the grandstand onto the field and began to dance methodically. The

Malekulan athletes circled around him. From somewhere they had retrieved *namele* leaves, which they fixed behind them in waistbands or tucked into their trousers. They chanted a Malekulan song, probably from the Big Nambas, though I couldn't really tell. Elsewhere on the field, a group from North Pentecost had produced a long, tubular drum, fashioned from thick bamboos bound together. The drum was held horizontally and beaten with sticks. They sang a number of tunes in Raga, the North Pentecost language; women and girls danced along with the men, and the Pentecost people seemed in general less dour than the Malekulans.

That night a disco was held on the field. I was exhausted and didn't go, but a lot of young ni-Vanuatu did, dancing and drinking *kava* and beer well into the morning despite heavy rains. I was told that the Malekulans didn't attend—the disco environment would have threatened Malekulan ideas of propriety—though I wonder if one or two didn't slip out to enjoy the lights and music.

■ A week or so later I flew from Vila to North Pentecost for a *bolololi*, the Raga word for a pig-killing ceremony. Through his sister, Hilda, Father Lini had suggested I go to the *bolololi* and, while on the island, interview him. I had spent much of the past three weeks trying to get an interview. I had networked shamelessly in a country where the word is unknown. The almost daily trips up the hill to Father Lini's Vila office began to feel like a Calvary, sweaty repentance for the sins of my ancestors (and contemporaries). Grace Molisa wasn't the only government official who disliked foreign journalists.

Hilda Lini had given me several ni-Vanuatu contacts on North Pentecost but, as often happened, I was sloughed off into the hands of local whites—a carpenter and a doctor, both from New Zealand. I stayed with the doctor, Margaret Neave, a tough and gracious woman in her sixties who had previously worked in Vietnam and Hong Kong, among other places. She was trying, against the odds, to run a small hospital on North Pentecost. Margaret, with her white hair, two cats, and stack of nineteenth-century English novels, had the vigor and impatient sadness of an experienced foreign-aid worker. The people who run aid programs are an almost uniformly repellent crew, but those who do the fieldwork, particularly if they're past middle age, can be remarkable. Perhaps they understand better what it's like to be outside the fast tides of history.

I spent a day and a half cooking up schemes to get from the hospital to Nambwaraniut, a tiny coastal village where the pig-killing was to be held. Going by "road" was hopeless, even if a car could be found; by footpath was a possibility, but Nambwaraniut was a long way away, I'd need a guide, and in any event I wasn't feeling too athletic. I made several trips on foot to the prime minister's village, Laone, several miles from the hospital. Unfortunately, Laone housed not only Father Lini but his brother, Ham, who was supposed to help me, and his Libyan-trained bodyguard, Peter, who explained to me (while clutching a copy of Fijian coup maker Sitiveni Rabuka's *No Other Way*) that he—Peter—just didn't like journalists. Ham made promises to help but was, in practice, unmotivated, whereas Peter was simply happy to obstruct. By my second evening at the hospital I was pretty depressed, and after dinner went to sit on the grass outside Margaret's house. Pentecost is a long, narrow island with a high ridge running north to south. Margaret lived a hundred or so steep feet uphill from a very tiny village called Abwatuntora, which was next to the sea. I lay beneath a low, spreading breadfruit tree on a rise. Directly below was a wide path that led to Abwatuntora. Sounds filtered up from the village—shouts, the quavering music of wooden flutes. Groups of children would walk by on the path with flashlights or burning torches; we'd say *rani* to each other ("hello" in Raga). I knew that across the water was the pyramidal shape of Ambae, but it was too dark to see. Jupiter glowed orange just above the ridgeline. Fruit bats glided overhead, and above them were thousands of stars. The wind came in gusts and I listened to varying sounds as it passed through the jungle: the thump-thump of banana leaves, the rustle of palms, the slightly deeper, more chaotic rustle of breadfruit leaves.

The next day I arrived early in the morning at the prime
minister's house, a quarter-mile walk along the beach from
Laone. Ham, under duress, found room for me on a small
outboard. When we reached Nambwaraniut the tam-tams
were already beating and the villagers dancing. It was a good
day for killing pigs: no rain, a cool breeze. Nambwaraniut is
separated from the ocean only by a few palm trees and a
narrow beach. Just in from the trees was the *nasara*, or dancing ground, filled with villagers dancing and singing. Men
danced at the center, facing inward; around them the women
danced, clockwise, some with umbrellas, some with feathers
in their hair, gently waving their arms at right angles to their
bodies. "It's a way of showing their happiness," Ham said.
Dancing counter to the mass of villagers were three men in
bright red loincloths. The oldest and the youngest—Samuel,
around forty, and his son John, eleven—would be killing the
pigs, both as a step toward attaining chiefly rank in their village and to stockpile wealth in the spirit world. This would
ensure a favorable place for them after death. There were
perhaps a hundred visitors from neighboring villages and
about two dozen pigs of various colors and sizes, tied to plants
or stakes, eating, sleeping, snorting.

At one end of the *nasara*, shaded by a few trees, Father Lini
sat in a folding chair, an uncomfortable seat that emphasized
his infirmity. His right arm was nearly useless and he often
held it in his lap; his damaged right leg stretched stiffly before
him. With him were Peter and an assistant, Lini's father,
Harper, various chiefs, and a friend—I think it was an uncle—
who would be acting out Lini's part in the ceremony. Father
Lini, who had his own, first *bolololi* in 1982, would be exchanging pigs with Samuel and John. His uncle-proxy would be
giving Lini's speeches for him. They involved pacing about
the *nasara* and declaiming ritual phrases as particular pigs
were given away and as Samuel and John acquired certain
privileges: for example, the right to wear *namele* and the scar-
let *faresangvulu* leaves in their waistbands.

For each pig, Samuel, John, and a man representing Samuel's deceased father would dance around the *nasara* in a

weaving, S-shaped pattern, waving one arm at their side, then
the other, now and then giving a medium-pitched shout. They
would virtually run during these dances; each dance culminated with their touching the leg of a man who stood by the
pig being given to Samuel and John. Those who were giving
the pigs would also dance: the man led and women of the
family followed. Other women would rush out to drape red
mats—which are used for burial and, like pigs, are a kind of
currency—over the arms of the dancing women. Sometimes
they would give fistfuls of change instead of mats. These pre-
paratory ceremonies went on for hours and I didn't understand them too clearly. The *bolololi* is exceedingly complicated
and seems to involve every person in the village, as well as
many from outside. Ham tried to explain roughly what was
going on but there was only so much he could clarify, particularly given his limited English and my feeble Bislama (not to
mention Raga). A strapping young man in Western dress
made notes on who was giving what to whom. He had a
clipboard and the demeanor of an aspiring accountant. After
each set of dances, the three principals, the accountant, Father
Lini's proxy, and the chiefs would huddle together to discuss
the deal. These conferences would often go on for a while;
when they did, Samuel would get up and pace nervously. The
bolololi is an opportunity to demonstrate chiefly abilities—
decisiveness, conciliation, intelligence—and a long haggle is
unchiefly. It became evident by midafternoon that Samuel was
not acquitting himself very well, and there were critical mur-
murings among the crowd.

The dancing and singing, the exchanging of pigs and mats,
and the tense negotiations took all day. The phrase in Bislama
is "business-pig." The *bolololi* reminded me of something I
couldn't quite place. Gradually I recalled scenes from the New
York Stock Exchange. Sitting with Ham on a log, the sea at
our back, watching the villagers with ash smeared on their
faces and feathers in their hair, I remembered standing with
my nose pressed against the glass of the NYSE viewing room
and seeing the traders with their different-colored coats, holding up slips of paper, staring at numbers, and shouting. People

can invest all sorts of things with cosmic value—chalices and books, figurines, swords, paper money, convertible debentures, junk bonds, pigs—shoring up cultural barricades, challenging oblivion for its control of time. The fact that many ni-Vanuatu complained to me of the tyranny of business-pig ("The pig is your master!" a young Christian woman in Vila said, shaking with anger) also called up memories of home, God, and Mammon.

The exchange ceremonies didn't wind down until sunset. Father Lini presented Samuel with a bracelet called a *bani*—it cost Samuel ten pigs—and another *bani* was given to John. Lini's proxy spoke on how to govern the people and be a capable chief. Samuel gave speeches too, sometimes faltering over the complex phrases; Lini's proxy would prompt him, irritably, from the sidelines. There was a lengthy ritual during which Samuel and John acquired the right to stand in the *tora*, a tiny space fenced off with boards alongside the *nasara*. Each speech, each change in the choreography, was marked by a beating on the tam-tams. Young men sat before the long hollow drums, shaded by branches stuck in the ground. Behind them was a formidable stone cross on a stepped cement platform. The people of Nambwaraniut, as on most of North Pentecost, are churchgoing Anglicans. The sight of an Anglican cross brooding over a pig-killing ceremony made my head spin a little, though after weeks in Vanuatu it was the sort of thing I'd come to expect.

There was a lull in the proceedings as the pigs were prepared for killing. A chief invited me to the *nakamal* for *kava*. After a day of sitting outdoors, a day of being observed by the villagers and having the occasional child, shocked by my whiteness, burst into tears, I was ready for the comforts of *kava*. The *nakamal* was about two-thirds the size of a basketball court, one large room with a high ceiling. Like most of Nambwaraniut's buildings, it was made of wood and had a peaked roof covered by thatch. The chief, an old, energetic man from a neighboring village, and I sat down with some other men in one corner and chatted for a while. He eventually realized my Bislama was limited, so a young man named

David, visiting from Vila, translated for us. *Kava* was offered.
I tried to get the rituals right; the key gesture was to say
tabeana ("thank you" in Raga) to the person offering the *kava*.
I felt I was being socially clumsy but everyone showed for-
bearance, as well as curiosity about my reaction to the *kava*.
I praised it profusely. It *was* excellent *kava*, prepared from
fresher roots than those used in Port Vila, and brewed strong.
North Pentecost is noted for its powerful *kava*. Raga-speaking
kava drinkers are also noted for their dramatic spitting. The
story is that *kava* originated from the vagina of a primordial
woman. That is why it tastes so bad, and why one spits so
vigorously after each drink to remove the taste; and, of course,
that is why the men return night after night to drink it. Tradi-
tionally, *kava* in this region was prepared with a coral stone.
Roots were held in the left hand, then ground with the stone,
which was about the size of a modest salami. The stone and
hand were meant to represent the preparer's penis and a ge-
neric vagina, respectively. The stone's dimensions were the
subject of much humorous repartee in the *nakamal*.

After my second shell of *kava* I began to feel a certain
mental thickening; I looked around the *nakamal* and was surprised to see women. "In the old days there were two *nakamals*, one for women, one for men," David explained in re-
gretful tones. "It changed with the church. This is one of many
things we have lost." We discussed the *bolololi* and Raga customs. David, who worked in the national statistics office in
Vila but was from North Pentecost, said this *bolololi* was
debased because so many people were dressed in "white-man
wear." I noticed that David was himself in white-man wear.
"I think most young people today, they don't think about
custom. They think about what's good for them. They go to
Vila for the boys and the girls, for the nightclubs, the movies,
the discos." We drank and talked then I decided I'd better
leave; the men I was sitting with seemed to be giving me
rather more than my share of the *kava*, and it was easy to
imagine myself, an hour or two hence, puking into the dirt
floor of the *nakamal* on hands and knees. David and I went
out back to urinate on a pile of pig fragments, discarded

coconut shells, played-out *kava* roots, and other garbage, and
I thought: drinking, talking, urinating—why is male bonding
so often the same?

By the time I rejoined Ham it was dark and I was stuporous.
Before us were pigs tied to a row of small *namele* bushes.
Father Lini had left—a sign of disapproval. In a good *bolololi*
the pigs should be killed before dusk. Hurricane lanterns and
flashlights were brought out to illuminate the *nasara*. There
was an enormous sounding of tam-tams. The village chief,
who had doffed his white-man clothes for a loincloth and
covered himself with ashes, led a single-file parade around the
pigs; following him were Samuel, his "father," John, and a
train of women who had smeared themselves with red stain.
Everybody sang and shouted. Then the group gathered
around a pig staked near the Anglican cross and John was
handed a steel-headed axe. There was just the sound of its
blunt end crushing the pig's skull. The lanterns and flashlights
were few and their light hectic so that our bodies were surrounded by trembling shadows. John swung and swung but
wasn't strong enough to kill the pig. An older man took the
axe, swung, and the pig ceased twitching. Everyone sang, the
women passed by and touched the pig with sticks. John
clubbed a second pig and succeeded in killing it. Then Samuel
took the axe and came to where Ham and I were sitting.
About six feet from us stood a medium-sized pig. Samuel
swung at its skull and the pig tottered. He swung repeatedly
and eventually the pig went down. Samuel moved on to kill
five other pigs tethered in a row. Blood ran from the nostrils
of the one lying before Ham and me; its breath made a gur-
gling sound. After killing the five, Samuel came back to this
first pig, which had tentatively regained its feet, and tried
again. Finally the chief took the axe and broke the pig's neck.
Most of the lanterns then went out and we all sat quietly there
in Nambwaraniut. You could hear the snuffling of the dying
pigs, the waves, wind through the palms, and faint conversations.

Soon Ham and I walked over to our boat. Two pigs were
being gutted. People poked at the stomach, intestines, and

other organs with sticks. "Peace, peace be with us," a young woman said, smiling; a man next to her laughed softly. I couldn't figure out if this was a pun or a joke and worried that I was imagining it. The gutted pigs were laid across the bow and our small launch slowly motored back to Laone, weighed down by twelve passengers and the pigs. Sometimes sparkling lights appeared in the dark water alongside us; Ham said they were from a type of fish that glitters at night.

■ Two days later Father Lini and I sat in folding chairs on his front lawn. His father sat nearby with an old chief. Peter the bodyguard cut pieces of fruit for us with his machete. "It was good that you saw the *bolololi*," Father Lini said. I apologized for not understanding much of it; he said there were parts he didn't understand either, that the speeches in particular require a great deal of instruction and practice and many men these days have trouble finding the time to study.

Father Lini spoke at length, in a somber monotone, about the intricacies of Vanuatu politics. Business deals, coalitions, why x got this construction contract instead of y. His remarks were rote, more or less; he seemed tired and distracted. I remembered that he had spent some fifteen years in the thick of politics, that he was the first prime minister of a new country and a prominent statesman in the region . . . that some of his former comrades were now battling his government, that he walks with a cane and fatigues easily. I wondered what it must be like to be Walter Lini, Red menace, father of his country.

Lini talked about his idea of success. "If I can spend the rest of my life to teach one of [my children] to be self-reliant and to develop whatever is necessary to help him face his own life and his family life after that, then I will have achieved the basis of the quality of life that I consider important." This, then, was the fire-breathing Walter Lini, apostle of Melanesian socialism, friend to Libyans, alleged communist. I fished around for some statement of ideology. This was as close as he came: "In a way, I think that people are going to be forced to go back. With the economic situation that exists in the world today, and

■ social problems that people face throughout the world, it
seems to me that if it continues for a number of decades it will
force people to change the system that has existed. . . . It is
clear that certain countries have completely overdone trying
to control their young, their society, and their people. I think
it is possible to help people, both men and women . . . to be
free and to be able to be masters of their own destiny."

I hadn't expected to see the inadequacy of Western political
rhetoric so vividly demonstrated by a head of government.
The politicians in Vila had always pushed rhetorical contradic-
tions to the limit, then left them hanging; Lini, by contrast,
seemed to have gone further, arriving at terminal language
fatigue. *In a way, I think that people are going to be forced to go back.*
It was with great relief that we turned to the subject of pigs.
Lini still owed three pigs from his own 1982 *bolololi* and was
eager to clear his account. "*Bolololi* is just like a business deal
in the European system. As soon as I have cleared those three
pigs, and if I have maybe six pigs or seven pigs with a tusk,
then I can make another *bolololi.* I do not have time to make
it when I am prime minister. If I stayed here, perhaps I could
concentrate more on paying back my accounts." Tusks are
key; the more curved the tusk, the more valuable the pig. We
talked about tusks and Samuel's performance during the ceremony. Father Lini became animated. He laughed and smiled
easily, he made little jokes. I ran out of cassettes for taping the
interview and didn't particularly care.

■ A few days before leaving Vanuatu I met up with my friend
Godrington in Vila. He invited me to a "custom dance" honoring the anniversary of the founding of North Pentecost's
local government. The celebration took place at an Anglican
church in Tagabe, an outlying district of Port Vila frequented
by people from North Pentecost. The church was very modest—two small buildings above an undulating, grassy slope.
The sun was warm and a cool breeze blew up from the harbor.
I went with two white friends; we sat alongside the church and
watched the dancing. There were five lines of about eight

dancers each, stepping up and down with deliberation, singing in Raga, their feet marking time on the grass. In their midst, one man held a pole topped by a model ship that sported a (nonfunctioning) white smokestack. In front of the dancers stood a tripod made from stout poles. The dancers, coated in black stain, wore loincloths, leafy headbands, ankle rattles and, in some cases, tennis shoes. Suddenly three men came running from behind the church. Children screamed and then laughed. One man wore a vintage military helmet; another wore an old, torn army shirt and gazed up and down through a huge pair of binoculars. The three ran around terrorizing the children, then enacted a play in front of the dancers. I couldn't understand the play; the three devil-men were somehow battling one another. Eventually they left. Moments later two more men appeared, wearing loincloths and leaves. One was clearly a devil. He grimaced, holding his hands before him and running about, ready to clutch any child who got in his way. The other man was, to me, more ambiguous; he carried a bow and a quiver of long, thin sticks. The two also acted a scene in front of the dancing lines, arrows arcing over the grass slope.

After the two men left, the dancers turned about and marched off. As they passed in front of the church I saw Godrington, waving and smiling. I hadn't recognized him before, smeared in black, his face tucked under leaves. He came over and we greeted each other; the blacking came off on my hand. A few minutes later Godrington returned, dressed like his old self in a casual shirt and jeans. We walked behind the church and down to a *nakamal* where we had drunk *kava* many times before. Godrington knew I was leaving and that this might be the last time we would see each other. We bought two cans of Foster's and sat on the rough benches. Around us dancers were relaxing, blackened, in loincloths, also drinking Foster's and smoking imported cigarettes. I asked Godrington about the first dance. He said it was meant to narrate the coming of white people to North Pentecost. The celebration was, after all, to mark the anniversary of local government. And since the purpose of local government,

184 Godrington said, was to interpret the white world and white customs, it made sense to create a dance about them. The dancing and singing prior to the arrival of the three men in military surplus was traditional, and intended to show those North Pentecost people who knew only Port Vila what life was like before white people arrived. The second dance was from a traditional story: A man goes fishing with arrows and catches a few fish. On his way home a devil attacks him and takes all his arrows. He runs to the nearest village and asks why this has happened. The villagers tell him it was because he didn't ask permission to fish, and the waters were *tabu* for him unless he asked permission.

Godrington said both dramas were composed specifically for this celebration. He had led a group of young men in planning them. They'd asked the old men for advice, but only one was willing to help. This man happened to be sitting next to us, so I was introduced and we shook hands. Godrington said the elders, by and large, hadn't liked the idea of young men coming up with new dances. "We could not just follow the old men. If we did a custom dance like they told us, after a while no one in Vila would come. It's good there was this old man who would talk with us." I wanted to know what the old man was thinking but he kept looking at the ground and seemed far away.

We bought two more beers and walked slowly back to the church. Godrington urged me to dance. I said, "But I'm white. Godrington, it would feel strange."

"No. The dance is fun. It's to express our happiness. You're my friend." Godrington smiled. "Come on. Let's dance." We approached the back of the church. "It's easy." Children saw me and shouted, *"Tuturani! Tuturani!"* Pointing and laughing. I was a bit addled by the beer. I was laughing. In front of the church there were several lines of dancers and thirty or forty people dancing counter clockwise around them. People held their hands perpendicular to their sides and shouted, "Ay, ay, ay," a high-pitched yowl. Godrington grabbed my arm and pulled me in, a giant smile on his face. I had a beer can in one hand and a cigarette in the other. I danced and tried

to yowl, but the cries got jumbled in my throat with the
laughter. Everyone was laughing, it seemed—at me, with me,
despite me, I couldn't say. I saw my two white friends under
a tree, alternately giggling, clutching their sides, and looking
embarrassed. After a minute or so I found Godrington and
said I had to leave. We embraced, then I walked off to join
my other friends for the drive back to town.

*In December 1988, Barak Sope and his uncle, President Ati
George Sokomanu, briefly took over the government from
Prime Minister Lini. Sope demanded allegiance from government members, the police, and the army. He said that if they
didn't pledge allegiance he would call in foreign military
help, mentioning Fiji in particular (Sope had met with Brigadier Rabuka two months before). Father Lini spoke to the
Army and had them round up the would-be government. Sope,
President Sokomanu, and their four "ministers" were jailed.
Various legal proceedings followed, and Sokomanu was replaced as president. Symbolic items, most importantly pigs,
were later exchanged among the coup-makers and their intended victims, and all of those arrested were freed.*

*The following year a large Taiwanese company, Tien Chu
Enterprise Ltd., convinced some traditional landowners on
the island of Malekula to allow logging. Tien Chu himself,
and his personal secretary, Johnson Wu, were later convicted
of bribing two senior Vanuatu government officials. Chu, Wu,
and the officials were all fined; Chu was deported, but he soon
sent a replacement to represent his company. The project is
going ahead, in an area whose people speak six different languages and where many valuable cultural sites are located.*

LA FRANCONÉSIE

■ " 'Who are we, where are we from, where are we going?'
*These questions that Gauguin, voluntary exile in the Pacific,
desperately sought answers to are perhaps French questions,
ones we ought to resolve in France and not in the antipodes.
But this, as Kipling said, is another story." So concludes the
historian and journalist Jean Chesneaux in his excellent book
*Transpacifiques. *Chesneaux coined the term "franconésie" to
describe France's three Pacific territories—New Caledonia,
Wallis and Futuna, and French Polynesia—whose total area
comprises some five million square miles of land and ocean,
mostly ocean. But "franconésie" also describes a state of mind,
a collection of dreams and desires. This state of mind is primarily French rather than Melanesian or Polynesian; it has
to do with France's dignity and plausibility as a world power,
the propagation of French as an international language, and
perhaps, in some subconscious way, the cultural memory of the*

190 *South Seas as a place of attainable happiness. As the first*
■ *Frenchman to visit the region, Louis Antoine de Bougainville,*
wrote of Tahiti, "I believed myself transported into the gar-
den of Eden."

What a strange fate it must have been for the Polynesians,
to be living in Eden and not even knowing it! The fate of
France's Pacific subjects has been strange ever since. New Cale-
donia, Wallis and Futuna, and French Polynesia are, along
with Mayotte, France's only substantial overseas territories, a
curious empire, farther flung than most. "France, a Pacific
power," French President François Mitterrand said in 1985,
"considers and decides with complete sovereignty whatever
touches on its national interests." With armed revolt in New
Caledonia and civil disturbances in Polynesia, French sover-
eignty has become increasingly problematic. Which is to say
that France continues to ask questions, of itself and others, in
the antipodes, though it has yet to resolve any of them.

New Caledonia

Three hundred miles southwest of Port Vila, Vanuatu, 850 miles east of Australia, the cigar-shaped, mountainous main island of New Caledonia, the Grande Terre, rises spectacularly out of the ocean. Captain James Cook, the first European to see the island, named it after his native Scotland—supposedly because of the plentiful pine trees. New Caledonia, comprising the Grande Terre and, farther north, the low-lying Loyalty Islands, was originally annexed by France in 1853. Its population of 145,000 is almost half indigenous Melanesians, known as Kanaks. The Kanaks have fought the French, on and off, for over a century. Since the early 1980s a Kanak-led mobilization for independence, and the distinctly unpleasant French reaction to it, have transformed this beautiful, pricey tourist destination into a battlefield.

■ On the plane to New Caledonia's capital city of Nouméa I sat with Morris, an overweight, balding man with dark curly hair and a Mobil Oil jacket. He was born and raised in the central Tunisian town of Sous; at twenty he left, penniless, for Australia. Morris learned English quickly, he worked hard. In New Caledonia he married a *caldoche*—the term for French people whose families are well established in the territory, as opposed to the *métropolitains*, those people who have more recently emigrated from France. Morris has lived "on the territory" for twenty years. Lately there's been a war and Morris isn't sure what to do. He certainly opposes the fight for independence and disdains the dark-skinned Kanaks, of whom a majority support the anti-French war. But, being neither white nor black, Morris is a confused case, a glitch in the chromatic algebra of New Caledonia's conflict. In the end he'll probably make his political decisions by the rules of the marketplace; independence wouldn't be good for business, or for low-level multinational functionaries like himself.

"Our real problem is Mitterrand. Oh, he's a bastard! It's just like Africa. He was in Algeria, he was the minister of something. If the French leave here it will be terrible. You must believe me." Out the window New Caledonia was breathtaking. Clouds wandered among peaks and steep, dark-green valleys; the Pacific was a washed-out, midafternoon blue, careless and placid. "France must stay, because if it doesn't the communists will come," Morris said energetically. "Oh la la, the Russians or someone else. Or if the Australians come, it will be very bad. If France left, it would be bad for *everybody*. You must believe me. If the French go, I will go, I think to Australia. The climate in Queensland is very much like here."

A lot of *caldoches* have emigrated to Queensland since the civil war, or *les événements* ("the events," an agile term), began in 1984. The Kanaks have made their white neighbors' lives uncomfortable—burning property, blockading roads, killing. Kanaks refer to *caldoches*, in a wonderful paradox, as "the victims of history." The insult gains credibility when *caldoches*, who sometimes express patriotism toward France, do their best to avoid ever going there. Jobs are very hard to find these days in France, and of course the European winters are much colder. *Caldoches* love to say how much they loathe, genuinely hate, Australians. But when they weary of "the events" they go to Queensland.

The Nouméa airport was flashy—illuminated color advertisements on poles, slowly revolving; a PA system that worked—and the soldiers were well armed. (New Caledonia is, effectively, under occupation.) The luggage arrived quickly on a conveyor. Morris offered to drive me into town. We met up with his dour wife and their two children, then got on the highway to Nouméa. It was an excellent highway. "It cost millions of francs!" Morris said. "In Vanuatu there are no roads like this. It is the French who pay for it. France gives New Caledonia forty-eight billion francs a year. If the French left, there wouldn't be one billion." A BMW passed—its white driver exchanged waves with Morris—followed by a lovely Peugeot sedan. "France gives all the money, but the black people—they want France to go. Now they have sugar on their table, and rice, soft drinks. They also want democracy. But where does the money for sugar come from? If France goes, there won't be any sugar. They can't have democracy and still have sugar on the table."

I couldn't stop gazing at the countryside. Each valley and hillside was different. Here a stand of young pines, then a field of grain, then a tiny forest of fragile, white-barked trees that looked like miniature aspens. Mountains eventually rose above the highway on either side, cut by verdant gorges. I kept remarking on how beautiful the landscape was but Morris seemed insensible to it. His wife and the kids remained silent in the back seat. "Here the black people get everything for free—hospitals, schools, helicopters to bring them in from the bush to Nouméa. They don't have to work. Everything is free. I'm telling you"—he lowered his voice—"these black people make more money than you and me. It's true. You see them driving big cars. You must believe me."

Outside Nouméa we came to a huge factory spewing orange smoke. I hadn't seen anything like it in over four months of Pacific travel, so the sight was jarring. I began to wonder if I were dreaming, a sensation that would continue for some time. Something felt fundamentally askew, as if I were in a

194 place that was tangible but didn't exist. "That is Société le
Nickel [SLN]," Morris explained. Nickel is, by far, the territory's major export (primarily sold to Japan); New Caledonia
has the second-largest nickel reserves in the world. Nickel
became a big deal in the 1960s. A number of French people
made fortunes in the industry; a larger number of Kanaks
made wages. It was *le boom de nickel*, and it fundamentally
altered the economic structure of New Caledonia. It is also
over, at least as long as international nickel prices remain low.
In the shadow of the SLN factory were four frightening apartment blocks. "You see those buildings? We gave them to the
black people. They were brand new. And very nice! Look at
them now. They are all dirty. Ah!" Morris, whose own features appeared to be mostly North African Arab, made a
French gesture with his left arm, a gesture that said: Oh well,
c'est la vie. Black people. What can you do?

We drove into town—tall office buildings, construction
everywhere, fine houses on tropical slopes overlooking the
bay—and slowed with the traffic as we passed Nouméa's new
port. "It cost millions of francs. France paid for that, too. Well,
our taxes paid for it." We drove on to the yacht harbor. It's
hard to say how many yachts there were, but the number
probably exceeded a thousand. *A thousand yachts.* Among
Kanaks, Nouméa is called *la ville blanche*, "the white city." I
told Morris how amazed I was by the yachts, and by how
staggeringly wealthy Nouméa seemed. "Mitterrand doesn't
like us because of them. We have a car *and* a yacht. He wants
to take them away—it isn't socialism! No, we are capitalists
here. I believe some people can do things, and some cannot.
If you want to do something, you go and work and do it.
You've seen Tunisia. One person works hard and does something, so a hundred people can sit and play cards all day. That's
socialism. Did you like Tunis?"

"Tunis is quite beautiful."

"Hah!" Morris turned to his wife. "Did you hear that? He
thinks Tunis is beautiful!" Morris's wife rolled her eyes and
said *"Bof."* Another flexible expression in the French language.

Geographically, Nouméa has no center. The older part of town is clustered around a rectangular plaza that rises from the harbor—rather like Tunis. But since the 1960s the city has sprawled, with former suburbs now part of the town proper, such that Nouméa spreads along the coast, with the SLN factory at one end and a Club Med at the other in the flashy beachside neighborhood called Anse Vata. It has become a city of layers, each economic era leaving its own sediment: colonial, *le boom de nickel*, and finally the French civil service immigration boom, which, after nearly two decades, is only now petering out. The city's colonial topography and architecture are largely gone; it is the metropolitan French immigrants who have given contemporary Nouméa its character, erecting steel-and-glass office blocks and mini-malls in search of *modernisme*. The yachts and BMW's date from this last immigration boom. French civil servants get considerable hardship pay for working in New Caledonia, as well as a tax holiday.

Apart from spending money, the French immigrants have a genetic role to play in the territory. In 1972, Pierre Messmer, then France's prime minister, presented in a letter to his secretary for overseas territories and departments a vision of New Caledonia that, in Nouméa at least, has come to pass:

New Caledonia . . . is probably the last nonindependent tropical territory in the world where a developed country is able to send its emigrants. It is necessary therefore to seize this last chance to create a supplementary French-speaking country. The French presence in Caledonia cannot be threatened, barring a world war, except by nationalist demands made by the aboriginal population, supported by eventual allies in other ethnic Pacific communities.

In the short and medium terms, a massive immigration of French metropolitan citizens . . . would permit us to avoid this danger by maintaining and improving the numerical balance of communities. In the long term, nationalist demands by the aborigines will not be avoided unless the communities from outside the Pacific represent a de-

mographic majority. Obviously one would not obtain the
slightest demographic effect in the long term without
systematic immigration of women and children. In order
to correct the imbalance of sexes in the nonaboriginal
population, doubtless it would be desirable to reserve
jobs for immigrants in the private enterprises. Ideally,
whatever jobs could be occupied by women would be
reserved for them. . . . The conditions are such that New
Caledonia, in 20 years, could be a small, prosperous
French territory comparable to Luxembourg and representing, evidently, in the emptiness of the Pacific, rather
more than Luxembourg does in Europe.

The success of this enterprise, indispensable to the
maintenance of French positions east of Suez, depends,
among other things, on our ability to succeed at last, after
so many setbacks in our history, in a populating operation
[*opération de peuplement*] overseas.

France's involvement in the Pacific—in Vanuatu, New
Caledonia, and the overseas territories of Wallis and Futuna
and French Polynesia—could probably be understood if one
were able to comprehend the mentality of Pierre Messmer.
That is, to put oneself in his shoes, really to understand how
anyone could imagine New Caledonia as "east of Suez." Another expression worth pondering is *métropolitains*. In New
Caledonia, France is referred to as *la métropole*, the French as
métropolitains. It is as if all France were actually Paris; the
humblest Auvergne shepherd would, in New Caledonia, find
himself a *métropolitain*.

I eventually arrived in the residential resort neighborhood
of Anse Vata—Morris dropped me off—and looked up a
Kanak contact, Fiz Xenié. We went and ate lunch on the
beach, a flawless strip of pale sand bordering calm water. We
gossiped about common friends in Vanuatu, and politics in
New Caledonia. I took advantage of Fiz's forbearing nature
and told him how disorienting Nouméa felt; how I'd expected
it to be reassuring to me because I'm white and from the
developed world and all that, but instead everything seemed

unreal. "Nouméa is a foul place," Fiz said. "But I stay here because my work is here. Sometimes I'd rather go back to my tribe." He smiled and laughed gently. His young son, David, played on the beach in front of us. The beach was covered with Caucasian bodies, very close to naked. Women went topless and had painted toenails. On the street at our backs people wore socks and shoes and even blazers. Everyone looked tanned, fit, and stylish. Was this the Riviera? Had someone in the projection room changed reels when I wasn't looking? David ran up and down the beach. His shirt was off and I was mesmerized by his dark skin, whirling at the center of this vista of white bodies. I felt something inside me give way. A strange feeling, not painful exactly, just an internal crumbling.

Fiz and I finished lunch and arranged to meet later for a drink. I wandered down the beach toward the Club Med. This was probably a bad idea. The sheer weight and expanse of undressed white bodies were overwhelming. Athletic young men shouted and romped, young women lay on towels, baking, silently displaying one side, then another. Getting dark. The effect was of a fleshy open-air market on sand.

I went poolside and sat down. Soon a Kanak man approached and asked deferentially, "Are you a member of the club?" I tried the journalist routine, saying I might write something about Club Med and this was part of my research.

"But this is a private club," he insisted.

"That must explain why all the people are white."

"No, they come from Australia. It's a private club. Caledonians can't come here either."

Back on the street, ejected from the Club Med, I wondered why a Kanak man wouldn't consider Australians white. Clearly the names people applied to each other were very important in New Caledonia.

∎ The word that defines Nouméa is *la brousse*, "the bush." It says nothing about the rural landscape, a diverse mix of tropical jungle, ranches, farms, and mountainous forest; but *la brousse* is a symbol, not a description. In New Caledonia you are either in Nouméa or *en brousse*. The bush is Nouméa's context, everything Nouméa is not—black, dangerous, "underdeveloped," and uncontrollable. Even white people in Nouméa realize that *la brousse* is "the real New Caledonia," which is one good reason why they avoid it. The bush surrounds Nouméa like unwanted memories. The key to living in the white city lies in forgetting, in trying to pretend you're really somewhere else. A Nouméa joke: "Why do all the cars have yellow headlights?" "For the fog." "What fog?" "The fog in France."

When Nouméa first became a colonial capital, in 1853, there was, of course, a tribe of Kanaks already there. They were displaced to a neighboring region and used as (usually unpaid) workers. "We're the most deracinated people in the territory!" a young woman from this tribe told me with an odd, rueful pride. "We only speak French." New Caledonia has about twenty-five indigenous languages that are still spoken; most Kanaks speak some French, and those who are better educated often speak it very well. Until recently, all education was in French, and this is still largely the case. (When Kanaks study history they learn about Charlemagne and Joan of Arc, not, for example, the nineteenth-century Kanak rebel chieftain Ataï.) It is a peculiar characteristic of French foreign policy that it emphasizes language. Former prime minister Messmer didn't just want New Caledonia to be a French territory, he wanted it to be French-*speaking*.

New Caledonia's earliest colonizers certainly spoke French, though, with the possible exception of missionaries, they didn't use the idiom of Racine or the Goncourt brothers. Apart from Irish, English, German, and Australian adventurers, the first Caledonians were mostly convicts. This was Napoleon III's idea. The lovely Isle of Pines, now a tourist destination, was occupied by veterans of the Paris Commune uprising and a few shipments of troublesome Arabs from the colonies. Later, penal settlements were established on the west coast of the Grande Terre. Facing a problem that would later worry Pierre Messmer, the French government pioneered two schemes aimed at getting white women to New Caledonia: shipments of female orphans were sent, beginning in 1863, and women prisoners were solicited in their French cells with promises of freedom if they'd agree to go to New Caledonia and marry freed convicts. Many of New Caledonia's older *caldoche* families are descended from convicts, a subject rarely broached among the local French, though the Kanaks like to remind them of it from time to time. Other, nonincarcerated colonizers also tended not to be French in the Gallic sense. They were often Basques, Bretons, or Alsatians, and always poor. They came mainly to farm and, since farmers prefer good land to bad, the Kanaks were systematically forced, with much blood shed, from the coastal plains onto "reservations" scattered among the central mountains of the Grande Terre, returning to their lost lands only as manual laborers for the white landowners.

Later waves of French immigrants were sometimes not from France at all, not even from Brittany. In the 1960s, several thousand *pieds noirs* fled Algeria and, instead of crossing the Mediterranean to France, crossed the planet and settled in New Caledonia. Also in the '60s, large numbers of emigrants from other French-speaking Pacific territories, particularly Tahiti and Wallis, arrived on the Grande Terre to work in the nickel factories and, à la Messmer, to reduce the Kanak share of the population (there are more Wallisians in New Caledonia than on Wallis). These francophone islanders were almost always pro-French; many of the right-wing militias that have been organized since the current armed conflict began are manned by Wallisians. Islander émigrés now make up about 13 percent of the population, providing—along with smaller numbers of Chinese, Vietnamese, and Indonesians—a crucial swing vote in referenda on New Caledonian independence.

This very motley population was augmented in the late 1960s and '70s by actual French people, come either to work in the nickel industry—not as laborers—or in government administration. Finally, in 1980 about a thousand frightened French colonists from Vanuatu hastily resettled in New Caledonia when Vanuatu achieved independence. At this point the

200
■

country's population probably would have stabilized, only the political situation had begun to degenerate. The French government dispatched platoons of bureaucrats, followed by troops, to pacify the population. These well-paid government employees gave Nouméa's retail, hotel, medical, entertainment, and real estate sectors a new lease on life. Serious conflict commenced in December 1984 with the Hienghène massacre, in which ten pro-independence Kanaks were ambushed and killed by local *loyalistes*. By 1986, there was one armed representative of the French state—soldier, gendarme, Foreign Legionnaire—for every twenty residents.

One might wonder why, with a French populace largely composed of people who have been avoiding France for decades and even generations, so much official rhetoric concentrates on the distinctly French nature of New Caledonia. I put this question to Henri Morini, main organizer of the country's militias, a compact and intense man who kindly agreed to an interview despite being in recovery from bullet wounds. He answered simply, "We are Europeans," though later on he would refer to himself as "Caledonian." This was surprising; Morini is high up in the Rassemblement pour la Calédonie dans la République (Rally for Caledonia in the Republic, or RPCR). As its name implies, the RPCR, led by a wealthy *caldoche* industrialist and plantation owner, Jacques Lafleur, is the main anti-independence party; Lafleur is the son of Henri Lafleur, who built a *caldoche* empire from nickel mines and ranches (worked by Kanaks, of course). Morini basically provides the RPCR with muscle—an ex-Army sergeant and current president of the National Karate Association, he's been organizing paramilitary groups since the '70s. But muscle for what? Clearly Morini, Lafleur, and the RPCR want to remain part of France, but it isn't at all clear why France exactly, apart from historical coincidence.

"No place will be independent in the future. The drama of this small country—*bof!* But unhappily it will certainly continue. We are pro-Free World. We are pro-French, pro-American. There are people here who are French because they came from France. But one shouldn't forget, it wasn't an

American who discovered America." Later Morini would emphasize that Caledonians are "99 percent pro-American," and that the key to New Caledonia's future lies in attracting foreign investment, which is difficult to do when people are shooting each other. Morini never thought to mention France, let alone French patriotism; as far as I could tell, France was a republic of convenience, little more than the only foreign nation willing to spend money on the protection of white Caledonians. Nor did Morini really explain why he thought the Kanaks had decided to fight for independence. Despite local and international media reports of foreign influence ("communist," Australian, and, yes, Libyan), Morini didn't believe that outside manipulation was relevant. He did say that young Kanaks in the bush didn't have much else to do. Perhaps they fought because of boredom, and a certain pre-civilized lack of discretion. "You and I, we have left the forest, we have been educated, but them!"

Henri Morini was shot while visiting Canala, a coastal nickel-mining town, with his militia. They were there, he said, to protect Kanak women and children who didn't support the Front de Libération National, Kanak et Socialiste (FLNKS). The FLNKS is a five-party pro-independence coalition, founded in 1984, and is the main opposition to the RPCR. The French National Front, which has a New Caledonia chapter, occupies a small but vocal position somewhat to the right of the RPCR, and is fiercely opposed to the FLNKS. The National Front, led by Jean-Marie Le Pen, is fairly popular in France, primarily because of its anti-immigrant "France for the French" rhetoric. In New Caledonia, the National Front usually attracts white settlers who find the RPCR too moderate. The chapter's membership tends to wax and wane dramatically, depending on how frightened the whites are at any given moment. The party lines among armed white militants are blurry. What unites them is more their willingness to shoot people than membership in any particular institution. Henri Morini, for example, might draw on the National Front, the RPCR, or other groups when he needs men to serve in his militias.

■　On April 24, 1988, there were both local New Caledonian and French presidential elections, and both were boycotted by the FLNKS. Morini's militia was supposedly in Canala to enable dissenting (that is, "loyalist") Kanaks to vote. He doesn't like the word "militia." "Militias are people who commit crimes." He prefers "civil protection." Morini laughed: "Maybe you could say we are like Robin Hood!" One group with which Morini was associated advocates efforts to "neutralize FLNKS action commandos or their sympathizers." In the following weeks I would meet a number of people, black and white, who fervently wished the next bullet to seek Morini would enter his head and not his chest.

When I first arrived at Morini's office, at his motel on Koindu Beach outside Nouméa, I noticed that the motel's bungalows were Kanak-style—the thatched, conical buildings called *cases*. Maybe this was just a pragmatic gesture toward touristic exoticism, but it was still striking. As Morini spoke, in his nervous voice, about internationalism and economic development, and not at all about France, I wondered what, exactly, he *was*. His office had but one decoration, a tacky painting of a white man with a laughing boy on his lap. "This is my country. I live here. I'll die here," Morini said at one point. "I had a little boy who died here. I want to be buried next to him." I imagined Morini sitting alone in his office by the beach, looking at his painting, and calling up his men for another trip into *la brousse*.

■　I was in Nouméa in the late summer of 1988. The conservative Jacques Chirac, who had been French President François Mitterrand's prime minister for two ill-tempered years—the president being Socialist—had lost his bid in the spring to unseat Mitterrand. Their two years of *cohabitation*, as it was called, were a triumph for the Fifth Republic, a proof of its stability. The triumph was not savored in New Caledonia. Chirac's Pacific policies had been repressive, undoing what few reforms Mitterrand put in place during 1981–86 when he had had more amenable, Socialist prime ministers. Chirac's

New Caledonia strategy had culminated on May 5, 1988, just before the second round of presidential elections, in the bloodiest incident of New Caledonia's postwar history—nineteen Kanaks and two French soldiers were killed on the island of Ouvéa, northeast of the Grande Terre. On April 22, two days before the first presidential round, the Kanaks had attacked an Ouvéa police post and taken twenty-seven prisoners after killing three gendarmes. By April 27, the Kanak militants were guarding twenty-three hostages in a cave. After extremely feeble negotiating efforts, Chirac sent special French troops to attack the cave. They killed all the Kanaks, some with a single bullet to the head. The story is complex and testimonies contradictory, but one clear result was that the Kanak death toll since 1984 had doubled overnight and was now twice that of non-Kanaks. The Ouvéa massacre was seen by many as a Chirac political tactic, a display of electoral machismo. Just before the massacre, Chirac's government had effectively paid $340 million to Iran in exchange for three French hostages from Lebanon, an action which, despite many statesmanlike photo opportunities, conflicted a bit with Chirac's election image as a man of strength and will. As it happened, Mitterrand beat Chirac. Mitterrand's own election image emphasized moderation and the president's avuncular qualities (his nickname was *tonton,* "uncle").

Mitterrand is a clever uncle. The Ouvéa massacre gave him an excellent opportunity to make Chirac look bad, and to prop up the weak public image of Chirac's Socialist replacement, Michel Rocard. Mitterrand sued for peace; by June, Rocard had brought the RPCR's Jacques Lafleur, FLNKS president Jean-Marie Tjibaou, and other New Caledonian politicians together in Paris's Hôtel Matignon to sign an accord. This happened quickly enough that Chirac looked, in retrospect, both cruel and inept, whereas Rocard now appeared to be a master diplomat. Of course, Mitterrand had already been president for seven years, and you might wonder why it took him that long to set up a peace agreement. It seemed to have a lot to do with French politics and rather little to do with New Caledonia.

By the time I arrived in Nouméa there hadn't been any killing for a few months, and none seemed to be in the works. Thousands of troops had returned to France. Right-wing leaders tended to act humble and mature—the Morini I met was probably different from the pre-election, pre-Canala Morini— while FLNKS leaders were a bit giddy from their newfound respectability. Léopold Jorédié, a dapper aspiring technocrat and number three in the FLNKS, spoke eagerly of a future New Caledonia full of small, entrepreneurial businesses and attractive to investors from Japan, Australia, and the U.S. He didn't mention socialism, any more than Morini had mentioned French patriotism (though Morini, too, had spoken eagerly about foreign investment). The Matignon accords— approved by French voters in a fall 1989 referendum—promised a training program for Kanaks, political reforms that would give them more power outside Nouméa, an independence referendum in ten years, and great sums of money. Jorédié was looking forward to spending the money. "It's necessary to profit from French money by building small businesses," he said. "It's necessary to create a *viable* independence. When the people sleep with a gun under their ears, ready to jump into the bush—that isn't viable."

I was only in Nouméa for a week, which was too long, particularly since I was staying in the overpriced, happy-tropics ghetto of Anse Vata along with the soldiers, *métros,* and tourists. I talked to politicians, journalists and officials, people I met on buses and in cafes and bars, friends and friends of friends. Always in the back of my mind lay *la brousse.* In Nouméa there seemed to be layer upon layer of falseness. White people tooled around in BMW's while inhabiting a Melanesian country; Caledonians of whatever color listened to European music, wore European clothes, drank European drinks at European clubs, and paid European prices (or higher); a New Caledonia peace accord was reached because of political rivalries halfway around the world; a right-wing leader never spoke of patriotism, and a left-wing leader never spoke of socialism. Every political conversation I had came back to the same point: politics is made in the bush, and played in Nouméa. FLNKS leaders admitted they knew little or nothing of the armed actions of Kanak militants, including the Ouvéa kidnapping. Whites inevitably spoke with mystified fear of "the young Kanaks in the bush."

Before I left for *la brousse*, Kanak friends gave me their home numbers and said to call if I had any problems. White friends joked about taking bets on my return; most had rarely or never been outside Nouméa.

■ The bus traveled north from Nouméa along the western coastline. The two-lane highway was excellent—it was originally constructed during World War II by American troops. We drove through La Foa, Moindou, Bourail, Poya, and Koné, small, whitewashed towns of 200 or so residents apiece. Each had seen fighting. Each had a small government administration building, a school, and a police station protected by barbed wire, usually with one machine-gun emplacement in front. Soldiers lounged in their fatigues in the dry heat, leaning against sandbags; a machine-gunner's head would be just visible above the barrier. Kanak militants weren't too well stocked with guns, but the French soldiers certainly were. When they emerged in groups for a patrol, or, perhaps, a trip to the market, they'd carry automatic pistols, a few light machine guns, and occasionally an assault rifle or two.

The fighting on the west coast followed a demographic pattern. The towns are white. They have been the strongholds of French colonialism from the beginning. The plantations and ranches that surround them are primarily owned by whites and worked by Kanaks. The land of the west coast is the best in the country and scenic in a well-tended way. The Kanaks who once lived there are now described as *en tribu*, "in the tribe," inhabiting the steep, wooded valleys that ascend from the coastal plain. Bands of young Kanak militants would come down from the hills, torching the homes of *caldoches* and Kanaks who were unsympathetic to the FLNKS, sometimes even raiding the towns. Places like La Foa and Bourail became bunkers, havens for harassed *caldoches*. The soldiers, armed settlers, and militias (like Henri Morini's) would make raids of their own, breaking out of the towns to go *en tribu* in search of militants, arresting, beating, or killing whomever they suspected.

As evening fell—by this time I was in the back of a pickup with a large, damp German shepherd—I passed the shabby, two-story Hôtel Koniambo, between Koné and the *tribu* of Oundjo. In the dimness I could see one sign, MOTEL, then another that said RECEPTION. Then I saw a watchtower with a soldier cradling his assault rifle, silhouetted against the pale gray sky, and everywhere rolls upon rolls of barbed wire. Not your usual idea of a motel. Most rural inns in New Caledonia had been taken over by the military as barracks.

I got off past the Hôtel Koniambo and walked a little ways to Oundjo. It lay in a clearing on swampy land next to the sea. One dirt road bisected the village; on my right the dark mountains loomed, to the left a white church stood outlined against the ocean, which seemed about to overwhelm it. The Kanaks lived in small, flimsy wooden homes and the occasional thatched *case.* Children were playing in the road and some adults were milling about, though most were inside preparing dinner or watching TV. I contacted Raymond Diela, a friend of a friend, and he took me into a nearby house with corrugated tin walls. A portion of deer carcass hung from a rafter, rats scurried here and there. Raymond was around fifty, a good-looking man with a grave manner. I presented him with a *manou,* an offering to be made upon arrival in a Kanak village. A *manou* typically consists of a few yards of colorful cotton cloth wrapped around a packet of cigarettes or stick tobacco, a pack of wooden matches, and from 200 to 1,000 Pacific francs ($2 to $10). Raymond said, "I thank you for this *manou* and for respecting our customs. As you have respected the traditional gesture, you are free to stay here, to eat with us, and to sleep in my home. *Vous êtes comme chez vous.*" You are here as if in your own home.

We sat together at a rough wooden table and drank instant coffee, with sugar and powdered milk, from glass bowls. "Before, we were on the land called Pignon. You have seen it, on the Koné road." I remembered—huge, open fields, one large ranch house atop a hill in the distance. "The whites pushed us from that land, hunted us. We came here. There were already some people from another tribe. Their language was different but more or less comprehensible. We have lived here since that time." I realized that he was describing events that occurred over a century ago.

"There was a man here, called Noël, who fought with the whites in the last century. It was 1878 when he was killed, just down there, at Koné. It was the same year that Ataï was killed, at La Foa. [The 1878 insurrection lasted over four months, resulting in 1,000 Kanak and 200 European deaths; Noël was actually beheaded in 1918.] Here one remembers Noël. Ultimately it is a question of land. The *caldoches* say they have paid for the land. But there were many battles, many conflicts between the Kanaks and the *caldoches*. *Eh bien*, to whom did they pay? *Bon*—politics here is hard. If there are deaths it is regrettable. But that's the way it is. *Bof!* That's war, that's life here.

"In 1983 we reclaimed the land, but we still haven't got title to the property. One works the land, but without title we can't finance investments. If we go to the bank, they say no, because we don't have title. Before the land reform [in 1982], it was the property of the large corporation Ballande—they're French. Ballande sold the land to the French government, and they made a lot in the exchange, *beaucoup*, *beaucoup*. And the government gave us the land, but without title. There were some *caldoches* who wanted to take the land a second time—it was in the Chirac period, in 1986. I believe that was the title policy of Chirac, to take the land a second time. But we said, forcefully, it was very clear: there would be a war. We said it would be impossible for them to take back the land."

Raymond spoke the way most Kanaks I knew did, especially the older men—with consideration, precision, and relatively few gestures. This was partly due, I suppose, to the formality of talking to a journalist in a non-primary language. Yet it is true that speech, *la parole*, played a special role in traditional

Kanak culture. A man proved himself by his ability to deliver a ritual speech with a single breath.

Raymond also conveyed a radicalism not usually associated with people his age. There is a very real generational aspect to Kanak life. The three main FLNKS parties are the Union Calédonienne (UC), the largest and most moderate group, led by FLNKS president Tjibaou; PALIKA (Parti de Libération Kanak), which has a youthful membership and more explicitly leftist politics; and the UPM (Union Progressiste Mélané-sienne), which mainly comprises Kanaks over thirty whose politics are more radical than the UC's. Raymond admitted that the *actions dures* ("hard actions," like the Ouvéa kidnap-ping) were carried out by young people with little reference either to FLNKS leaders or to local elders—a sharp departure from Kanak tradition, in which the influence of the chief was considerable and submission to elders a basic principle of social order. Even in a small village like Oundjo, with a few hundred people, an older person like Raymond might not know where, for example, the guns are kept. "The young people keep their secrets," he said.

This is in part a result of French policy. When the Kanaks were relocated *en tribu*, the existing social structures were severely undercut; colonial administrators appointed tribal chiefs and paid them a salary. So the new "tribes" were sad-dled with two competing hierarchies, the "real chiefs" and the "official chiefs," a strange duality that continues today. It was rather like white South African policies in the 1950s and '60s, which organized urban black South Africans into so-called tribes whose new members hadn't previously thought of themselves as, for example, Tswana or Xhosa.

We spent the evening chatting about politics and life in New Caledonia, drinking bowl after bowl of instant coffee. At one point a relative of Raymond's entered and began cutting a chunk from the deer carcass. "*Voilà*, it's like that, Melanesian life," Raymond said triumphantly. "He can come here and take what he wants, and if I need something I can go to his house." The relative smiled, nodded, and hacked away. "It is reciprocal," Raymond said. "One never lacks for anything. I believe there are beggars and poor people in other countries. I've seen beggars in Nouméa. But that is not Melanesian. We live at the same level, one like another."

Raymond talked like one who believes in something and also has to make it believable. "Truly we have a happy life, it is a happy life here. One grows manioc, yams. There's always something to eat. One doesn't work much, one works when it's necessary, and one shares everything. When there's a party or something like that, we all eat together at the communal house. It really is a happy life." One new aspect of this happy life is television. Most people in Oundjo have regular access to TV. They are, Raymond said, gradually losing the habit of conversation. And the children, watching TV, learn about things like crime and the material world outside the tribe. "It's a mode of education, ultimately."

In the last ten years, Oundjo has grown accustomed to conveniences like electricity and piped water. Raymond attributes this partly to American influence. "When the Americans were here [during World War II] everything changed. Before the Americans came, the *caldoches* forced us to work from sunup to sundown, with an hour for lunch. Often they didn't pay us. We were like slaves—they thought that we were completely like slaves. But the Americans said, 'No, that isn't right.' They said that to the *caldoches*. The Americans spoke with us like equals. They slept in our homes, ate, discussed things, they paid us." The refrigerator still used by Oundjo for preserving fish was a gift from the Americans. "The awakening of the Kanaks, I believe, dates from the war. The experience changed their mentality. It was only after the war that the French administration began to construct schools, good roads, and water pipes. And little by little the Kanaks thought that the relationship between whites and blacks ought to change."

Oundjo's pastor was away that night so I slept in his bed, surrounded by Bibles and evangelical literature. In the morning Raymond appeared at my bedside, rather early, and we had coffee and bread together at the communal house. One man joined us, but the rest stayed away; at the other end of the long table, a group of girls sipped their coffee, occasionally stealing glimpses.

After breakfast, Raymond and I went and sat by the church, on the site of an old *case*. You could still see a large circle denting the earth. On one side of us the ocean spread out in gracious morning light, on the other side green mountains reared up; there was a cool, moist breeze. Raymond said the *case* had belonged to the people who originally occupied this land, before his own tribe was forced here by the whites. I asked about ancestors; Raymond responded by bringing up sorcery. Sorcerers are the only people who can speak directly with the dead. "There aren't many sorcerers here, maybe sixty out of a population of sixty-one thousand Kanaks. They have dreams that enable them to talk with the ancestors. They've asked the ancestors what they think of independence. Because . . . *bon*, it's an important question, and the people want to know their opinions. The ancestors said 'Yes' to independence. This is more important for the old people than the young. The young have their own ways of thinking about politics."

■ The leading right-wing figure in Koné is Robert Seggio, an RPCR member of the local assembly and chairman of the regional soccer committee. Seggio is a typical "French" *caldoche* in that his father was Italian and he grew up in the Algerian desert speaking Arabic. We met at a soccer match just outside Koné, where he was providing commentary over a radio hookup between playing periods. He was easy to find. There were maybe a dozen whites at the match, most of whom were either referees or involved in the radio transmission. All of the players were Kanaks, as were most of the spectators. Seggio was next to the radio table, high up in the back of the stands. He sat in a folding chair, legs carelessly crossed, wearing loafers and silk stockings and smoking cigarettes in a holder. Scrawled on the wall behind him, in large letters, was "Le Pen dans le Cul," a play on the name of French National Front leader Jean-Marie Le Pen, whose frankly racist demagoguery has had such ill effects on the social peace in France (*dans le cul* means "in the ass"). Having heard a number of stories involving Seggio and guns, I wondered why he was still alive and so comfortable among Kanaks. His chubby young son was there too, playing with a small colorful ball that regularly went astray, bouncing down upon the heads of the Kanak crowd.

It took Seggio a long time to warm to the idea of an interview. We talked about the soccer games and his son. Hours went by. I sort of imposed myself on Seggio, going to his house after the games, meeting his Indonesian wife and the other children, drinking a beer while the kids watched cartoons. On the wall was a certificate naming Seggio a member of Kiwanis International. More hours went by. Eventually, after a late-night meeting between Koné's hard-core RPCR members and French visitors from Jacques Chirac's Rassemblement pour la République (RPR, the RPCR's mother ship), Seggio and I sat down in the local assembly's hall for a chat.

He was reasonably optimistic about the Matignon accords and the possibilities for peace. "I don't mind working with them [the Kanaks] as long as they respect the accords." He gave the football match as an example of interethnic cooperation. "We have always believed that this is a country where people can work together. Each to his own political opinions. Racism didn't exist here before. It is politics that has set one group against another." Seggio gave a convincing impression of someone trying to be nice. He said the main problem, with or without accords, is the economy, particularly the issue of owning land. The RPCR, he said, favors individual land titles. Kanak custom is more complicated. Tribes "own" land; it is disposed of by the chief, or the chief and his advisers, or in other ways depending on the play of forces within the tribe. "It's hard to know who owns what. Custom damages the economy. You can't mix custom and the economy. The Melanesians have exactly the same chances as everyone else, but they don't want to work. That's the number-one problem in New Caledonia."

After talking with Seggio I went to a tiny hotel run by

Javanese—a few rooms on the second floor, a cafe down-
stairs—and watched the Olympic Games on the cafe's TV.
New Caledonia receives a special overseas transmission from
France. For me it was a funny sort of program. The Olympics
are a supremely nationalistic event. The TV broadcasts concentrated on French athletes, which made the coverage
skewed and somewhat pathetic, since the French weren't
doing too well. At this point France was tied in the gold-medal
tally with New Zealand. The news announcers were searching
frantically for competitive French athletes. There was one
good team in small-boat sailing, and two other talented com-
petitors in judo and dressage. These events were covered
exhaustively. I wondered if it didn't rankle the French a little
to be tied with New Zealand. After all, France, unlike New
Zealand, has a seat on the UN Security Council, three colonies
on the other side of the globe, and an independent nuclear
force, the *force de frappe* (*frapper* meaning to knock, hit, or
strike). So you would think that, as a great and powerful
nation, France would be able to do a little better in international athletic competition. Sitting there in the dusty cafe nurs-
ing a beer, I wondered, somewhat incoherently, if the fact that
France was tied with New Zealand for gold medals was the
reason why it has an independent nuclear force. The idea may
seem absurd, or at least irrational. But you never know. Ab-
surdity and irrationality are often leading characteristics of
nationalism. Perhaps someday, when France no longer has an
independent nuclear force, or when everybody does (even
New Zealand), it will lose its seat on the UN Security Council.
And what would that imply for French athletes? *Hélas*, they
could only get better.

The Olympics coverage was followed by a movie, *How the
West Was Won*, dubbed into French. It was a group film,
directed by John Ford, George Marshall, and others for
MGM, and starring John Wayne, Gregory Peck, and Karl
Malden. After the opening credits, the camera eased forward
like the prow of a ship, dollying over open plains, through
forests, up magnificent alpine valleys. A deep male voice de-

scribed how pioneers had first penetrated these lands, coming
to "conquer nature and primitive man."

■

■ I caught up with Patrick Ardimani, a friend of a friend, at
his ranch outside Koné. It was dominated by a single-story
home that could have been lifted directly from Arizona or
Texas. Patrick puts on rodeos and takes tourists on trips into
the forest. He looks like Gérard Depardieu would look if he
were a real person. Patrick wore boots, jeans, and a denim
jacket unbuttoned to the stomach, no shirt underneath. He
was big and well tanned, *bronzé*; he liked to make gestures, talk
fast, and say *merde*. When I arrived, Patrick's hunting dogs,
kept in a pen near the house, jumped around and barked.

We went for a drive, passing his wife, who was heading back
to the house in their other car—his wife, a mixed-blood Kanak
from Oundjo. "I love it here," Patrick shouted over the rat-
tling of the truck. "To stay, you have to deal with Kanaks. If
I am here it's because the Kanaks accept me. If Robert Seggio
is here it's because the Kanaks accept him. If one day the
Kanaks decide to get rid of us, we'll be gone just like that.
Here in Koné, there are two thousand Kanaks *en tribu*, and
two hundred whites. *Voilà.*"

There used to be more whites, but they've left for Queensland and Nouméa—the *dures,* the "hard ones," whose burnt
homes are scattered here and there around Koné, and other
whites who couldn't take the fear anymore. I suppose they got
tired of talking each other through the nights on the CB, tired
of keeping their guns clean and listening for sounds before
sleep. Tired of dreaming of black faces and torches. Patrick
figures *la brousse* is better off without them. "Nouméa, it's a
white city. But the future of Caledonia, it's here in the bush.
Where the Caledonians and the Kanaks live together. The
future of Caledonia, it isn't in Nouméa!"

We rode to an outlying ranch where a white *colon* ("colo-
nist"; the term is still used) and two Kanak ranch hands were
corraling cattle. The four of us sat on high wooden fences and

talked about Kanak custom. "The problems here are custom and the lack of jobs in the bush," the rancher said. "We must move toward having private property. Economically it's necessary. But of course private property is a European custom." He smiled faintly. "You know, it's taken the Gauls two thousand years to adjust to the idea of private property."

I tried to get the ranch hands to join in the conversation, but they were reluctant. One said that he recognized land ownership was a problem, adding agreeably that "customs are very strong here. We aren't losing them." The rancher spoke at length of grievances against the French administration—his property didn't have electricity—and praised the Americans, who "did more in one year than the French have done in ten." The ranch hands and Patrick all nodded. "I always voted with the right," the rancher said. "Most of the whites here are rightist by habit. But things are changing. If in ten years the country is independent and I am still welcome, I'll stay. I live here, I work with Kanaks every day, I'd like to stay."

Driving away from the ranch, Patrick was even more animated than usual. His hands rarely touched the steering wheel. The whites, he said, are at last changing their mentality—at gunpoint, sure, but *quand même*. "It took long enough. It's fifteen, twenty years they've thought like that, always opposing the Kanaks. So now maybe they've spent two or three months thinking differently. But we have a saying in French—Better late than never!" Patrick drove me to a road that traverses the Grande Terre. "I've known since I was a child that the Kanaks want independence, even then they spoke of it. But above all, I believe, they want to have an identity." Patrick grabbed my leg, gazed at me. His voice was almost quiet. "The Caledonians also want an identity. Me. I want an identity too."

I left Patrick and wandered up the road. He had said the hitchhiking would be good—the road was too rough for buses—and he was right for an hour or two. After that I just walked. The road led through tropical forests at the base of the central mountains. The moist, heavy trees eventually gave way to open hillsides. The road would tack across slopes then drop sharply into narrow gullies choked with stands of bamboo rubbing and creaking. Here and there, the road passed through miniature forests of wispy, white-barked trees, their pale green leaves fluttering. For hours I walked alone into the hills and gradually the clouds came closer. Sometimes it rained lightly. Clusters of small pines sheltered in depressions on the mountainsides. I wondered if walking here was dangerous. Geographically, this was the heart of *la brousse*. The last great Kanak insurrection, in 1917, had taken place here, a revolt during which FLNKS president Jean-Marie Tjibaou's grandmother, along with some 200 other Kanaks (and eleven whites), was killed. The valley is now almost entirely empty of people, but there was the occasional *case*. Every kilometer I would see a few Kanaks, washing clothes in a stream or farming. People would always wave when I waved, even if we were on opposite sides of a valley. I can't imagine what they made of a tall white man with reddish hair and a backpack wandering about alone. In any event, I didn't sense any hostility and couldn't feel anything but happy about spending a day in such a landscape.

The road eventually crested, then, after many ups and downs, reached Bopop, a lovely village of two dozen plastered houses, brightly painted, each one set amid grass and shade trees. From there on it was downhill. The road followed along the Tiwaka, a very lazy greenish river. I'd encounter people—always Kanaks—from time to time. They were usually reserved beyond a wave and a smile. The river slowly broadened until I was walking through bottomland. The road left the riverbank for half a kilometer; when I again saw the Tiwaka it seemed very wide. Darkness had fallen, and wide rivers at night always seem huge to me. A full yellow moon rose above coastal peaks. I'd been walking for eight hours and was tired. The river in moonlight was from a dream and faintly frightening. I heard gunshots—spaced, single shots from one gun, as if someone were shooting at a target or trying to get used to the recoil. At the river's mouth was the Tiwaka Bridge, the moon shone above it, in and out of black clouds.

■ That night I went to stay with Alfred Tein, a tall, lean, soft-spoken schoolteacher in his thirties, and his family in the *tribu* of Touho, just north of the Tiwaka Bridge. I presented my *manou,* which surprised Alfred a little. He is from Oundjo, where he had been active in politics; Raymond Diela, among others, had suggested I talk to him.

We sat down for dinner—Alfred, his round, cheerful wife, Lola, two of their kids (Jessika and Ludovic), and me. A third child, Sephora, was still an infant and lay sleeping in a bassinet. Before dinner, Jessika sang a prayer in French. She was a little embarrassed. Lola had prepared pork chops, a salad, and french fries. Alfred and Lola's house was Western-style and spacious; the only furnishings were two picnic tables. The living-room walls were almost barren save for a landscape poster that said "The Savior is my rock, my fortress, my liberator." We ate and Alfred talked about his days as a Kanak militant.

"Before 1984 I was living in Nouméa, working but also politically active. At that time, political action consisted mainly of demonstrations, meetings, publications. After the events of 1984, I returned to my *tribu*, to Oundjo, and engaged in politics full-time. At that time the older people were incapable of organizing serious political action, and particularly harder actions, you see. Everything was done by the young people. The events of 1984 had changed our attitudes. The leaders in Nouméa, and the older people, thought we ought to moderate our actions after 1984. But we, the young people, wanted to become harder. So we organized ourselves, we held meetings, we divided into small cells. For the *actions plus dures* [literally "harder actions"], there was no overall coordination. These actions were planned and carried out by the small cells, and one cell didn't know what the other was doing—and, of course, the FLNKS leaders in Nouméa had no idea at all. There were meetings of all the young people, and hints were dropped, one heard little things, so that two cells would not be carrying out the same action.

"Though my father was politically active, I didn't talk with him about what I was doing. We never consulted the older people about our actions. I don't just mean the *actions dures*. For example, Oundjo was blockaded—there were blockades between Oundjo and Voh, Koné, and like that, on all the roads. So we organized ourselves to distribute food, we started the communal house. All that was organized by the young."

Alfred spoke very softly and had a habit of inhaling sharply after a series of sentences. He would take in breath and say *oui* as a kind of forlorn coda; it reminded me of a tiny cloud scuttling too fast across the sky. Lola did it too, though less dramatically. They said it was a traditional way of speaking, an old pattern hanging on in their voices.

Lola washed up and put the kids to bed. Alfred and I sprawled on the floor and talked—I was too tired and sore to sit up on the picnic-table benches. Alfred tried to explain why he'd left the barricades. "I've been living here since March. This is my first job since 1984. I've retired from politics." His retirement had something to do with the Matignon accords and the approaching referendum, in which all French citizens would vote whether to accept the accords. "It was France who staged the accords, it is the French who are voting in the referendum. But, for us, France should not be part of anything. We must plan and direct our own future. We can't arrive at socialism when things are being decided in France."

I told Alfred about meeting Henri Morini and FLNKS leader Léopold Jorédié, how their plans for New Caledonia's future sounded almost identical. "Yes, it's true," he said with resignation. "The FLNKS leaders in Nouméa, they have their positions, their cars, their houses. They are negotiating our future with France. But if they want to create what is basically capitalism, we will have to change leaders. Many of the young people want to have socialism. And it's evident that the *actions dures* of the young are what have brought us this far. The leaders in Nouméa know nothing of such actions; they are informed after the fact, or hear about what has happened from others. It's quite possible that they will forget about socialism,

■ that they have forgotten the demands of the young. Though, at the same time, it might be good if investors from Japan, Australia, New Zealand, from other countries . . . if they invest here when there is independence. It seems very likely." I was given Jessika's room for the night, and slept on the floor surrounded by more fundamentalist posters—"my rock, my fortress, my liberator."

In the morning, over coffee, Lola said, "I don't get involved in politics. No one in my family is involved in politics. We're Christians, and we follow the Lord." Lola exuded contentment. It was broken only by a distant melancholy that came when she played her Christian cassettes, which were in French and usually decorated with pictures of blond children standing in fields. In contrast to Alfred's tense leanness, Lola's body was full and relaxed. "I've gone to meetings of the young people of the *tribu*, and they really don't like whites. But it says in the Bible that we are all equal before the Lord. The young people have arrived at a type of racism, ultimately. But we are all children of the Lord. For a long time they thought that my family was RPCR. But for me, one day it's the RPCR, another it's the FLNKS, they come and they go." She got up and started washing dishes. She smiled. "The young people don't trust Christians, because our hearts are divided."

Perhaps her political heart was divided because her attitude toward violence was not: it comes, she pointed out, from both sides. Lola related the familiar stories of Kanaks being threatened by other Kanaks, their *cases* being burned because they didn't support the FLNKS. She also noted that Kanak militants have chased a lot of whites from the towns along the east coast—Hienghène to the north, Poindimié, Ponérihouen, Canala, and Thio to the south. On the other hand, in May a young Kanak, Albert Kaehne, had been killed on a road a mile or two from Lola's house. French soldiers fired on him and a friend after the two shone a flashlight in their direction. Lola said things have quieted since then.

Alfred spent the morning at the school, which was right next door, while I chatted with Lola. Over lunch he seemed tired. "In 1984, we had our goals, and we would set out to achieve them. We were motivated by our goals; we had a clear political consciousness. Now many of the young are no longer motivated. They are tired of making war. They see that certain goals can be achieved yet life doesn't change that much. Like me, I've decided to follow the Lord."

After lunch Alfred went back to the school, Lola washed dishes to French Christian music. A young cousin of hers was there, singing along—he'd been at a Struggle Committee meeting the night before. The Struggle Committees are the only formal organizations of grass-roots militants. National FLNKS leaders like to think of them as "FLNKS Struggle Committees." Certainly it's true that, at the regular national congresses, these committees struggle a lot with the FLNKS leadership, which they often see as overbearing, too moderate, and uninformed.

I walked over to the beach, just across the road from Alfred and Lola's house. Palms leaned toward the sea. Beneath them canoes and boats sheltered, propped up on logs. The tide was out, the white strip of sand merging into a broad flat expanse of flotsam and wet stones. Low breakers crashed over the reef. Three small dogs chased a large bird flying lazily over the tidal shallows. I set to reading the French anthropologist Jean Guiart's excellent book on New Caledonia, *La terre est le sang des morts* ("The land is the blood of the dead"). Alfred brought the primary school students to the beach for relay races. The kids seemed to have a great time, laughing and shouting. Even Alfred let out the odd smile. Above their heads were the mountains near Poindimié.

That evening the mayor of Touho, Raymond Pabouty, dropped by the house. Alfred presented a *manou* on my behalf. The mayor gave a speech, then I gave one in response. We sat on the floor. Mayor Pabouty, a vigorous man approaching middle age, cheerfully verified that it was the young people who ran the revolution and that older people like himself didn't much know what was going on. Pabouty was from the same generation as most of the FLNKS leadership, the generation that, broadly speaking, had conceived of fighting for independence. "I think, personally, that the real cause of all this is unemployment. One has all these young people with nothing to do, so they fight a war. There are no jobs for them, there's nothing to do."

But what, I wondered, about Melanesian socialism?

The mayor smiled. "In principle, there is no unemployment for Melanesians. There is plenty of land, our population is very small in relation to the land available for cultivation. As you've seen, the forest is virtually empty."

"So why don't the young people want to work the land?"

"*Bon*, there are many things people want other than something to eat. And I think people—the Europeans with their cars and all that . . . people feel like they're strangers in their own country. Like they don't have control of things. What we really need here is development; the Kanaks have to start working. But there are many problems. The biggest problem is motivation. You don't have to work, and you can still have enough to eat. Also, Kanaks are afraid to start businesses— they're afraid they'll fail, so they don't try to do anything. We are well colonized! We're used to working for someone else and getting paid—*Kanaks de service!*" The mayor laughed. *Kanaks de service* is a pun on *homme de service*, which could be translated as "right-hand man." It is also an insulting term for Kanaks who support the whites.

"Custom is a big problem," Pabouty said. "If one is going to develop the country, it will be necessary to get rid of the customs." Alfred interjected the story of a tribe near Voh that had taken back land from the whites but, instead of classifying it as tribal land, they took it as private property—then gave each family a share and worked the land collectively. By doing this they were able to get bank credit for investment. Pabouty just nodded and gave examples of various Kanak businesses that had failed.

It was late when the mayor left. Alfred and I went outside and squatted on the porch in front of the two-room schoolhouse. Despite his decision to follow the Lord, Alfred clearly thought a lot about politics. I was still curious why he'd given up the late-night cell meetings, the *actions dures*. Maybe it was because of Lola and the kids, or maybe, as Alfred had said of

others, he simply got tired of war. In any case, it seemed that
Mayor Pabouty was an example of the sort of leadership Alfred's generation had struggled against. "For me, custom is a
false problem," he said after a long silence. "As they've done
at Voh, it's possible to develop without abandoning custom."
It was a cool night. There were very few cars on the road, so
you could just hear the ocean. "It's quite possible that we'll
struggle for independence against capitalism then become an
independent capitalist country. It's quite possible."

The next morning Lola walked me to the bus, which
stopped in front of the schoolhouse. She was holding Sephora,
a beautiful happy baby, in her arms. Through a narrow band
of coconut trees we could see that the tide was in.

"It isn't like this in New York, is it? So tranquil?"

"No. There aren't many trees. One walks among buildings
of thirty or forty stories."

"I've seen Paris and the United States on TV. The people
there are all very rich."

"It isn't like that really."

Lola hesitated for a moment. "And there are a lot of people
and cars?"

The bus came. Lola and I kissed on both cheeks. I kissed
Sephora, then waved to Alfred, who was standing in the doorway of his classroom.

■ I took the bus through Poindimié to Ponérihouen, a town
with maybe 200 people remaining, virtually none of them
Kanaks. It looked as if it had been shelled. A good third of the
buildings were ruins, fragments of wall jutting from the undergrowth, or roofless structures with barren window frames
like eye sockets. In the center of town was a once stately home,
now charred and crumbling, with the memory of a garden out
back complete with stagnant green pond. It looked like once
there had been white children in white clothes tripping about
the lawn and taunting their nannies. It looked like the set for
a TV movie about the gracious, lost past.

But Ponérihouen hadn't been shelled. These houses and

shops had been burned one by one, and the people who burned them knew exactly who was living where. On most of the walls graffiti were scrawled: "America," "La Nouvelle Calédonie, 51ème Etat des Etats-Unis" (New Caledonia, 51st state of the United States), "U.S.A."

I went to the post office and contacted André Gopéa, a founder of the UPM, active in the FLNKS, and Ponérihouen's postmaster. We made an appointment for that evening. I left the post office and walked to Ponérihouen's only hotel, which had a few rooms and a primitive restaurant. The hotel was run by a Japanese woman; a geisha maquette stood in a glass display case in one corner. At noon the Olympics appeared once again on TV. Most of the hour-long program was devoted to Marc Alexander, a Frenchman who had won a judo match. There was also some brief footage of Ben Johnson winning the 100 meters. Later a tennis match in Nouméa was televised. I sat by a window writing notes and letters, trying to stay cool. Across the street a shop catered to the occasional white person who drove up, and to soldiers who came over from their barracks to get groceries and gas canisters for their stoves.

In the evening I went to André's house and presented a *manou,* which he received without ceremony. André, who seemed like a once vigorous man whom circumstance had quickly aged, wandered about the house while his wife, Mikaela, fried something to snack on and talked about recent events in Ponérihouen. Like all the east coast towns, Ponérihouen had experienced various acts of violence and extended blockades over the last four years. All or most of the ruined houses belonged to whites who were hostile to the FLNKS. The biggest local *caldoche* landowner, a man named du Bois, is associated with the National Front. The house with the green pond belonged to his son, who no longer lives in Ponérihouen.

Prior to the spring elections, the National Front visited Ponérihouen in force. A young man named Sangarné, who worked for du Bois, was shot to death on June 7 (the case remains unsolved). On the evening of June 10 the National

Front arrived. Their first action was to harass the FLNKS people, or those perceived to support the FLNKS, who still lived in Ponérihouen. It was a short list. At the top were André and Mikaela. In fact, André and Mikaela made up half the list—the others were the local schoolmaster and doctor.

Mikaela told her story in a voice I hadn't heard before in New Caledonia. Large and forceful, she seemed very much like a tough suburban housewife describing how bad the traffic was coming home from the market. "They threw stones on our roof," she said. "They'd come up to our windows with their guns, pointing them in at us and shouting things. They broke the door out back. We were surrounded." André, Mikaela, and their two young children left the next day, a Sunday, escorted by French soldiers. The doctor, the schoolmaster, and their families also fled. Soldiers had been called the previous evening, but somehow weren't able to negotiate the few kilometers from their post to Ponérihouen until the following day. The National Front remained in Ponérihouen for nearly two months—as did the military, there to "restore order." The NF kept the town blockaded; only whites and sympathetic Kanaks were allowed in, though André did visit on several occasions, carrying his own gun. Kanak militants, in turn, blockaded the roads into the tribal villages that surround Ponérihouen. There were frequent armed clashes but no more deaths.

André, Mikaela, and I went to visit Ponérihouen's mayor, a Kanak named Richard Poarairiwa. He lived in one of the tribes outside town, in a modest Western-style home that nevertheless had three televisions. Mikaela sat in the kitchen with the mayor's wife, while we men lounged on sofas in the living room. André and the mayor sat next to each other and joked easily like old friends or a contented couple. For people who had fairly recently been threatened with death they were extremely chipper. After the presentation of a *manou* we settled on what was evidently a favorite topic: New Caledonia's white people and their strange ways.

"Above all, the Europeans are materialist," André said, smiling. "If you speak of dignity or identity they don't know what you're talking about. They think the Kanaks are savage, incapable."

Richard laughed. "They speak of France, but they don't know anything about France!"

André: "They're pro-American, but they're also loyalist!"

Richard: "They're lost! Hee, hee! They're the lost ones!"

André: "The lost Americans!"

André and Richard were beside themselves, giggling away on the sofa. So this was the reason for the American flags. There was a group of people in Ponérihouen who were part of a "pro-American" organization.

"They want New Caledonia to be the fifty-first state of the United States." André chuckled. "Their leader here is Patrick Song. He has pictures of Reagan all over his shop. You should go see it!"

Also among the lost ones, Richard said, are those Kanaks who either support the pro-American party or support the pro-French whites—the famous *Kanaks de service*. "They are *really* lost. They can't return to their tribes. They aren't allowed back in."

André: "They're a bit like the slaves in America. They work for the boss. They get paid to do what he says."

Richard: "Hah! They're lost!"

If humor is a valuable weapon against power, then André and Richard were amply armed. For years, FLNKS publications had been describing the *caldoches* as "the victims of history." I was only now coming to appreciate the subtlety of that phrase. Like so many ideas in the Pacific islands, it is a complete overturning of *tuturani* logic. In the colonial era, whites tended to treat the indigenes as people without history—timeless beings suddenly come into contact with the true actors and subjects of history, the people of destiny, that is, white people. The phrase "victims of history" and the wry amusement of André and Richard, giggling away *en tribu*, simply reverse the equation. It is the whites, and the nonwhites (Kanaks, Wallisians) who support and emulate them, who have lost their grip on time and history. They're fish out of water, emperors without clothes. And what makes their situation both pitiable and hilarious is that they don't realize it, that, on the contrary, they actually believe they're in control of history and their own destinies.

"You know, the *caldoches* are going to have to start talking about roots," Richard said with some seriousness. "They're all mixed anyway."

"Only four or five percent of them are pure-blooded French," André said. More laughter. I mentioned Patrick Ardimani and how he'd said he wanted to have an identity too.

"Well that's it!" Richard said. "They have to speak about these things."

"But aren't the Kanaks all mixed too?"

"Of course. The difference is that the mixed-blood Kanaks are accepted," Richard said. "They don't have any complexes, they are part of the tribe. Mixed-blood whites have to hide their roots, they're afraid of them, they have complexes. We don't have complexes. If we can talk openly about our histories, then we can live together. The whites have to talk about these things."

The conversation continued through several hours and numerous topics. Richard and André mused at length over the distinctions between their generation, born in the 1950s, and the current one of youthful militants. "When we saw the police, we were a little afraid," Richard said, "but the young today"—he made a gesture—"they're not afraid to say, 'Fuck off.'"

It was dark when we left the mayor's house and drove back from the tribe to the ruins of Ponérihouen. André and Mikaela were in front, gossiping about friends. I sat behind and watched the dark drooping trees crowding the car's light. I thought how much nicer it would have been to spend the night *en tribu*. Richard's house was nestled amid tropical foliage; André's was protected by a Cyclone fence and the windows were kept shuttered and bolted, the doors carefully locked. Outside, fluorescent lights were kept on all night long.

Back home, Mikaela headed immediately for the television. It was quite a TV, "programmable," with built-in video games and a VCR. Mikaela couldn't get it to work, so she swore at it. "To get it fixed we'll have to go to Nouméa. There's no one here who can fix a TV. It's like that here. We're a bit far away from things." Mikaela, a brusque woman who wore city clothes rather than the long Mother Hubbards favored by rural Kanak women, fondled her videos sadly. "We import everything from Australia. Imports from France are too expensive. Rice, sugar, milk, cheese, even coffee. The old folks used to grow rice near Pouebo, north of here, but no more. And we used to grow our own sugarcane. It's the policy of importation. It's crazy. We buy everything at high prices when we could make them ourselves."

Mikaela fiddled listlessly with the TV some more, then went to the kitchen to fix dinner—fried chicken, rice, french fries from a package, canned beans mixed with franks. It was odd to sit at the long kitchen table with all the windows shuttered. Mikaela talked about their children, who were eleven and nine years old. "The kids are used to life here and the events. It doesn't surprise them when they hear shooting, rocks thrown on the roof, when they smell tear gas—not at all. My little son was still a baby when he cried from his first smell of tear gas, at a demonstration in Nouméa. They're really used to it."

The family and I sat down to our quasi-suburban meal. It wasn't very good and reminded me of meals I'd had when growing up, which was disorienting. But then everything in Ponérihouen was disorienting. Outside, four dogs—"our guardians," André called them ruefully—rummaged about in the fluorescent glare. His home was an overlit bunker surrounded by dark tropical mountains.

After dinner André and I discussed development economics while Mikaela did the dishes and the kids more or less did their homework. André said it is necessary to develop the country in order to satisfy basic needs like sugar and rice. I tried to ask, sensitively, why sugar and rice were basic needs in a country that had only had them for eighty years or so.

"Look. Progress, as it's called, comes," André said evenly. "If one leaves the tribe, if one follows the Western life, it's a kind of death, that's true. It used to be we ate yams, manioc, bananas, not refined sugar and coffee. We cooked with wood, not gas. Yes, one could stay in the tribe, but that too is like a death. If you stay in the tribe, then everything outside the tribe will be French, or Western. That way we'd lose *control*— and evidently there would be a war. That's what has happened. It's necessary to master development, to develop at our own rhythm. Because Kanaks, you see, we have our own rhythm. We don't work all week so we can live on weekends. We live each day. Tuesday is like Saturday. One day is like another. It won't work to rush-rush all week then live on weekends. We must *master* development, not become slaves of it."

Mikaela had finished cleaning up. "You two can stay and discuss socialism," she said. "I'm going to bed." She grabbed her cigarettes, went to the bedroom, and turned up the stereo. It was a Nouméa rock 'n' roll station. André and I talked until our heads drooped and the sentences turned into numb little fragments, then we tottered off to sleep.

■ The next morning I was woken by the shuffling sounds of André and Mikaela's daughter, who was up preparing for school. She wore a New York Mets T-shirt and carried a copy of *OK*, a kind of French *Tiger Beat* fanzine. She set it down by my bed—I had slept in the living room—and I leafed through, trying to wake myself up. There were photo specials on French heart throbs I'd never heard of and a special section on acne, featuring semi-porn photos of well-developed young women squeezing spots on their faces. André came by and peered over my shoulder. "Oh la la," he said, "the things people read." His daughter looked out from her room, the walls of which were covered with posters of French pop musicians, and composed her features so as not to give André the pleasure of a reaction. Then it was off to school to learn about Charlemagne and Joan of Arc.

I left the house with a young man I'll call Gaston. I didn't know it at the time, but he was my bodyguard and was carrying a pistol in a shoulder holster. Gaston was with the FLNKS, though he seemed to have some sort of deal worked out with the local military. It was all rather vague but I didn't feel like prying. Gaston said he was one of the Kanaks who'd been sent to Libya for "training," an experience he recalled with macho fondness—apparently it involved bread, water, and a lot of empty sandy desert. The "Libya connection," dating from the mid-1980s, had been carefully attended to by the EuroAmerican press, as had the much more imaginary "Soviet threat." Apparently several dozen FLNKS militants, like Gaston, have visited Libya and been trained to look fierce and handle weapons. Of course, these are skills easily acquired without ever leaving New Caledonia. The trips were conceived by Yann-Céléné Uregeï, a Libya enthusiast and former FLNKS foreign minister; Uregeï was suspended as minister by the FLNKS after his contacts with Libya were reported overseas, though he remained an active leader.

We walked through Ponérihouen and Gaston pointed out the sights. This burned house belonged to that *facho* (slang for "fascist"), this shop, Stars and Stripes fluttering, belonged to one of "the lost Americans." I enjoyed ambling around with Gaston—tall, wiry, scruffily dressed, he had a manner at once lighthearted, cocky, and quite serious, a vigorous combination I've encountered elsewhere among young men and women during wartime. Clearly there is a real thrill in feeling that you're making history.

Occasionally other Kanaks would walk by and Gaston would say hello. Then he'd turn to me and say "She's a fascist," or "She's one of us," or "He's a *Kanak de service*." We passed the tiny hotel I'd been in earlier—Gaston said it had lodged some of the National Front men during the occupation—then arrived at a cooperative store just outside town, one of three shops still operating. Two were run by "loyalists." This was the FLNKS store, and something of a gathering point for militants. In front was a burned-out car that Gaston said had been torched by the National Front.

Inside we met with a rather cool reception. Several young Kanak men were working the store. We waited for a while until a man in his thirties named Marcel appeared, then we all went into a back room to talk. I wanted to hear what the younger people had to say, but they were extremely reluctant to speak and deferred to Marcel, who headed their Struggle Committee. Gaston sat to one side, getting up often to check the door. "In 1940, people were afraid," Marcel said. "There was a complex of colonization and superiority—whites above, blacks below. We worked the land from 1940 to 1984. The young people were more or less under control until 1981, when Pierre Declerq was assassinated. [Declerq, a Frenchman, was general secretary of the *indépendantiste* Union Calédonienne; he was gunned down in Nouméa, a murder that remains unsolved.] There were meetings, and then a certain evolution, a coming to consciousness [*prise de conscience*]. When 1984 arrived, the young people were ready to fight."

I asked the others their opinion of this and they just nodded. Marcel said many whites had left Ponérihouen, though the elder du Bois continued to live on his ranch outside town. The remaining whites probably would be allowed to stay: "That depends on them, not us." The interview wasn't going too well; everyone seemed unhappy with my presence. There was, however, one point that Marcel wanted to emphasize. "It's important to have discipline. When there is danger one has to put traditions aside . . . but that doesn't mean they are abandoned. Each Kanak has his customs within himself. There has been an evolution of the customs in relation to the world. They have had to change."

Gaston and I left, and it was nice to be outside again. He laughed about the games he and other Kanak militants used to play when the National Front was here. The *caldoches* communicated by CB radio because many didn't have telephone service and were afraid to leave their homes. The Kanaks did the same, but they could speak in tribal languages that the whites didn't understand, whereas most Kanaks could understand French. "The *caldoches* would swear at us when we spoke in our language! Sometimes we would call each other over the CB and say, 'Hey, let's go to the village and massacre all the whites like dogs!' But we never did attack the village in force.

Though it would be perfectly easy. There are a hundred of them and twelve hundred of us, and they're surrounded." Once again I asked the question that had been bothering me for weeks, a question that becomes extremely obvious after two or three minutes *en brousse*: If you want to get rid of the whites, why not just kill them? And Gaston gave the answer I'd heard before. He shrugged and said, "It wouldn't be hard." Then he smiled, because Gaston has a lively sense of humor.

We stopped in front of André's house. I had another appointment, but Gaston looked like he had something on his mind so we stood around kicking the dirt and smoking cigarettes. Then he said: "What you were asking earlier about custom—it's true what Marcel said, that custom evolves. We haven't modified custom, you can't do that. You just"—he smiled—"forget some parts and remember others. You understand? Customs of marriage, births and deaths, customs with the yams, we still do that. Yams are the roots of custom, they're the ancestors. Respect for elders is also a custom, and we've had to forget some of that. You know, during the Chirac-Pons period the government used the customary chiefs to control the people. Many times we wanted to really *push* things"—he struck out with his fist—"and Marcel said no. And we respected him and didn't attack. That kind of respect for elders is custom. We still have that custom. If we didn't there would be war everywhere. Everywhere."

Gaston gestured with uncharacteristic solemnity toward the hills surrounding Ponérihouen. "You know, each coconut tree and *sapin* [fir tree] that you see planted here and there, those were planted for a specific ancestor. Custom continues. It's in our heart." Gaston held his hand to his chest. I looked up at the hills, picked out the pairings of coconut and pine, tried to imagine what it would be like to believe each one of those represented an ancestor and realized I couldn't. Every culture engages in a dialogue with its dead but this was one I knew I couldn't hear, or else only as the faintest whispers.

Gaston took me over to meet Patrick Song, the sallow, agitated leader of Ponérihouen's would-be Americans, then

left us alone in Song's cramped general store. American paraphernalia covered the walls, with a special display of old cov-
ers from *Time* and *Newsweek* featuring President Reagan and
the bombing of Libya. Patrick asked if I wanted some beer and
when I said yes he allowed me to pay for it, a sure indication
that I was no longer among Kanaks.

"We are completely finished with France," Song said.
"Look at Hawaii, or Guam. Skyscrapers everywhere. Here?
Nothing! Nothing at all!" We sat on the floor of a little auto
repair garage appended to the store. A young Kanak man and
two whites were there; one of the whites was extremely old
and withered, the other was in his thirties. I gathered this was
the core of the Ponérihouen group. There are two official
pro-American groups in New Caledonia, Song explained,
L'Amicale des Etats-Unis (Friends of the United States) and
AMERICA, the younger of the two, whose acronym stands for
Association Multi-Ethnique pour une République Indépen-
dant avec l'Amérique (Multiethnic Association for an Independent Republic with America). Song's group apparently
pertained to AMERICA, though the lines of organizational
loyalty were not clear. The key factor was that members of
both groups want the United States to take over New Caledonia.

Song and his friends filled me in on the history of pro-
Americanism. They said that New Caledonia's pro-Americans
were in contact with representatives of eighteen U.S. states.
Evidently the contact didn't go beyond "Thank you for writing" letters; nevertheless, it was a source of pride and solace
for the pro-Americans. In 1985, a delegation went to visit
President Reagan and took with them a maquette of a proposed memorial to U.S. soldiers in World War II. Unfortunately, the president wasn't able to receive the delegation or
see the maquette, though a lower-level official did meet briefly
with the Caledonians. World War II seems to have played a
major role in inspiring pro-Americanism. The U.S. occupied
the country from 1942 to 1945, leaving one lasting *caldoche*
perception: that the U.S. knows how to take care of business
and France doesn't. Also, as one pro-American said, "My

grandfather told me stories about the American soldiers. They were very big, they were everywhere, everywhere. He said their breast pockets were full, *full* of money."

Patrick Song, thirty-two, was born and raised in Ponérihouen. He's pure *caldoche*, and his greatest dislike was for the French, not the Kanaks. "Our goal is simple. Multiethnic Association explains it. We would rather live with the Kanaks than the *zoreilles*. Because there's no solution with those guys. The second-largest producer of nickel in the world, and there's nothing here." *Zoreilles* is another term for the *métros*. No one could really explain its derivation, though *les oreilles* means "the ears." "The whites here," Song said in his frenetic voice, "are all in accord with us, underneath, because if you look at history there's nothing else. There's no country that's independent. Look at Vanuatu. It's independent and nobody wants to finance it. Every country needs another country to lend a hand. Hawaii, before the war, was in exactly the same position as us. Lifou [an island north of the Grande Terre] is the same size as Hawaii. But in Hawaii there are skyscrapers. And here?"

The young Kanak man leaned forward to explain his own position. "I'm a friend of the U.S. That's all. All the words, it's a big bag of hot air. I just want a president like Reagan, and I'll shut my mouth. There will be cars everywhere, there will be skyscrapers."

I worried about whether the pro-Americans would be able to make the transition to President Bush. George Bush could never be a cult figure like Reagan. But then in Vanuatu there's a group that worships Prince Philip. Compared to Prince Philip, George Bush is a virtual Napoleon. You just never know.

The conversation went on for some time and we drank another round or two of beer. The pro-Americans tended to blurt rather than talk. I had this feeling that I had come suddenly, from another planet, to land on a garage floor in the middle of a village nearly destroyed by war; and not just any planet, but *the* planet, the cargo cult's promised land. None of Ponérihouen's pro-Americans spoke any English nor had they

been to even an outpost of the U.S. (The 1985 delegation
hadn't included anyone from Ponérihouen.) Maybe this was
why I sensed that they were afraid of me. I had a responsibility
I didn't particularly want. Should I tell them that the Japanese
are buying Hawaii and the native Hawaiians are often bitter
and unhappy, as are the Chamorros on Guam? Ponérihouen's
pro-Americans seemed both harmless and desperate. The lost
ones, as the mayor had said.

At one point Patrick asked furtively, "Why haven't officials
from the U.S. come here yet?" I said it was difficult to explain,
but maybe they were worried about offending France.
"France is not here!" Patrick said, trembling. "This is the
fifty-first star! This is part of America now!" (I later met the
pro-Americans' chief ideologist, Roger Ludeau of La Foa; with
the help of charts and graphs, he explained his theory, which
draws on certain Mayan texts, that New Caledonia *actually is*
part of the U.S. Only through the uncontrollable exigencies
of continental drift—and, culturally speaking, the stubborn
weakness of human memory—has New Caledonia become
orphaned at the other end of the globe. All this was explicated
by the diminutive Ludeau in a few minutes' time, during
which he also played, at high volume, a Sousa march that was
intended to convey his cultural Americanness. Our conversation was all in French. I made an appointment to return for a
fuller explanation of his theories; but later I was overcome by
a bad mood and never went.)

I spent the evening with Mikaela and Gaston. We had a
little party in Mikaela's kitchen. I'd heard in Nouméa that
alcoholism is a serious problem in the bush. The FLNKS has
taken various steps against it—forbidding alcohol at meetings,
for example. Gaston laughed about the many strategies for
evading these prohibitions. During the occupation of
Ponérihouen, the Struggle Committee, he said, used to buy its
booze from none other than Patrick Song—who also sold to
the National Front militants. "At the last Struggle Committee
meeting everyone got completely drunk. But at the tribal
Council of Elders it's the same! They get drunk too! It's really
bad, people drink a lot here, even our own FLNKS leaders.

234 They don't set a very good example." Mikaela said there's a local type of marijuana that's also popular among the young. Gaston pulled out a guitar with one string missing and Mikaela left when he and I started to sing. Gaston liked reggae. The only song we could both remember well was Bob Marley's "Is This Love?" so we sang it over and over until the words became too slurred for even us to enjoy them.

In the morning Gaston chased his hangover with beer while I tried coffee. We caught an early bus heading back to the west coast. The countryside was lush and colorful as ever—rural Kanaks love to garden. In the towns Gaston would give me a rundown on the local military, the FLNKS, and their relative strengths. An odd sort of tourism. I thought often of Ponérihouen as we rolled along, and particularly of its school-master, whom I'd met shortly before leaving. He was sitting in his car outside the school, staring at soldiers milling about the small town hall. He rolled down his window to talk and eventually even stood outside leaning against the car. He was of an exceptionally slight build and considered "white" by the Kanaks. His origins were a complicated mix of Asian and European; in most parts of the world he wouldn't be called white, but this was New Caledonia. He spoke with the droll irony of an educated man. "What happened to me wasn't as bad as what they did to André and Mikaela—shooting off guns, threatening them with rifles at the windows. With my family it was more psychological. Surrounding the house, throwing stones on the roof, cutting off the water supply and the phone. We left in a convoy on the twelfth of June." His family hadn't been back since, and the schoolmaster visited only occasionally. He kept glancing at the soldiers; he seemed afraid to leave his car. "We'll have to wait and see what attitude the authorities take. You know, when I called the regional captain of police and asked him for help, all he said was 'When are the FLNKS going to attack?' " He vividly remembered the National Front men who had come to Ponérihouen. "There were thirty or forty, most of them out of shape. They were well armed, well excited, and rather fat."

The schoolmaster went back and sat in the driver's seat with his door left open. "It isn't very pretty what has happened to Ponérihouen," he said softly. "It's like a museum. A living museum."

■ Gaston and I spent the afternoon on the west coast, visiting friends of his and going together to various white cafes and bars. We imagined ourselves as the Racial Combination from Hell—strangers, ill-kempt, young and healthy and gratingly self-confident. We chose places where we knew we wouldn't be welcome and made a point of looking chummy and fearless. *Epatez le blanc.* Toward the end, Gaston's nerves started to wear thin. We were in a hotel bar in La Foa, one of the more notorious white enclaves. He wanted to drink some water and wash his face but was afraid somehow of the white woman who ran the bar. So he went across the street and found a tap. Before boarding the bus back to Ponérihouen, Gaston gave me his ring, a death's head that looked like something from a perverse gumball machine. He had tears in his eyes. We embraced repeatedly and he said I must return and then we'd travel the world together.

I spent the next two days among *caldoches* in and around La Foa. Eventually I went to find Jean-Charles Moglia—yet another Italian father—who was elected on the National Front ticket to the Western Regional Council, a provincial deliberative body, and was among the NF militants who had occupied Ponérihouen. He lived outside La Foa, and I found myself walking toward a farmhouse from which issued the pulsating strains of a Casio electronic organ (tabletop model). A handsome truck and a BMW were parked outside; inside, seated at the Casio, was Moglia, olive-skinned and thin in an unhealthy way, absorbed in his music. I stood in the doorway to listen. It took him a minute or two to realize I was there. He seemed slightly embarrassed to have been caught in the creative act, but we laughed off the awkwardness.

"I'm friends with everyone here, including the little natives," Moglia said, ushering me to a chair. He was around thirty and gracious in a rough, ungainly way. "We understand the Melanesians very well. In the bush they call us 'the white Kanaks.' " Moglia tried to explain that the National Front's visit to Ponérihouen wasn't an occupation as such. "We were there to eat with the people, talk with them. Help out our friends, basically."

He also noted that the Ponérihouen action had been led by a representative from the relatively mainstream RPCR, not by the National Front, and that such actions "are always led by an RPCR leader." It seems that the distinctions among New Caledonia's white organizations are extremely blurry, whether they are "legitimate," like the RPCR, or marginal, like the National Front. It was, however, quite clear that the RPCR had used certain less than savory Caledonians like Jean-Charles Moglia (or Henri Morini) to carry out its own "hard actions." Moglia had been an active pro-American before he joined the reputedly French-patriotic National Front; he knew Patrick Song, who he said had been helpful during the Ponérihouen occupation.

Despite the extreme national chauvinism that characterizes the French National Front, Moglia showed no signs of patriotism. "In my heart I'm not proud to be French. But with a man like [NF leader Jean-Marie] Le Pen . . . Le Pen for us is like Reagan has been for you. I love Reagan. Le Pen is a personal friend of mine." All Moglia had to say about France, which he apparently had never visited, was that "she is terribly generous, terribly generous. She has given a lot of money to New Caledonia."

Moglia believed the whites' greatest hope lay in arms and economic power. "The war is quiet now—the war is fought now with paper. But if paper doesn't work, there will be fighting again. We are ready for battle. There is no question of ending up like Vanuatu, Fiji, Tonga, and Samoa. They are in misery. The economy is us. The Melanesians don't do anything. Nothing, nothing, nothing. We have a big advantage." He went on to characterize the FLNKS as a terrorist organization, and said that if the 300 or so hard-core leaders were killed "everything would be fine."

Moglia's mother, a Breton, asked me to stay for lunch. I said

I had another appointment. She produced a photo album. Moglia showed off photos of himself variously positioned next to American flags and talked about how much Caledonians love the U.S. I flipped through the pages and came across photos of white men standing around with automatic rifles, smiling, as if posing playfully during a late-night party. Moglia turned the pages for me after that.

I left Moglia's farm on foot and walked slowly toward La Foa; it was a hot afternoon, interviewing Moglia had left me somewhat dazed, and I decided it was time to return to Nouméa. Then an old Alsatian kindly offered me a ride in his battered Citroën. He smoked Gauloise Disque Bleu, loved to talk, and invited me to share a beer with him at his home in town. There we found his wife—a *caldoche* whose family had been in La Foa for generations—a refrigerator stocked with Kronenbourg (an Alsatian beer, from Strasbourg), and a TV. The *caldoche* turned on the Olympics and we chatted as obscure, but French, athletes competed determinedly on the screen.

The Alsatian emphasized that New Caledonia was a land of opportunity where one didn't have to work very hard and could go to the beach any time. He had tried returning to France after twenty years overseas, but found it difficult. He worked as a garbageman for a year then was unemployed for five months. Once, when he went to the old market in his hometown, he was shocked to find that "everyone was wearing turbans on their heads!" France, he said, was lost; there was no more France.

And yet the land of opportunity has its problems, too. Kanaks, he said, don't like to work, and the French Army is ineffective in controlling them. "They run around trying to fight Kanaks, then on their way back to the post they see a Kanak by the side of the road and wave, 'Hello there, pretty little Kanak!' If it were me, I'd just point my gun out the window and shoot him." His wife laughed. She seemed to enjoy it when her husband got outrageous. On the TV were, as I remember, some French gymnasts, and they were losing despite the announcer's enthusiasm.

FLNKS leader Jean-Marie Tjibaou traveled to Ouvéa in May 1989 to mark the first anniversary of the massacre there of Kanak militants. The Hôtel Matignon accords had been approved the previous fall, setting a ten-year period to prepare for a vote on independence, and Tjibaou was busy organizing government reforms and programs mandated by the accords. Among those attending the Ouvéa ceremonies was Wea Djoubelli, a former Protestant pastor and schoolteacher. Djoubelli's elderly father allegedly had been tortured by French soldiers during the Ouvéa events, and died soon thereafter. Djoubelli opposed the Matignon accords; according to one FLNKS leader, he believed that "the body of my brothers"—that is, the nineteen Kanaks killed by the French at Ouvéa—had been "sold" to procure the accords. On May 4, Djoubelli shot and killed Tjibaou's deputy, the veteran politician Yeiwené Yeiwené, then was himself killed by Tjibaou's French bodyguards. According to some eyewitnesses, it was another gunman who killed Tjibaou. Numerous conspiracy theories have been proposed since to explain the killings.

French Polynesia

"No doubt the reader is looking for the idyll in all this," an embittered Paul Gauguin wrote in his Intimate Journals, *"for there is no book without an idyll. But . . . this is not a book." The first European to land at Tahiti was British Captain Samuel Wallis, in 1767. He and his crew were greeted by, among others, local women who "played a great many droll, wanton tricks." Polynesia's international reputation began in that moment, though its greatest architects would be Wallis's successors Captain James Cook and Louis Antoine de Bougainville. The latter named Tahiti "La Nouvelle Cythère," Cythère being the birthplace of Venus. Today Tahiti is part of French Polynesia, a vast overseas territory with a population of 189,000—66 percent "pure Polynesian," 11 percent European (i.e., "white"), 5 percent Asian, and 17 percent* demi, *or of mixed blood. The influential class is overwhelmingly* demi, *leading to the term* demicratie, *with substantial*

portions of French and Chinese. The territory provides the site for France's nuclear-testing program; its capital, Papeete, has also been the site of rioting by Polynesians.

■ "In your stupidity I found/ The sweet hush after a sweet sound," Rupert Brooke wrote in his poem "Retrospect," dated January 1914. Judging from the rest of his lyric, the reference was to a sexual adventure he had with a local Tahitian woman. I read "Retrospect" at the Musée de Tahiti et des Iles, a center for research into and promotion of Polynesian life, just outside Papeete. The museum was founded through the energies of a local missionary, and the efforts of his predecessors are recognized with a prominent plaque—in French, Tahitian, and English—that reads, "They loved us, taught us, and gave us good rules to live by. We accepted their God, the true God, who has protected us and loved us for these past 170 years, and who has made a new people of us."

I toured the museum with a Tahitian acquaintance who'd worked there as a volunteer. She asked not to be identified. (Papeete is a small place.) "Polynesians don't come to the museum. It doesn't interest them," she said. "That's good. You see, our culture is a living culture. It would be sad if they came to the museum. They can go to the valleys, the mountains, the beaches. Why should they go to a museum? It's more for students, and tourists." Compared to other Pacific museums, Tahiti's *musée* was extremely well appointed; some of the exhibits even involved pushing buttons so that various things would light up. The modern building was air-conditioned and spacious, with picture windows at the rear offering views of a pretty garden.

"The museum is here to affirm our original culture, faced with foreign cultures. Polynesian culture is a *living* culture," she repeated, noting the resurgence of interest in traditional tattooing—most hip young Polynesians in Papeete have tattoos—and in walking on fire. "Though all these things from the past, we get them out of books. Usually the classic work of Teuira Henry, *La Tahiti d'autrefois,* who was a missionary."

She looked at me with what felt like distant anger. I think I must have appeared unconvinced. "But the really important thing is attitude, a sense of community, of being relaxed, being Polynesian. It's difficult to define, obviously."

■ Just over half of French Polynesia's population live in Papeete, a crowded, noisy, unattractive city huddling beneath breathtaking tropical peaks and gorges. One evening I went out on the town with Manouche Lehartel, director of the Musée des Iles. I had my own thoughts about the museum but kept them to myself. I'd been told that Manouche didn't really want to be the director. She had studied history at the Sorbonne, and hoped to pursue an academic career; but her degree had put her among the very few well-educated Polynesians, and the government badly wanted an *indigène* to head the museum. So in her late twenties Manouche became one of the most prominent women in a country ruled exclusively by men.

We drove to an art gallery in central Papeete. An older, white French woman with close-cropped gray hair and an animated expression was displaying her watercolors. The paintings were of Polynesians in various relaxed attitudes— sitting under trees, sitting on a beach. Apart from Manouche and several slender young women, the watercolor Polynesians were the only ones in attendance. As at gallery openings all over the world, the people at this party mostly stood with their backs to the pictures, drank, and talked. The men tended to dress with a casual elegance, in light cottons and linens; white leather moccasins were the fashion in footwear. The women wore Western dresses—risqué ones, by Pacific standards.

Manouche's outfit was particularly revealing. She was an arrestingly beautiful woman, very much along *Mutiny on the Bounty* lines. A *vahine*, a fantasy object, her head wreathed in flowers. I was struck by this because I already knew Manouche a little, and her Polynesian pride was strong. So why play *vahine* in a room full of white people? Then I saw her in conversation with one of the elegant Frenchmen and it all made sense. He was voicing his opinions about art in confident, ironic tones, one hand holding a glass of wine, the other casually nestled in a trouser pocket, his face wearing a suggestive smile. Manouche listened pleasantly for a bit then leapt in, snatching one comment or another, slicing it into little pieces, then scattering the man's confettied confidence at his feet. Manouche repeated this process with a number of people. I watched, fascinated, as she worked the room. She was exacting her vengeance, the *vahine* Manouche, for 200-some years of objectification by Europeans, and she was good at it.

Finally we went back to her car and drove out of town. "There were a lot of jokes about the flowers in my hair," she said. Her *tiare* was of a traditional type: not one of the soft, colorful strings of hibiscus and bougainvillea you find in airport terminals, but a green and rather spiky wreath. Manouche seemed outraged that people had made fun of it. "There were a *lot* of jokes about the flowers in my hair," she said again, gripping the steering wheel.

We drove to the Auberge du Pacifique, a posh restaurant outside Papeete, overlooking the sea. Many opportunities exist in Tahiti for fine living. We met up with the other members of Manouche's dance company. The troupe was her main activity outside the museum. They performed every Friday night at the Auberge.

Tables covered in white linen arced around a central dance floor. The women dancers, six or so, were all slender and beautiful, the men were muscular and beautiful; neither sex wore much clothing. Their dances were intricate, intensely athletic, and arousing. Manouche smiled constantly and with apparent sincerity. I was relieved to see her looking so happy. The diners were, for the most part, indifferent to the performance, except during those dances when Manouche and the others would wander among the tables and invite people onto the floor. Those selected seemed to enjoy the lascivious movements they were urged to perform; I remember one young woman who had to be ushered back to her table, she was having so much fun.

After the performance, Manouche's group retired to a back

room to pack their instruments and change into street clothes.
I talked to Pierre, who earlier had played a brilliant percussion
solo on three small logs. "The problem for us is that we
naturally dance for ourselves," he said. "Manouche has to
remind us to pay attention to the audience."

Manouche and I drove back to Papeete, then down along
the wharf, where lunch wagons called *roulottes* serve shish
kebab, Chinese food, hot dogs, and most everything else. We
sat at one and ate pizza. I remarked that the Auberge diners
didn't seem to care much about the dancing unless they were
dancing themselves. "If I were sitting down to a nice dinner
I wouldn't want to watch a bunch of dancers either,"
Manouche said testily. The wharf was crowded with cars and
pedestrians; the *roulottes* were doing a brisk business. I asked
where the dances were from.

"I made them all up. I'm the choreographer. The songs
were made up by the musicians."

"What about roots? What about traditions?"

Manouche glared at me. "For a hundred years the missionaries were here, and it was absolutely forbidden to dance.
Only in the fifties did we begin to dance again."

"Well, then it's hard to see what's Tahitian about it."

Manouche laughed. "It's hard to see what's Tahitian!"

She stared into the distance and munched on her pizza. I
gazed toward the harbor. Actually you couldn't see the harbor
because next to the wharf floated the *Wind Song*, an enormous
American sailing vessel, run by computers, that offers expensive cruises of the South Pacific. In technological terms, the
Wind Song is at the high end of Tahiti's tourism market. Its
sails are trimmed according to elaborate electronic calcula-
tions. I found it extraordinarily ugly, though impressive. I
imagined a tattooed Yankee geek, the last sailor, crouched
deep in the hold, poring over printouts and monitoring subtle
shifts in wind direction on his video display.

■ The October 23, 1987, riot in Papeete alerted many people
to dissatisfaction among younger Polynesians. The date was

244 christened "Black Friday," and Pacific newspapers carried ■ trouble-in-paradise stories. Eight buildings were gutted, twenty-three shops and offices burned, and many others looted; the value of destroyed and lost property was estimated at between 70 and 100 million Australian dollars. The proximate cause for the riot was a strike by dockers and sailors. Such strikes are taken seriously because the dockers load and unload ships from Moruroa, the distant Polynesian atoll where France tests its nuclear weapons. A week before the riot, 150 *gendarmes mobiles*, elite troops trained in handling civil disturbances, were flown in from Paris to help break the strike. The appearance at dockside of these heavily armed gendarmes brought a hail of stones from the strikers, who had been playing cards and chatting. Sympathizers, mostly young men from the poor surrounding neighborhoods, joined in, and a riot was born. More troops were flown in the next day, from Moruroa and elsewhere. They occupied Papeete, which was placed under curfew; alcoholic beverages were banned. The more *loyaliste* wing of French Polynesia's Territorial Assembly quickly passed a law making the dockers public servants, and thus forbidden to strike. The assembly's meeting was televised, and an opposition spokesman took advantage of the air time to blame the riot on policies of the French government and the ruling party—which, through gerrymandering, had a voting majority despite having won only 40 percent of the actual poll. During his speech, however, a technical accident caused the transmission suddenly to disappear.

I met Pierre Chanut, an adviser to the assembly's president, at his comfortable government office in downtown Papeete. He explained that Polynesians "have undergone a radical change in mentality over the last five or six years." The nuclear experimentation program, which began in 1963, brought millions of francs (as well as soldiers and radiation) into Tahiti, touching off, eventually, a service-sector boom. Thousands of young Polynesians came to Papeete to make money, see the bright lights, and meet other young Polynesians. Wealthier people arrived in Papeete to set up businesses and trade in real estate, which had become quite valuable. A

second boom occurred in 1983, after seven devastating cyclones hit the islands. The French government poured money
into reconstruction, raising land prices still further, temporarily employing more Polynesians, and swelling the administrative bureaucracy. "People were enriched very quickly, and
got used to living above their means. Since then, personal debt
has become enormous. Big companies came in and bought out
smaller ones. *Enfin*—we have become a society of very rich
people and poor, with few in the middle. The Army, and later
the cyclones, completely destabilized the economy. In 1962,
maybe seventy percent of the people were farmers; now it is
about seven percent."

I left Chanut and went for a walk, meandering along the
docks, past the well-fortified military post, and into Tahiti's
slums. Since the riot, much had been made, among opponents
of the French and Polynesian governments, of these slums.
Simply using the word "slums," in the context of Paradise
Island, carried political weight. The housing didn't look all
that bad—most homes had a yard, though I'm sure the buildings themselves were crowded. What really struck me was
how divided it all seemed. Many homes had forbidding
fences, some with barbed wire, and most had *chien méchant*
("dangerous dog") signs. I had hoped, somehow, that it might
be possible to lounge around and have a chat. I'd even hoped
that my whiteness and maleness would not prohibit conversation. But people's reactions were distinctly hostile and reserved; they stayed behind their fences with the *chiens mé-
chants*.

I crossed the slums and hiked up into a gorge. The gorge
was divided by a drainage canal. On one side were two-story
tenement blocks, stained and covered with laundry; on the
other, where I walked, was a cordoned-off housing development of detached, single-family homes. I wandered up private
roads then across open ground onto the mountainside, eventually reaching the ridge. With careful concentration I was able
to avoid seeing the tenements below, the stretch of slum, the
appalling modern structures being built on the ridge, the low-
rise congestion of Papeete, the industrial docklands, and the

246 *Wind Song*, and I realized just how gorgeous Tahiti was. Across the bay rose the dark green crags of Moorea, the sea sparkled, I inhaled warm moist air and the scents of a thousand flowers. Unfortunately I was still surrounded by houses in various stages of construction, and the odor of fresh concrete intruded on the frangipani.

Wealthy residents of Papeete like to live in the heights, and it was in this neighborhood that, some days later, I had lunch *chez* Pierre Chanut. His home was spacious and attractively decorated in a minimalist, glass-and-black-leather way. Out front were two BMW's; inside were the dapper Pierre, his white, ex-stewardess wife (Pierre is *demi,* or mixed-blood), a large dangerous dog, and a fax machine. We ate outdoors on a terrace with a stunning view of Papeete and Moorea. "The key to Polynesia," Pierre said, "is the magic of the mountains and the sea, religion, and *fiu. " Fiu* is what you say when you're tired of working and decide to leave it for tomorrow. Pierre said that Polynesian culture is very much alive. However, the independence movement, which began in earnest after World War II and has suffered consistent French repression ever since, was weakening. "People are more concerned with the economy now than with philosophy." Over postprandial drinks I told him what one Tahitian had told me, that "all Tahitians are *indépendantiste* in their soul. Polynesians are not a servile people. But the money comes from France." Pierre smiled and nodded. His whisky was good and expensive. As he'd said before, "*Enfin*—we have become a society of very rich people and poor, with few in the middle."

■ France started testing nuclear devices in 1954. Seventeen open-air tests took place in the Sahara Desert, ending in 1963. Two years before the last test, the French government, worried about Algeria's impending independence, looked to the Pacific as an alternative site. The French minister for overseas territories said at the time that "no nuclear tests will ever be made by France in the Pacific Ocean." He may not have been lying, but he was certainly mistaken. Similar mistakes would

be made by French representatives in the years to come—a
history of deception carefully told in Bengt and Marie-Thérèse Danielsson's fascinating book *Poisoned Reign*. In 1963,
French Foreign Legion troops occupied Moruroa and Fangataufa atolls over the unanimous objection of Polynesia's
Territorial Assembly. In September 1966, French President
Charles de Gaulle flew to Moruroa to witness the first test. The
winds, unfortunately, were blowing toward occupied islands.
But de Gaulle's schedule was tight, so the device was exploded
anyway.

From that day to this, the French have maintained that their
test program poses absolutely no health risks. The claim has
been made plausible only because fallout statistics, public-
health figures, and even private medical statistics have been
studiously withheld by the government. Cancer statistics,
available or not, weren't even recorded in Polynesia until
1980, and only after 1983 were private physicians required to
state causes of death. Polynesians with cancer are regularly
shipped off to France for treatment, often in military hospitals.
Others, distrusting the French system, choose to go to New
Zealand or Australia. Abundant anecdotal evidence, usually
published in the New Zealand and Australian press, suggests
that radiation-related cancers have increased among Polynesians. But without reliable statistics it is difficult to prove a
trend.

To some extent, however, statistical vagueness can be clari-
fied by common sense. If the tests are safe, then why is basic
information about radiation and its possible effects, including
health records of workers on Moruroa and Fangataufa, being
kept secret? Why were the tests, after 1974, moved under-
ground? The French blame international pressure for the latter decision; but the U.S. and the Soviet Union banned open-
air tests in 1963 because of acknowledged health dangers, not
international pressure. And finally, as a Polynesian assembly
member once said, "If there is really no danger at all, why
doesn't the French government conduct these tests in Mar-
seilles Harbor or in the center of Paris?"

In any event France continues to explode nuclear devices in

248 Polynesia. The prevailing mythos in Paris connects nuclear
■ weaponry, the *force de frappe*, with both France's international
credibility and its desire to partake of *modernisme*. The credibility question is not something that preoccupies many people
outside France, but within *la métropole* it is vexing. A former
prime minister stated in late 1985 that "Whatever the costs,
the overseas territories provide us with a world dimension that
is fundamental to us"; a French Army report declared, in that
same year, "At the dawn of the 21st century, France plays its
role as a middle-sized world power in the Pacific hemisphere."
Such statements can't simply be dismissed as delusions of gran-
deur, even when they reach the parodic level of writer and
political adviser Régis Debray's belief that opposition to
France's Pacific policy extends from a "conspiracy of the customary law of Pacific islands and the Biblical morality of London missionaries." Geopolitical *amour propre* (literally "self-
love," usually translated as "pride" or "vanity") is a serious
matter among the French elite. A consultant to President Mitterrand once explained it this way: "We would risk losing our
seat in a Yalta of the Pacific to come, and even in the [UN]
Security Council, if we were not able to express our economic,
political and military power with the utmost determination."
Readers will note the similarity between "Yalta of the Pacific"
and Messmer's "French position east of Suez."

France's hopes of being a medium-sized world power (*puis-
sance mondiale moyenne*, a term of jargon) stay alive at some cost
to Polynesians. But then, Polynesian hopes for independence
would have a cost too. French money has brought a situation
in which 85 percent of Polynesia's food is imported, and its
commercial deficit runs at 99 percent. Two-thirds of
Polynesia's budget is provided by taxes on imports, which are
of course passed on to consumers. And, meanwhile, every
year 3,000 more young Polynesians enter the labor market to
look for jobs. If Polynesia became independent, where would
the money come from?

• • •

■ After a week in Papeete I was eager to travel, so I flew to
Rangiroa, an atoll in the Tuamotu Archipelago, 180 miles
from Tahiti. While there one afternoon I visited Gustave San-
ford, a mild-mannered *demi* in his thirties who was administer-
ing an agricultural program on Rangiroa. The French are
trying to get Polynesians to leave Papeete and return to the
outer islands. To this end elaborate policies, and an elaborate
bureaucracy, have been created. For example, Gustave
pointed out that the world market price of copra was fifteen
Pacific francs per kilo. The official, subsidized price was sixty-
five francs, plus a five-franc premium paid directly to farmers.
On Rangiroa, the government also subsidized housing, boat
purchases, various small-scale development projects, and the
distribution of videotapes (there was no television service as
yet in the Tuamotus).

"The project of the government is to send all the Polynesians from Papeete to the Tuamotus," Gustave said. "The
government even gives them housing here, because of the
present lack of work in Papeete. Some have come back,
though most of the new residents are not from here but from
other islands. People here speak Tahitian, not Paumotu [the
language of the Tuamotus]. One big problem is that, after the
sixth grade, there are no schools here, so all the kids go to
Papeete. After ten years there, they don't want to return,
because they've adapted to life in Papeete. The last time reset-
tlement was tried, in the mid-seventies, people came back until
the bon-bons ran out. Then they returned to Papeete."

We went outside Gustave's modest, modern house to look
at his garden. Earlier, he had introduced me to his wife, but
then she disappeared. I'd tried to make contact with his fif-
teen-year-old daughter, but she would hide whenever I caught
her eye. "She's ashamed," Gustave said. "Tahitian women are
very *pudique*." *Pudique* means "modest" or "chaste." Gustave's garden was small but productive. He was attempting to
show the local people that it was possible to grow unfamiliar
crops, particularly vanilla, which takes less space than coconut
trees and is more remunerative. He also grew native trees—

kahaia, aito, none, miro. Gustave confessed he hadn't had much
success in convincing people. "The difficulty is that everyone
has become separated. In the sixties, the community began to
fall apart. There is no community now except for the Church.
Until 1962 land was cultivated communally, led by a chief.
Every three months the land was rotated. Then a mayoral
system was installed, and people divided into political parties.
Now they can't work together on anything. The possibility of
individual gain—subsidies go to individuals—destroyed communal activity. If one fine day I were mayor, I'd start the old
system again." We ran our hands through the soil, talked
about crops, gazed at the septic tank, surveyed the compost
heap. "People are building barriers around their homes. I've
just built one myself. It's a question of mentality. If I see you
with a television, then I absolutely must have a television. It
doesn't matter if your kid is dying! There is a French proverb,
'Each for himself, God for all.' That is not a Polynesian proverb."

We went back to Gustave's house and ate some fruit in the
kitchen. The conversation returned to Papeete. "The problem
starts when people feel invaded. You see it now in Papeete—
the Europeans have all the good land, while the Tahitians get
pushed into the mountains, like Indians onto a reserve. It's
partly because of the French administration. The officials get
paid so much, they can afford the shops, and to buy the best
land. One day there will be no more Tahitian race. People are
beginning to resent it. I am also beginning to feel that way."

Gustave drove me to a small dock, where I took a speedboat
across a narrow channel to the village of Tiputa, population
300. I was staying there at a *pension*—three tiny cabins behind
a house—run by Lucien Pea and his sons, Ralph and Angelo.
It was an idyllic spot. Every morning I'd sit on a stone wall in
front of Lucien's house and watch dolphins swim by in the
channel. The dolphins passed twice a day, morning and evening. Villagers from Tiputa went out daily to fish from open
motorboats. No particular regimen governed these trips.
When the seas looked good and you needed fish you went
fishing. Lucien's table, set outdoors under a thatched roof by

the sea, was always laden with sushi, ceviche, lobsters, everything fresh from the ocean around us.

I spent much of my time with Lucien's son Angelo, playing *pétanque* and pool (they had a small, ramshackle table), bicycling around Tiputa, and above all sitting by the beach and talking. He'd gone to high school in Papeete but had failed his final exam; now he was biding time until beginning the compulsory year of military service. Angelo was handsome and vigorous, and chafed at the lack of distractions, particularly female distractions, in Tiputa. "The problem is that the girls here are all pregnant by the time they're fourteen. And once they're pregnant, they stay pregnant." He said there were two or three girls in Tiputa approaching fourteen, but they'd soon be grabbed up. "It's different in Papeete because there are lots of European women. It's better with the European women. They like the color of our skin. And the Tahitian women, you see, are . . . *pudique*. It takes much longer to get to the, uh, question." I had noticed that young Polynesian women in Tiputa tended to walk with their eyes cast downward; they only looked straight ahead when gazing through a window, and even then, if I caught a woman's glance, she would invariably shy away.

We talked about how Europeans—which, in this context, included Americans—come to Tahiti assuming that the Polynesians are enthused about casual sex, when in fact it's the Europeans who are casual. We had a good laugh over this common misunderstanding. "In Papeete there is much more freedom, and more choice—that's why so many young people go there," Angelo said. "Well, that and jobs, because there's no work here. You can fish, and plant a little, but there's no way to get cash, except for tourism. Though in Papeete, too, it's become really hard, there isn't much work. And you have to live so fast, always looking at your watch. Nowadays a lot of young people just go to Papeete to work for a while, buy a radio/cassette player, and return to the islands. It's too hard to live permanently in Papeete."

One evening we had a party. Actually the party began that morning. A boat had come in bearing the French administra-

tor for the Tuamotus. He was a thin, straight-backed, middle-
aged man who smoked a pipe and made the rounds in a
bright-white, high-colonial uniform. His wife wore stylish
Parisian clothes, had coiffed hair, and plucked her eyebrows
(or perhaps someone did it for her). I met them in the house
of a Tiputa police officer, a Polynesian. It was 11 A.M. and we
sat around drinking whisky. The administrator spoke of
France: "The problem in France now is blacks and Arabs," he
said, packing his pipe. "They sell drugs, and they are favored
by government programs over the French!" His wife nodded
and gestured violently. I asked about New Caledonia. "Listen,
the problem there is subversion by New Zealand and Australia. They [the Kanaks] are not ready for independence."

I didn't stay long with the administrator, his wife, and the
policeman. I wasn't accustomed to drinking whisky at eleven
in the morning and didn't want to be sick. But, as it turned
out, they appeared again that evening at Lucien's, along with
several others representing Tiputa's European contingent—
essentially a group of cops and their wives. The only really
profitable business in Tiputa was civil service. I gathered that
Lucien wanted to be on these people's good side. Also he'd
been drinking their whisky all afternoon. How he managed to
fix supper I don't know, though the food was abundant and
delicious. At table the French guests dominated the conversation, even when it was about Polynesia. I felt that during the
afternoon a century of world history had somehow dropped
away.

After dinner the French left and I joined Lucien, Angelo,
and several other Polynesian men in the pool room. More
alcohol was consumed—bottles of whisky, rum, vodka, and
bourbon. The idea was for the six of us to go through them
one by one. This was a level of drinking I'd never encountered
before. It was the kind of drinking that I thought killed people. Gustave was right; Polynesians are very competitive. We
played pool and drank until all the bottles were empty, at
about three in the morning.

After a night's sweaty rest I stumbled out into the bright
daylight and found Lucien, Angelo, and Henri, who'd been

with us the previous night, sitting on the beach eating raw fish
and drinking beer. The fish had just been caught. Angelo
picked one from a pail, killed it by bashing the head against
a rock, cut its skin just below the gills, peeled the skin back,
and handed me breakfast. Holding the head and tail, I pulled
the flesh off with my teeth. I refused beer and put up with their
taunting.

Though we'd seen each other many times during the
preceding days, Henri, a tall and gaunt man whose features
suggested European blood, had not been forthcoming. But
then Tiputa was not the sort of village where you could just
strike up conversation with a stranger. This morning, however, he was suddenly voluble, perhaps because of our intense
male bonding the night before. He said he'd been born in
Tiputa, so I asked what he thought of all these Polynesians
immigrating from Papeete. "It's fine having them here. The
problem now is Europeans. I think racism is beginning among
the Polynesians. The French come and ask, 'What do you do?'
And I say, 'I'm a *paysan*, I make some copra, I go fishing.'
After that they don't think again of talking with me. I think
the French are a bit, uh, snob."

Angelo broke in and reminded me of our conversation
about Papeete.

Henri: "There's a lot of racism there among the Polynesians."

Angelo: "A lot."

Henri: "Papeete's full of racism, and now it's beginning to
come here."

I was intrigued by this idea of racism, treating it like a
disease or a contagious infirmity—something that just happens. "When we were in France last year," Angelo said, "we
saw bars with signs that said '*Chiens et Tahitiens Au Dehors*'
[Dogs and Tahitians Outside]. It was full of places like that."
The shared -*iens* endings make the phrase a kind of alliterative
pun.

"It wasn't like that in the forties," Henri noted, "during the
war, when the French came to us and said, 'Help! Help!'"

Talk turned to geopolitics. Henri felt the French were here

254 because of geopolitical competition ("Tomorrow we might
■ have to learn Russian"), while Angelo and Lucien believed
their presence was due to their needing a bomb-test site, and
Angelo added, "If it's safe, why test it twenty-one thousand
kilometers away?" All agreed they wanted independence but
couldn't afford it.

Later that morning Angelo suggested we go swimming by
the fish trap near his house. We trooped over with our masks
and snorkels and slipped into the warm flowing channel. The
trap was about fifteen feet high and thirty wide, a circular
enclosure made with Cyclone fencing that reached from the
sea floor to above the surface. It was filled with an amazing
variety of fish: long thin blue fish; strange multicolored ones
at the bottom; beneath them, in the mud, flat brown fish.
Angelo swam into the trap, dove to the bottom, and touched
the flat ones to show me where they were. There was also a
shark in the trap, swimming at a leisurely pace. Angelo swam
back toward me and we broke surface. "The sharks here aren't
dangerous," he said confidently.

We left the trap and swam off, against the current, toward
the house. Angelo angled toward the middle of the channel
and I was alone. There were so many fish I thought I could
gather a handful without much effort. A shark swam beneath
me, then another one, riding the current out from the lagoon
and into open ocean.

■ "Little of the ancient customs of the Otaheitans remain.
. . . It is difficult to get them to speak their own language
without mixing a jargon of English with it, and they are so
altered that I believe in future no Europeans will ever know
what their ancient customs of receiving strangers were."
These were the words of Captain William Bligh on his second
trip to Tahiti, in 1792. His first trip, as is well known, went
awry. But Bligh was not a person easily put off. His goal was
to acquire Tahitian breadfruit plants and transport them to
West Indian plantations, where they were to be used to feed

slaves. (As it turned out, the slaves refused to eat breadfruit,
and Bligh's five years of work were wasted.)

It's remarkably sad to hear Bligh mourning the end of Tahitian life some 200 years ago. Only de Bougainville and Captain Cook, and their respective crews, seem to have found what they wanted in Tahiti. As de Bougainville's naturalist, Commerson, wrote, "It is the only corner of the earth where men live without vices, without prejudices, without needs or dissension. Born under the most beautiful sky, nourished by the fruits of uncultivated land . . . they know no god but Love. Each day is consecrated to him, all the island is his temple, all the women are his altars, all the men his sacrificers [*sacrificateurs*]. And what sort of women, you ask? The rival of Georgians in beauty, and sisters of the Graces, completely nude. There neither shame nor modesty [*la pudeur*] exercise their tyranny: the lightest of veils floats always at the mercy of the winds and of the desires." After more in this vein, Commerson notes that a cynic might consider such behavior to be merely dissipation. "But he would be grossly mistaken in not recognizing the state of natural man, born essentially good, exempt from all prejudice and following, with neither suspicion nor remorse, the soft impulses of an instinct always sure, because it has not yet degenerated into reason."

It has been said that happiness was a new idea to eighteenth-century Europe. Louis Constant, in his introduction to a recent edition of de Bougainville's *Voyage autour du monde*, writes that "without wishing it, and perhaps contrary to his intimate convictions, de Bougainville brought back to his own people, to Europe, evidence with which to believe for two hundred years that *happiness exists.*" In de Bougainville's writings, and those of various crew members, *sacrificateurs* often comes up with respect to Tahitian men, and *victimes* with respect to women. It is of course impossible to determine the extent to which this rhetoric, like the idea of happiness, was distinctively Tahitian or distinctively French. In any case, the belief that happiness could be real, present in the landscape and in the bodies and souls of Polynesians, has been Polynesia's most influential contribution to modern mythology, despite the disappointed remarks of Captain Bligh and his many successors.

■ My next stop after Tiputa was Raiatea, one of the Society Islands (along with, most famously, Mooréa, Bora Bora, Huahine, and Tahiti). The Society Islands are, excepting perhaps the Marquesas, the most spectacular in Polynesia, and the most heavily touristed. Polynesian tourism has been stagnating; prices are simply too high, and the capital can no longer be described reasonably as the "dear old Papeete town" of tourist brochures.

So the territorial government has mounted a propaganda effort, launched in April 1987 with a report by Alexandre Leontieff, then minister of economy, tourism, and the sea (he later became president of the Territorial Assembly, after the 1987 *événements*). "What we offer is originality," Leontieff argued in his poorly translated conclusion, "the difference of a unique character that is 'the Polynesian world.' . . . The mythical image of the Polynesian world is known throughout the world, and has become a reality for those who have discovered it. . . . Concerning tourist animation, too often the visitors have a first impression of being bored in Polynesia. And yet there are existing and potential activities based around nature and nautical sports, plus the discovery of the natural and cultural heritage of Polynesia. But what is missing is an effective system of commercialization, where these activities can be put at the disposition of the tourists. Also missing are Polynesian animators who are proud and happy to help others discover their country." *Animateurs* ("animators") is here an untranslatable term meaning people who make things happen; it isn't meant to convey a sense, as in English, of artists who draw cartoon characters.

On Raiatea I stayed with a white Frenchwoman and her Chinese husband at their modest *pension*. It was off a narrow road overlooking the Faaroa River, whence, according to some authorities, the original Maoris embarked for New Zealand (the legend is disputed by anthropologists). One Sunday

I borrowed a bicycle and rode off toward the *marae*, or ceremonial ground, of Taputapuatea. The gravel road was empty, the air moist and heavy; I experienced one of those corporeal epiphanies that are possible in a place like Raiatea, pedaling as fast as I could, reveling in the heat and perspiration and dense fragrances, the blur of dark undergrowth passing by, above me steep mountainsides. After an hour's effort I arrived at Taputapuatea. Raiatea was once called Havai'i, the legendary name for the Polynesians' place of origin. According to some traditions, all of the *maohis*, or Polynesians (including the Hawaiians, Micronesians, Maoris, Easter Islanders), came from Havai'i, and the most sacred site on Havai'i was Taputapuatea.

I nearly missed the *marae*, as it was marked only by a worn picket fence and a tiny sign. The first prominent feature was a tall stone, under which four guardians are said to have been buried alive. Beyond the cairn lay the heart of the *marae*: a flat area, about sixty feet square, paved with large stones. At its far end stood a platform perhaps six feet high and fifteen deep. Beyond the platform were palm trees and, on the horizon, the lush pinnacles of Huahine. There were no markers or signs of any kind to indicate what these monuments might mean; what little I knew had been gleaned from an earlier conversation with a French woman on Raiatea. At the base of the raised platform sat a stone figure. I suppose it was a god.

I climbed atop the platform. Looking back toward the road, across the field of stones, I noticed to my right a small tree by a large flat stone. According to my source, two infant heirs to the throne were once placed on this stone and carefully watched over until one had died. Other stones, here and there, were supposedly sacred rocks that women could not pass except on pain of death. I clambered down and walked through the palms to stone slips where, centuries ago, canoes were docked. Two young Polynesian men sat among them, listening to Cyndi Lauper sing "Girls Just Wanna Have Fun" on their portable cassette player. I said hello and asked if they knew any stories about the place. "No," one said grudgingly. "It has to do with the old people [*les anciens*]." Neither man

seemed eager to talk so I wandered back to the *marae* and
entertained incoherent thoughts about antiquity, the sacred,
and the language of stones. Next to Taputapuatea stretched a
rustic barbed-wire fence and, beyond it, more monuments. A
group of Polynesians walked in from the road bearing picnic
supplies and a red radio. The hefty man with the red radio
broke away and stopped before the platform to write DANAI
on a facing stone. He left, then reappeared and began writing
other names. I couldn't bear to watch him write "Jean ♥
Isabelle" or some such thing so I quickly left.

On the ride back I saw many missionaries plying their trade
at roadside homes. For decades the Catholic and Methodist
churches have dominated Polynesia, but recently other
groups—Mormons, Seventh Day Adventists—have been cultivating followers. I passed an enormous church of no apparent denomination, painted red and white like a barn, beside
the water. Occasionally I would see Polynesians walking home
from church in their solemn Sunday best, or a missionary in
someone's yard, his weighty book opened to this page or that,
explaining.

I stayed on Raiatea for only three days. People naturally
regarded me as a tourist, which made conversation nearly
impossible unless some transaction was involved. Just before
leaving I lounged around the airport's deserted restaurant and
chatted with the Polynesian waitress. She was helping her
young son with his homework—a French reading lesson about
Tunisia. "I used to be ashamed of being a waitress, but now
I'm proud of it," she said. "There are a lot of young people
here without jobs. If you don't have a diploma you can't get
a job. A lot of people don't have diplomas because they didn't
work in school. If you want to get a job with the government
you either have to do it through family connections or be very
pretty. If you're pretty and make an effort you can get a good
job as a secretary, if you know what I mean."

I told her a bit about my experiences, and she said, "Everybody comes to Tahiti with ideas in their head. But once you
stay here for a while, it's quite obvious, this isn't paradise."
She figured the old way of life started going bad sometime in

the 1960s or '70s. "Now you can live in Tahiti, as a *Polynesian*, and not know your neighbor. It's almost like France." I asked about the image of Polynesian women, and what it's like to be a *vahine*, an internationally recognized object of desire. "But that's all publicity! That's all in the heads of the men who visit here. Sure, maybe a Frenchman walks down a beach and sees a Tahitian girl and says to himself, 'Ooh, a *Tahitian girl*! In paradise!' But it really isn't like that." I said it must be strange, growing up in a place where the cultural image is so divergent from reality. "Yes, it is bizarre," she said with a half-smile, then looked away toward her son.

■ One night in Papeete: I had dinner at the home of a white Frenchman and his Polynesian wife; with us were several of their children and an old Polynesian uncle. We talked about sex. The wife told a story: Once, when still a young girl, she made some European friends at the Club Med. They took a Polaroid of her at the club one night dressed in a swim suit. She took the picture home to show off to her parents, and they burned it.

Everyone at dinner agreed that it was the mixed-blood *demis* who kept the myths of Tahiti alive—"it's the *demis* who go topless [*titi à l'aire*]." I mentioned the early explorers' accounts of a happy land where people worshipped no god but Love. The wife said, "Who knows what they really saw? Maybe they exaggerated, maybe they lied. No one knows what it was like." The old uncle nodded sadly: "Things have changed a lot since I was young. We used to go to church every morning and evening, all the young people, every day." And the wife said, "We really don't think much about our culture. Have you been to the Musée des Iles?"

Another night in Papeete: A white French artist and I went drinking at the Hôtel Tahiti, which stands where Queen Pomare, Tahiti's last monarch, once had her palace. Next to the bar was a dais, on which several young female *mannequins* ("models") were slinking about in practice for a fashion show later that night. They wore European clothes and had Euro-

260 pean mannerisms. In appearance, none was Polynesian but
■ they were rather *demi*. They were extremely thin and flirta-
tious. Pop music played from a stereo. In his 1918 *Essai sur
l'exotisme*, the French poet and traveler Victor Segalen wrote,
praisingly, "The [Polynesian] woman possesses above all else
the quality of a young man: a slender, adolescent beauty that
she maintains right until old age."

A third night in Papeete: In the few days before leaving
Polynesia I imposed on the hospitality of a middle-aged
French woman living outside town. I'll call her Christine. Her
comfortable, one-story house was set back from the road and
had its own small stretch of beach. On this particular evening
she hosted me, her daughter, and a thirty-ish Frenchman I'll
call Alain.

Over drinks I spoke about my travels and impressions. The
general picture I offered was not cheerful. "But the landscape
is beautiful," Christine objected gently. She'd lived in Tahiti
for some thirty years. "And the people are nice when they're
simple. When they get ambitious there are problems. The next
two generations will be problematic. But they'll enter the
modern world eventually." Alain noted that Polynesians are
still happier to take orders from French people than from
other Polynesians.

After a delicious dinner, Christine and Alain wheeled a
television out to the veranda, where we sat at table, caressed
by a warm breeze. The television brought us an unexpected
glimpse of the modern world. It was *Apostrophes*, an intellectual talk show broadcast from Paris. This particular episode
began with various recognizable intellectuals walking, one at
a time, down a Paris street. Each smiled happily upon seeing
a familiar chef standing before a fashionable doorway. After
these preliminaries a different set of intellectuals appeared,
grouped around a dinner table laden with silver and crystal.
They were at the Drouart, a restaurant used by the Goncourt
Academy to meet and announce literary prizewinners. The
Apostrophes writers were gathering there as part of the runup
to the year's Goncourt ceremonies. They had not come to eat,

for this was not a dinner party qua dinner party—no food was served, and the guests drank only what appeared to be water. But the *impression* of a dinner party was clearly made. The eight guests that night were all men, including the dashing young thinker Bernard Henri-Lévy, the novelist and critic Hervé Bazin, and a writer named Philippe Labro. "This is the best program on television," Alain said excitedly. *Apostrophes* had been a surprise success on European TV; a French poll named its host, Bernard Pivot, as the most important intellectual in France. Each guest (or contestant) has a few minutes to explain his or her latest work, then the others ask questions. I was disappointed to find that the questions always came in the form of attacks. The show was very competitive, and its guests seemed quite insecure and defensive. It reminded me of the Australian sport in which two men sit on a raised wooden rail and hit each other with pillows.

At one point Philippe Labro introduced his new book, *Un Eté dans l'ouest* (*A Summer in the West*). Labro had traveled in the American West in the 1950s. While there, he had met some of the rough-hewn folks who inhabit that region—"simple," "hard [*dure*]," and "savage" were the words he used to describe them. He encountered "Indians," and studied their myths and ideas of the supernatural. For once, the other guests responded not with scorn but with a jolly fellow feeling. Ah, *l'Amérique pure!*

I found myself undergoing a spell of dizziness, and realized it was due to my having, suddenly, thanks to Philippe Labro, become a primitive. I was born in the American West and grew up there; I had traveled where Labro had traveled. Was I then simple? Hard and savage? Had I, there in Tahiti, left civilization behind only to find that I'd never been in it at all, that I was, in fact, born a primitive?

At the end of the program, Bernard Pivot produced a daunting stack of books intended to be that week's reading for his viewers. I thought this a wise move on his part. For if his viewers were to neglect their reading they might find time to wonder why there were no women on this special program;

why eight human beings were able to pass an hour without
ever saying "I don't know," "I'm not sure," or "I'm afraid";
why eight white men of letters in 1988 chose to arrange
themselves around an *haute bourgeoise* table in a room from the
last century, if not the one before. They might have stopped
to wonder about civilization and the meanings and values it
conveys, often without intention.

Christine had not exactly invited me to stay at her home. We
had a friend in common, and I had simply appeared one day,
presenting myself as a well-mannered indigent. That night I
slept on the veranda with her dog, a German shepherd. After
some initial tension he accepted me. At sunrise we awoke,
walked to the beach, sat beneath a palm tree, gazed at Moorea,
and listened to the gentle morning surf.

Select Bibliography

INTRODUCTION

Geertz, C. *Works and Lives: The Anthropologist as Author*. Stanford: Stanford University Press, 1988.

PALAU

Barnett, H. G. *Being a Palauan.* New York: Holt, Rinehart and Winston, 1960.

Bowen, A. M. "Philippine Bases: U.S. Redeployment Options." Washington, D.C.: Congressional Research Service, 1986.

Butler, W. J., G. C. Edwards, and M. D. Kirby. *Palau: A Challenge to the Rule of Law in Micronesia*. New York: International Commission of Jurists, 1988.

Clark, R. S. "Self-Determination and Free Association—Should the United Nations Terminate the Pacific Islands Trust?" *Harvard International Law Journal* 211, no. 1 (Winter 1980).

264 ——— "The Republic of Palau." *Constitutions of Dependencies and*
■ *Special Sovereignties.* Dobbs Ferry, NY: Oceana, 1988.

Clark, R. S., and S. R. Roff. *Micronesia: The Problem of Palau.* New
York: Minority Rights Group, 1987.

McHenry, D. *Micronesia: Trust Betrayed.* Washington, D.C.: Carne-
gie Endowment for International Peace, 1975.

Smith, D. R. *Palauan Social Structure.* New Brunswick, NJ: Rutgers
University Press, 1983.

Stanley, D. *Micronesia Handbook: Guide to an American Lake.* Chico,
CA: Moon, 1985.

U.S. General Accounting Office. *U.S. Trust Territory: Issues Associated
with Palau's Transition to Self-Government* (report to Congressional
requesters and supplement). Washington, D.C.: U.S. General Accounting Office, 1989.

GUAM

Berg, M. L., and F. X. Hezel. *Micronesia: Winds of Change.* Saipan:
U.S. Trust Territory of the Pacific Islands, n.d.

Guthertz, J. P., and D. Singh. *Government Ethics and Corruption on
Guam.* Mangilao, Guam: University of Guam, 1986.

Rogers, R. F. *Guam's Search for Commonwealth Status.* Mangilao,
Guam: Micronesian Area Research Center, 1984.

Souder-Jaffery, L., and R. A. Underwood. *Chamorro Self-Determination.* Mangilao, Guam: Micronesian Area Research Center, 1987.

Webb, J. H., Jr. *Micronesia and U.S. Pacific Strategy: A Blueprint for
the 1980s.* New York: Praeger, 1974.

SAIPAN

Ballendorf, D. A., and B. G. Karolle. "Prospects for Economic
Self-Sufficiency in the New Micronesian States." *Center for Southeast
Asian Studies Occasional Papers,* no. 25 (1986).

Joseph, A., and V. F. Murray. *Chamorros and Carolinians of Saipan:
Personality Studies.* Cambridge, MA: Harvard University Press, 1951.

Kahn, E. J., Jr. *A Reporter in Micronesia.* New York: W. W. Norton,
1966.

Past Achievements and Future Possibilities: A Conference on Economic Development in Micronesia. Majuro: The Micronesian Seminar, 1984.

MARSHALL ISLANDS

Bradley, D. *No Place to Hide: 1946–1984.* Hanover, NH: University Press of New England, 1983.

Bulletin of Concerned Asian Scholars 18, no. 2 (April–June 1986).

Dibblin, J. *Day of Two Suns: U.S. Nuclear Testing and the Pacific Islanders.* New York: New Amsterdam, 1988.

Hayes, P., L. Zarsky, and W. Bello. *American Lake: Nuclear Peril in the Pacific.* Harmondsworth: Penguin, 1987.

Lutz, C., ed. *Micronesia as Strategic Colony: The Impact of U.S. Policy on Micronesian Health and Culture.* Cambridge, MA: Cultural Survival, 1984.

Marshall Islands: A Chronology: 1944–1983. Honolulu: Micronesia Support Committee, 1983.

FIJI

Ali, A. *Plantation to Politics: Studies on Fiji Indians.* Suva: University of the South Pacific, 1980.

Amratlal, J., E. Baro, V. Griffen, and G. B. Singh. *Women's Role in Fiji.* Suva: South Pacific Social Sciences Association, 1975.

Dean, E., and S. Ritova. *Rabuka: No Other Way: His Own Story.* Suva: The Marketing Team International, 1988.

Derrick, R. A. *A History of Fiji.* Suva: Government Press, 1974.

Durutalo, S. *The Paramountcy of Fijian Interest and the Politicization of Ethnicity.* Suva: USP Sociological Society, 1986.

Hagan, S. "Race, Politics, and the Coup in Fiji." *Bulletin of Concerned Asian Scholars* 19, no. 4 (Oct.–Dec. 1987).

Nayacakalou, R. R. *Leadership in Fiji.* Suva: University of the South Pacific, 1975.

Ravuvu, A. *Vaka i Taukei: The Fijian Way of Life.* Suva: Institute of Pacific Studies, 1983.

266 Routledge, D. *Matanitū: The Struggle for Power in Early Fiji.* Suva:
■   Institute of Pacific Studies, 1985.

Sahlins, M. *Islands of History.* Chicago: University of Chicago Press,
1985.

Schütz, A. J. *Say It in Fijian.* Sydney: Pacific Publications, 1984.

Tinker, H., N. Duraiswamy, Y. Ghai, and M. Ennals. *Fiji.* London:
Minority Rights Group, 1987.

Wright, R. *On Fiji Islands.* New York: Viking Penguin, 1986.

VANUATU

Lini, W. *Beyond Pandemonium: From the New Hebrides to Vanuatu.*
Wellington: Asia Pacific, 1980.

Molisa, G. M. *Colonised People.* Port Vila: Black Stone, 1987.

Paton, Mrs. J. G. *Letters and Sketches from the New Hebrides.* New
York: A. C. Armstrong and Son, 1897.

Toupouniua, S., R. Crocombe, and C. Slatter. *The Pacific Way.* Suva:
South Pacific Social Sciences Association, 1980.

NEW CALEDONIA

Burchett, W. G. *Pacific Treasure Island: New Caledonia.* Philadelphia:
David McKay, 1944.

Chesneaux, J. *Transpacifiques: Observations et considérations diverses sur
les Terres et Archipels du Grand Océan.* Paris: La Découverte, 1987.

Contribution à l'histoire du pays Kanak. Nouméa: IKS, n.d.

Coulon, M. *L'irruption kanak: de Calédonie à Kanaky.* Paris: Messidor,
1985.

Dornoy, M. *Politics in New Caledonia.* Sydney: Sydney University
Press, 1984.

*F.L.N.K.S.: La charte du FLNKS, les motions de tous les congrès, les
décisions du gouvernement provisoire de Kanaky.* Nouméa: Edipop, 1987.

Guiart, J. *La terre est le sang des morts: Nouvelle Calédonie du passé au
présent.* Paris: Anthropos, 1985.

Investir en Nouvelle Calédonie. Nouméa: Institut Territorial de la Statistique et des Etudes Economiques, 1987.

Kircher, I. A. *The Kanaks of New Caledonia.* London: Minority Rights Group, 1986.

Leenhardt, M. *Do Kamo: La personne et le mythe dans le monde mélanesien.* Paris: Gallimard, 1971.

Spencer, M. C. *New Caledonia in Crisis.* Canberra: Australian Institute of International Affairs, 1985.

Tjibaou, J. M., and P. Missotte. *Kanaké: The Melanesian Way.* Papeete: Les Editions du Pacifique, 1978.

Weingärtner, E., and F. Trautmann. *New Caledonia: Towards Kanak Independence.* Geneva: World Council of Churches, 1984.

FRENCH POLYNESIA

Alpers, A. *The World of the Polynesians.* Auckland: Oxford University Press, 1987.

Beaglehole, J. C. *The Life of Captain James Cook.* London: The Hakluyt Society, 1974.

Danielsson, Bengt, and Marie-Thérèse Danielsson. *Poisoned Reign.* Harmondsworth: Penguin, 1987.

De Bougainville, L. A. *Voyage autour du monde par la frégate* Boudeuse *et la flûte* l'Etoile. Paris: La Découverte, 1985.

Gauguin, P. *The Intimate Journals of Paul Gauguin.* London: KPI, 1985.

Rognon, F. *Les primitifs, nos contemporains.* Paris: Hatier, 1988.

Segalen, V. *Essai sur l'exotisme: une esthétique du divers.* Paris: Le Livre de Poche, 1986.